Carlton Ware
The Complete Guide
(including a Price Guide)

Dr Czes & Yvonne Kosniowski
ckyk publishing

Limited Edition 241/777

Czes   Yvonne

Carlton Ware

Acknowledgments

Whilst most of the pictures in this book were photographed by us, many were supplied by others and we would like to thank them for their contribution.

Bruce Nichol has supplied a large number of pictures from the "Parnell Collection" and the "Dulcie Agnes Joyce Memorial Collection". There is a short piece describing these collections in the chapter "Collecting Carlton Ware". Bruce has also sent us some pictures from the "Margaret Jones Collection" and the "Lexi James Collection".

Thanks go to Will Farmer from Fielding Auctioneers (www.fieldingsauctioneers.co.uk) who has provided some pictures from his archives. Will Farmer regularly appears on the BBC Antiques Roadshow and has kindly written a Foreword to this book.

We have included some pictures of Carlton Ware from old advertisements and from the original Carlton Ware Pattern and Shape books that have survived. Some of this material is in our possession but the majority is held at The Potteries Museum & Art Gallery in Stoke-on-Trent. We would very much like to thank them as well as the owners of the material, Frank Salmon (Francis Joseph) and John McCluskey.

Our friends, Ian Harwood and Jerome Wilson, have supplied several pictures from the "Ian & Jerome Collection" for which we would like to express our thanks.

Denise Burningham from Zeichen Antiques (www.zeichen.dsl.pipex.com) kindly supplied us with several pictures of Flow Blue as well as some Glacielle Ware and Stone Ware.

Derek and Jane Towns from www.carltonchina.info run a web site devoted to Carlton China and have supplied us with some pictures of Carlton China as well as some Figurines.

Mike Maunder has supplied some pictures of his Blush Ware from the "Mike Maunder Collection".

The images of the Crested Ware were taken, with kind permission, at the Goss & Crested China Club Museum in Horndean (www.gosschinaclub.demon.co.uk).

Two other collectors that have supplied some pictures from their collections are Rodger Aitchison and Stephen Garratt-Frost.

We would also like to thank the collectors, dealers and auction houses that have supplied us with one or two pictures. These include Mario & Betty Hart, Nicholas Pine, Peter Meyer & Gary Jessup, Jackie Casey, Allan Bellamy, Charterhouse Auctions and Kent Auctions.

Pictures have been credited although where no credit is mentioned it is a photograph taken by the authors.

Published by ckyk publishing

ISBN 978-0-9549558-2-3

Contents

Foreword

I remember as a child digging around my late grandmothers house, snooping, nosing and generally investigating, as I always did. It was a house filled with antiques and interesting items, some proudly on display, others tucked away in the back of cupboards.

One day, around the age of eleven, I remember stumbling upon a wonderful coffee service, bright, bold and splashed with colour. The cups had funny shaped handles and the coffee pot was smothered in bold little flowers. It was my grandma's Shelley coffee service, a wonderful and incredibly stylish wedding gift to her back in 1935.

After many months of begging and pleading I was eventually granted custody, and so marked the moment when ceramics, and more importantly 20th Century ceramics were to take over my life.

An early interest grew into a passion and soon I was the bane of my poor parents. Every weekend and spare moment was handed over to long car journeys all over the country in pursuit of the next find.

One of my favourite haunts was the Art Deco Fair at the Commodore rooms in Nottingham. This wonderful old building used to be a buzz with dealers from all over the country, each setting up their stalls on the many tiered rows. In those days (and I'm talking about the early 1980s) it was all so new, so exciting with everyone still finding their way!

The stalls were awash with jugs, plates, vases, and tea sets from all manner of factories, Shelley, Poole, Clarice and of course Carlton Ware! Bold shapes and bright colours sung from each and every stall. Unknown pattern names were guessed at, or better still invented, either way it didn't matter. One thing was clear, a sense that we were all part of something very new and very exciting!

Many said it wouldn't last, Art Deco was a fad, 20th Century Decorative Arts a 'flash in the pan'…some flash!

While scouring the Fair for what became my first love, Clarice, I was increasingly aware of the beautiful ceramics of

Carlton Ware. The myriad of patterns, techniques and glazes all brought together to make some of the most exquisite pots ever made.

I have few regrets, however one of them is not collecting Carlton Ware. I have been fortunate to own a few select pieces of Carlton Ware in my time but nothing that would constitute a collection. Fortunately I can now satisfy myself with the pieces that grace the pages of this book…. and what a book!

Of all the Carlton Ware my first love has to be the amazing pieces of the 1930s, the abstract patterns, luxurious glazes and daring enamels of Enoch Bolton and the great-unsung lady of Art Deco, Violet Elmer. From *Jazz* to *Floral Comets* the wares just exude the essence of the era and in an instant they jettison you back to the glory days of the 1930s.

Today I'm in the fortunate position of working with antiques on a daily basis, from the many thousands of items that pass through my saleroom to the countless pieces I see at the Antiques Roadshow. In either of these environments the arrival of a piece of Carlton Ware lifts the spirits on what can be long and tiring days.

Only a few years ago while filming the Antiques Roadshow at St Georges Hall in Liverpool I remember a lovely lady who had spent some three hours in the queue. Out of her carrier bag she pulled a glorious and rather large vase in…Jazz! You can imagine my delight, a delight that was eventually eclipsed by the owners when I revealed both the history and more importantly the price! Her Grandmothers vase took on a whole new identity and she returned home clutching the vase far more safely than when she arrived!

Whilst that lady vowed never to part with her wonderful vase there are people who do part company with their inheritance pieces. As my late grandmother taught me, we never own anything; we merely look after it, being custodians for the next generation.

As an auctioneer I'm at the front line of managing this custodial responsibility and this is how I first met Czes and Yvonne. Some eight or nine years ago they pulled up outside my offices to collect a pair of rather large *Mikado* pattern temple jars they had purchased at my sale. To this day I recall thinking….'now there's a pair of collectors', their passion, knowledge and dedication were both instant and infectious.

Over the past few years Czes and Yvonne have gone beyond the call of duty for what is expected of a collector. Most of us are happy just in the company of our pots, but not them! They have created a database, manage a web site and produced numerous books, all for their love of Carlton Ware.

Although there may be several books on the subject we now have a book which is long overdue, a luxurious tome which will grace the coffee tables and shelves of collectors all over the world. This book not only shows the immense diversity of the factories output but also reflects the energies of two collectors whose passion for Carlton Ware is as charming and infectious as the pots themselves.

Will Farmer - ASFAV

Introduction

This is the third book that we have written about Carlton Ware, the most comprehensive to date. We have spent a great deal of time over the last decade researching and logging information about Carlton Ware. Our aim has always been to share what ever we discovered with other collectors to improve interest and knowledge, some of this may be found on our web site www.carltonware.com. We are very excited about the launch of this new book and know that the world of Carlton Ware is ready for it.

Why the fascination with Carlton Ware? For those of you that are already collectors know the wonderful pieces produced and so the answer is obvious. We hope that you enjoy this book and that it will serve to increase a greater interest in Carlton Ware. Also we hope that this book will serve to enlighten new collectors and the rest of the world to its beauty and to give some of the other manufacturers a run for their money. We are glad to be able to showcase many beautiful designs and show some of the vast diversity of pieces that Carlton Ware produced over a period of production that lasted for over a century.

One of the Carlton Ware advertisements stated:

"For many centuries man has created pottery of utilitarian value to assist in eating and drinking, but in this enlightened age, his inherent desire to create artistic things has led him to produce pottery of aesthetic value, which will beautify and adorn the home and contribute to our modern ideas of gracious living."

Carlton Ware have certainly succeeded in producing beautiful pieces as we trust that the contents of this book will testify.

We have included many pictures, we know that Carlton Ware collectors love to see them, and of course as always they are a great way to identify unfamiliar designs.

With each picture we have included the source and a guide price for the item. Most of the pictures are from our own collection - the "Kosniowski Collection". We make no excuses for this; we have collected many pieces for research over the last decade. Other sources of pictures are detailed in the Acknowledgments on page 2. Some pictures are ones

that we have photographed but the owner wishes to remain anonymous. Some of the pieces may not necessarily still remain in the source's collection as pieces are bought and sold.

The price guide with each photograph is based on the assumption that the item is not damaged or restored. It is possible that one or two of the items photographed are either damaged or restored, however for clarity, the guide price indicated against the piece ignores this! Obviously the value of a damaged or restored item may be lower than indicated. Also, the guide price shown against an item does not necessarily mean that the owner is willing to sell the item, although if you are interested then please contact the owners or the authors!

The subject of price guide is a difficult one to agree especially as market values can vary greatly from time to time and of course once one has gone to print it is to late to include amendments or make adjustments. So we have had to make decisions and be dammed for any inadvertent errors. Also there are of course the considerations of the condition, size, colour, availability, rarity and desirability that can change along with current vogue and fashions, so we will never please all of the people all of the time.

When we first started to collect Carlton Ware the information available in the market place was sketchy. How we would have coveted such an excellent source of reference as the contents of this book. We have included a comprehensive list of pattern numbers. There is also a list of shapes that were produced from number 1,000 onwards. Unfortunately we are not able to include a picture of every different pattern and shape, as the book would be the size of a coffee table!

The chapters have been divided into what we feel influenced Carlton Ware to produce the design. Some designs fall into different categories and we have had to place the pictures within just one chapter so please do not be disappointed if you do not agree with the placement. For example, Fantasia, which has an exotic bird with swallow like tail amongst exotic flowers and foliage, could have been placed in the Influence of Nature - Birds section but we decided to include in the Art Deco and Best Ware section.

One of the sad aspects about Carlton Ware is the amount of records that have been destroyed, lost or stolen. Patterns and shapes sometimes appear which do not exist in any of the known records. Also, the records show patterns and shapes that, to our knowledge, were never produced. We have done our best to present the information in an accurate and informative way. Occasionally mistakes may occur and we apologise in advance for any errors. Please accept this book and the information included in the spirit of friendship in which it was written. We have put together pieces of past history and produced this book for the love of Carlton Ware and for your enjoyment.

Czes & Yvonne

The Carlton Ware Story

Our story starts in 1890 when James Frederick Wiltshaw was keen to have his own pottery works after working for his father and so he set up a company in partnership with brothers James Alcock Robinson and William Herbert Robinson. The Wiltshaw & Robinson Company began life at Carlton Works, Copeland Street, Stoke on Trent. This gave birth to a company that lasted for more than a century, albeit with several changes of ownership. By 1894 the name "Carlton Ware" appeared as part of the new Crown back stamp and this replaced the old W&R Ribbon or Bluebird logo. However, it wasn't until 1958 that the company officially changed its name to Carlton Ware Ltd.

Nowadays the Carlton Ware name is well known all over the world. The extensive range that was produced over the long history of Carlton Ware has created a great variety of superb designs to suit all interests and tastes.

The early Carlton Ware products were variants of designs that were popularised by the likes of Wedgwood, Crown Devon, Royal Doulton and Royal Worcester. Many fashionable homes were adorned with the Victorian Blush Ware and Flow Blue in an array of tableware, dinnerware, etc. Wiltshaw & Robinson obviously wished to tap into the growing demand of the eclectic Victorians. As always the designs that Carlton Ware emulated and adapted were done with a sincerity of style and quality in design and finish. These were, and indeed remain, popular.

At the turn of the 20th century Wiltshaw & Robinson once again seized an opening into the very popular "Crested Heraldic China" lines and were probably one of the first competitors for the Goss factory. Production was prolific and included many ranges of seaside souvenirs which were collected with passion during the latest craze for travel. Production of crested Ware lasted for about twenty years.

In 1911 the original partnership was dissolved and J. F. Wiltshaw proudly announced that he was now the sole owner. It seems there had been difficulties with the directors especially as Harold Taylor Robinson had taken over his uncle William Herbert Robinson's directorship. This created a clash of personalities and aspirations between James Wiltshaw and the Robinson family.

The Oriental and Persian designs were introduced between the two World Wars along with many designs containing blossoms and birds. This combined with a series of lustre finishes that Carlton Ware had perfected and proudly announced put Carlton Ware at the forefront of the market.

Tragically, James Frederick Wiltshaw died in 1918 under a train at the Stoke Railway Station. After this terrible accident his son Frederick Cuthbert Wiltshaw, still in his early 20s, took over the reigns of the company. Arguably it was he that shook the company and moved it into a new productive era with talented designers.

The momentous opening of the tomb of the boy king Tutankhamen was a perfect opportunity for the designers to capitalise on the enormous interest generated by the media. This was accomplished with magnificent depictions of the artifacts revealed within the burial chamber. The treasure that was to carry the boy king to eternity made for grand designs on ceramics, elaborately decorated with Egyptian symbols, gods and even a copy of Tutankhamen's death mask as a finial. This was masterfully used to its full potential by Carlton Ware with some fabulous collectable pieces.

In 1925 the first of the embossed Salad Wares appeared, these contained vivid red painted Crabs, Lobsters and Tomatoes. These ranges were and continued to be very popular with the public so consequently remained in production, albeit with slight changes, until the 1970s.

The back stamp changed again in about 1925 moving from the Crown Mark to the Script Mark. One can surmise that as new designers took over then new back stamps were introduced to reflect a new era.

Wiltshaw & Robinson produced a China range under a Carlton China back stamp. In 1928 Wiltshaw & Robinson merged with the manufacturers of Savoy China; Birks Rawlins & Co of Vine Pottery. The bone china designs of Savoy China were incorporated into the Carlton China range. The range was further extended to include many new patterns under the influence of the Carlton Ware designers.

At the same time, by the late 1920s, the range of Carlton Ware had expanded to include more modestly priced tableware. And, Carlton Ware was the first manufacturer to offer the very popular "Oven to Table" wares in 1929.

Arguably the most celebrated period of production was during the 1920s and 1930s. Most of the "Best Wares" were designed during this period. Good in-house designers made this possible with new innovative designs that pushed the boundaries of excellence. During the innovative period of the 1920s freehand hand painted designs appeared. These were usually stamped "Handcraft" and they tended to be more abstract simplistic floral patterns. This move was probably to follow the trends of the modern free hand painting at that time. This was being set by the likes of Clarice Cliff and her contemporaries. These early hand painted designs were of a simplistic interpretation of abstract floral themes, with only a few colours being used on such patterns as *Floribunda*, *Shamrock* and *Flowering Papyrus*. The advantage was that

6

a design didn't need the expensive outlay of lithographs or transfers and so could be discontinued or changed without too much waste.

In contrast, the next phase of Handcraft moved away from floral and into more adventurous use of bold colours with a geometric, angular and zig-zag designs. Some of the designs include *Russian, Chevrons, Mondrian, Chevrons, Intersection* and *Lightning*. These designs were now truly moving into what is now known as the Art Deco period. Some designs did include the use of transfers and were finished in a high lustre glaze, for example, *Anemone*. This period arguably saw some of Carlton Ware's most sought after designs that are highly valued by collectors today.

This heralded the advent of Carlton Ware's journey into beautiful Art Deco designs. They had been very competitive with intricate Chinoiserie, Egyptian and lustre designs, and now they needed to once again come up with their own adaptations of the Art Deco movement rather than merely copy others. This they did with fabulous complex patterns that were without parallel. These would include *Geometrica, Fan, Floral Comets, Explosion, Awakening, Sunflower Geometrica, Rainbow Fan* and *Ziggarette*, etc. These masterpieces of design and excellence took them forward into the Jazz age with lustre designs to render you speechless - designs that without dispute were to become some of the most collectable Art Deco designs ever produced by Carlton Ware.

In the early 1930s beautiful embossed patterns such as *Fruit Basket, Anemone, Gum Nut, Oak Tree* and *Rock Garden* were introduced. These were multi-coloured and very popular. Even these utilitarian pieces were completed with the usual high quality of finish that was the hallmark of Carlton Ware. By the mid 1930s, Carlton Ware's success led to other firms, especially those overseas, copying their designs. In order to protect the overseas markets, in particular in Australia and New Zealand, Carlton Ware applied for patents and registered a large number of designs in Australia. This explains the Registered Australian Design back stamp on many of these wares. The early Australian Design back stamp read "Registration Applied For", which was removed at a later date.

World War II effectively stopped the production of anything except utility wares. However, during this period, new production methods were introduced and the very popular lustre ranges were produced in the Royale range of colours. The Royale colours were called Bleu, Rouge, Vert and Noire (Blue, Red, Green and Black respectively). Apart from black, these new colours were much more uniform and were easily distinguishable from the pre-war versions which tended to be mottled and have some visual texture. New hand-painted decorations were also added to include *Spider's Web, New*

Mikado and *New Storks*. In parallel with these finer wares, fruit and floral designs also continued to be made and the range was expanded to include *Hydrangea, Vine, Grape, Poppy* and *Daisy*.

The 1950s was probably the most productive period in the Carlton Ware history in terms of output but unfortunately the intricate and complex designs of earlier years were too time consuming and expensive to replicate. Restrictions because of World War II on the pottery industry were finally removed and this prompted most of the Carlton Ware being produced to contain the word "Handpainted" on the back stamp, regardless of whether it was or wasn't. *Windswept, Leaf* and *Pinstripe* were added to the range and a steady production of lustre wares was maintained. In 1958, the company officially changed its name to Carlton Ware Ltd.

The owner F. C. Wiltshaw died in 1966 and the company was taken over by Arthur Wood & Company (Longport) Ltd the following year. They continued to produce Carlton Ware as well as re-introducing the Apple Blossom range and producing a Flow Blue range. In addition, the 1970s led to the introduction of the Walking Ware range. This novelty ware gained immediate popularity and probably kept the company afloat.

CARLTON & KENT
Carlton Ware Ltd and James Kent Ltd

MIKE FORD
Sales Representative

462 & 468 King Street, Fenton, Stoke-on-Trent ST4 3DH
Tel: 0782 599544, Fax: 0782 599382, Telex: 367144

In 1987 County Potteries bought both James Kent and Carlton Ware. The combined companies were named Carlton & Kent. Some literature survives from those days and the Salesmen sold James Kent Pottery in unison with Carlton Ware.

With the recession in the early 1980s the Receivers were called into the Copeland Street works in 1989. Grosvenor Ceramics temporarily saved the company and there was a short period of production of Carlton Ware between 1990 and 1992. The Company and name then remained dormant until 1997 when Frank Salmon from Francis Joseph acquired it together with a number of moulds and a few pre-production models. He continues to produce Carlton Ware.

The Early Years - Victorian Blush

One of the earliest ranges produced by Carlton Ware was what is now known as the Blush Ware range. The Royal Worcester Company was believed to be the main instigators of the original blush ivory ware designs. This style was an adaptation to their previous designs that were influenced by the wave of Japonisme that had swept through Europe in the 1880s and 1890s.

Wiltshaw & Robinson introduced this range after it had been popularised by other manufacturers such as Royal Worcester, Royal Doulton and Crown Devon. The owners of Carlton Ware obviously wanted to be part of what was very popular with the Victorians. Their range began early in the company's conception in 1890 and remained in production for about twenty-five years and so not surprisingly the vast quantities produced ensure that there is still a lot of it around today.

The Blush name refers to the subtle shades of pink, yellow, blue and green that were used in the decoration. The designs usually depicted naturalistic flower patterns. These were created initially by a transfer print onto a white or cream ground and then often finished by hand with the subtle colours to create the blush effect. The pieces were then decorated with varying degrees of gilt. The gilt was usually more prolific on the handles, borders and the base of the pieces. The overall effect was a very ornate and opulent piece of pottery.

The range of designs and shapes produced was vast and consisted of tea sets, biscuit barrels, dressing table sets, claret jugs, fruit bowls, sweet dishes and many exquisitely shaped vases. Some of the items were finished with EPNS rims, lids and handles which enhanced their opulence. Utilitarian wares were included in the range; such as sardine pots, cruets and butter dishes. Some of the patterns are actually named on the underside of the piece. These include *Peony, Chrysanthemum, Poppy, Arvista, Petunia, Honfleur* and *Catalpa*; which, apart from Honfleur, are a replication of their floral name.

Some Blush Ware patterns also have an element of Flow Blue and vice-versa. It is not surprising that Carlton Ware sometimes combined several ideas in a design.

Heather - Pattern 1166
Large Cake Basket from the Kosniowski Collection
£70 - £90

Blush Ware - Picottes - Pattern 624
Tray from the Parnell Collection
Image courtesy of www.nicholnack.com.au
£50 - £100

Marguerite - Pattern 1655
Biscuit, Tobacco, Handled Vases, Lidded Urns, Teapot
(made 1894 - 1900) from the Mike Maunder Collection
*£70 - £100 (biscuit), £60 - £80, £180 - £220 (vases), £200 - £230 (urns),
£50 - £80 (teapot)*

Blush Ware - Camelia
Plate from the Parnell Collection
Image courtesy of www.nicholnack.com.au
£60 - £80

Daffodil & Carnation
Vases from the Parnell Collection
Image courtesy of www.nicholnack.com.au
£100 - £150 each

Blush Ware - Cherry Blossom - Pattern 2406
Biscuit Barrel from the Parnell Collection
Image courtesy of www.nicholnack.com.au
£70 - £100

Gladioli - Pattern 1750
Pair of Tall Vases from the Parnell Collection
Image courtesy of www.nicholnack.com.au
£200 - £250

Poppy (left), Petunia (right), No Name (all others)
Vases (made about 1895) from the Mike Maunder Collection
£70 - £90 (left), £180 - £220 (handled pair), £160 - £200 (centre back), £80 - £100 (right), £120 - £180 (squat vase)

Blush Ware - Victorian Girls
Biscuit Barrel from the Parnell Collection
Image courtesy of www.nicholnack.com.au
£250 - £300

Blush Ware - Poppy
Tea Set (made 1890 - 1894) from the Mike Maunder Collection
£180 - £250

Cornucopia, Dahlia, Petunia, Carnation
Claret Jugs (made about 1895) from the Mike Maunder Collection
£200 - £250 (left), £300 - £320, £230 - 280, £200 - £250 (right)

The Early Years - Flow Blue

Flow Blue pottery and china were very popular in Victorian England but were also produced and collected prolifically in many countries around the world. It was an important collectible in the United States back in the 1800s.

Early Pottery designers had copied the very popular Chinese Porcelain designs and colours which consisted of Cobalt Blue on a White background. Most discerning ceramics companies were producing some form of Blue and White and Flow Blue patterns such as Wedgwood, Crown Devon, Royal Doulton and Royal Worcester to mention a few. This is apparent by the copious amount still available to collectors today. The wares tended to be based on tableware or dinnerware which included an enormous array of plates, serving dishes, bowls, jugs, biscuit barrels, bon bon servers and of course vases etc.

Flow Blue was another of the designs that Carlton Ware copied from other manufacturers of the time. The term Flow Blue refers to designs that have softly flowing transfer-printed decorations on durable, white, earthenware bodies. The designs were produced on hard, white-bodied earthenwares decorated with underglazed transfer printed designs that were allowed to bleed or "flow" into the undecorated portions. Some believe that this process of flowing the colours to have been unintentional initially but it obviously caught someone's imagination. The process was produced by the addition of lime or ammonia chloride into the protective shell of the fire-clay sagger surrounding the wares whilst firing the glaze, which produced the desired "flowing" effect.

Flow Blue was popular even though it was criticised at the time. Hudson Moore, wrote in his 1903 edition of "The Old China Book"; *"There is a certain style of design known as 'flow blue', which has nondescript patterns, flowers, geometric designs, and which has nothing whatever of beauty or interest to recommend it..."*

Although we have written separate chapters on Blush Ware and Flow Blue, many Victorian pieces have a semblance of each; so please don't treat the categories as gospel.

Flow Blue
Tea Pot from Jackie Casey's Antique Showcase (www.flowblue.co.uk)
£100 - £150

Flow Blue - Iris (left), no name, Penstemon, Nigella
Vase, Biscuit, Vase, Vase from Zeichen Antiques
£550 - £650, £250 - £300, £190 - £220, £190 - £220

Dragons & Unicorn, Carnation, Multi-Flowers
Patterns 2787, 1981, 1941
Claret Jugs from Zeichen Antiques (www.zeichen.dsl.pipex.com)
£600 - £850, £750 - £1,100, £500 - £700

Flow Blue - Chrysanthemum - Pattern 1635
Pair of Large Footed Vases from the Kosniowski Collection
£300 - £500

Green Dahlia
Two Tone Bowl from the Parnell Collection
Image courtesy of www.nicholnack.com.au
£150 - £200

Flow Blue - Petunia - Pattern 534
Tea Pot from the Parnell Collection
Image courtesy of www.nicholnack.com.au
£100 - £150

Marguerite
Biscuit Barrel from the Parnell Collection
Image courtesy of www.nicholnack.com.au
£70 - £100

Marguerite
Vase from the Parnell Collection
Image courtesy of www.nicholnack.com.au
£70 - £100

Flow Blue - Patterns number unknown, 1619
Biscuit Barrels from Zeichen Antiques (www.zeichen.dsl.pipex.com)
£200 - £250 each

Flow Blue - Flower Garland, Honfleur, May - Patterns 586, 1639, 876
Water Jugs & Sweetmeal Barrel from Zeichen Antiques (www.zeichen.dsl.pipex.com)
£150 - £200, £150 - £200, £75 - £100

Flow Blue - Carnation
Reticulated Plates from Zeichen Antiques (www.zeichen.dsl.pipex.com)
£180 - £220 each

Carlton Ware *Flow Blue*

CARLTON WORKS COPELAND STREET STOKE-ON-TRENT Tel: (0782) 44205

In the mid 1970s Carlton Ware, under the ownership of Arthur Wood, introduced a new range of ornamental sized Flow Blue pieces. The illustration above is of an advertisement for the re-introduction of Flow Blue during the Arthur Woods Period.

The Early Years - Crested Ware

W H Goss, at the Falcon Works, introduced Heraldic China for universities, public schools and colleges as early as the 1870s and so it is believed that they were the originators of what we now call collectively Crested Ware. In 1883 Williams' son Adolphus Goss joined the company and with great determination eventually convinced his father to extend the ranges of Heraldic China to appeal to the general population. By 1887 they had procured permission to produce miniature models of British Historical artefacts decorated with the coats of arms of towns and cities. This caught on in a big way and by the turn of the century had become a collecting craze. Virtually every town and city in the land now had its arms produced and sold by a Goss appointed agent.

By the late 19th century the Goss factory decided to further take advantage of the new niche market of seaside souvenir collecting by producing miniature copies of Greek and Roman pots and vases. They decorated these with the coat of arms of coastal towns and sold them as "seaside souvenirs". This was the result of the new wave of tourism by Edwardians and Victorians discovering holidays.

It is believed that, in 1910, some 95% of homes in Britain had a piece of 'Crested China'. Obviously this great appetite for crested china was now also being met by other potteries that desired to be part of the success of W H Goss namely Shelley, Arcadian and Willow Art.

Wiltshaw and Robinson entered the crested china market in about 1902, which probably made them the first company to compete with W H Goss. They were presumably very eager to enter another fast growing sector of the ceramic market. An advertisement at this time announced their latest speciality 'Carlton Heraldic China'. They had been busy completing orders for the coronation and this seemed like a suitable progression of their fancy goods.

The extent of the ranges of Crested ware are too numerous to list especially as this has been documented so aptly by others. For further information see the books by Nicholas Pine (for example *The Price Guide to Crested China*) and the Goss Crested China Club run by Lynda Pine.

By the 1920s Carlton Ware was, according to an advertisement in the *Pottery Gazette*, offering their new range of lustre finishes which were available in twelve colours. Most of the crested ware produced by Carlton Ware after this date was completed with the lustre finish. Crested Ware began its decline in popularity after the first world war and was completely out of vogue by second world war. Its popularity today still survives and collectors have a vast amount of miniature wares in many numerous designs to satisfy all tastes and pockets.

Crested Ware
Goose from The Goss & Crested China Club
£30 - £40

Crested Ware
Bi-plane from The Goss & Crested China Club
£200 - £250

Crested Ware
Sailing Boat from The Goss & Crested China Club
£35 - £40

Crested Ware
Time Glass & Judge from The Goss & Crested China Club
£20 - £30 each

Crested Ware
Golf Ball & Floating Mine from The Goss & Crested China Club
£25 - £30 & £125 - £140

Crested Ware
Cigarette Holder from The Goss & Crested China Club
£50 - £55

Crested Ware
Doll from The Goss & Crested China Club
£120 - £140

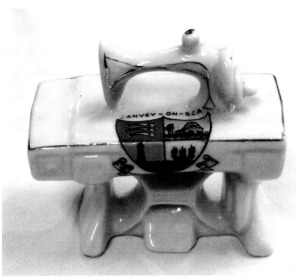

Crested Ware
Sewing Machine from The Goss & Crested China Club
£35 - £40

Crested Ware
Felix the Cat from The Goss & Crested China Club
£650 - £700

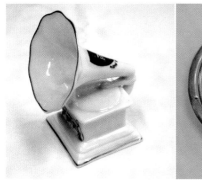

Crested Ware

Gramophone & Silver Rimmed Pin Dish from The Goss & Crested China Club

£50 - £55 & £15 - £20

Crested Ware

Wallace Sword from The Goss & Crested China Club

£150 - £180

Crested Ware

Drunkard leaning on lamp-post Ashtray from
The Goss & Crested China Club

£75 - £90

Crested Ware

Felix the Cat from The Goss & Crested China Club

£650 - £700

Crested Ware

Charabanc from The Goss & Crested China Club

£50 - £55

The Early Years - The Greek Connection

Carlton Ware were renowned for making fashionable earthenware. In the early 1900s this included sprigged ware that is reminiscent of Wedgwood. It was produced in a variety of colours. Other manufacturers including Spode had produced sprigged ware but suffice to say that the most famous was Josiah Wedgewood's Jasper and Basalt examples. Sprigged ware is a term used to describe raised relief images, which are made in moulds and applied to the form before firing.

Ancient Greece is considered to be the cradle of Western civilisation. It is not surprising that Carlton Ware used ideas from Grecian urns to produce some Carlton Ware patterns. Two well known designs are *Grecian Figures* and *Dancing Figures*.

Grecian Figures contains a number of figures, usually six. These figures include the Greek god Apollo and some of the nine muses, daughters of Zeus.

The *Dancing Figures* pattern shows six draped maidens holding hands. The pattern is probably based on the Wedgewood Jasperware 'Dancing Hours', which is still produced today. The Wedgewood design is attributed to John Flaxman Jnr (1755-1826).

Some pieces, such as plates, spoons and forks come with just a frieze. Close-ups of two of the frieze variations are shown here. Other sprigged ware designs include hunting scenes which again were popular with many potteries as well as the public.

Grecian Figures - Pattern 602
Tea Pot from the Kosniowski Collection
£50 - £80

Dancing Figures - Pattern 602
Salad Bowl and Servers from the Kosniowski Collection
£80 - £120

Grecian Figures - Pattern 601
Tea Pot from the Parnell Collection
Image courtesy of www.nicholnack.com.au
£50 - £60

Dancing Figures - Pattern 604
Biscuit Barrel from the Parnell Collection
Image courtesy of www.nicholnack.com.au
£100 - £150

The Oriental Influence - Chinese

The name Chinoiserie is a term used to explain the style of decoration reflecting a Chinese influence. The patterns are normally very elaborate and intricate. Chinoiserie patterns were very fashionable in the 17th and 18th centuries. Carlton Ware introduced their Chinoiserie between the two World Wars from about 1916 onwards.

A common form of Chinoiserie is the well known *Willow* pattern. Usually this is a blue Chinese design on a white background depicting a willow tree, a river and a pair of lovebirds in flight. This design has been used by most potteries and it's not surprising that Carlton Ware also produced this. They introduced the *Willow* pattern into their portfolio quite early in their lifetime, and they produced it in a number of different colours.

Willow Pattern (not Carlton Ware)

The *Willow* pattern was the basis for a number of other Chinoiserie patterns produced by Carlton Ware. The *Willow* pattern is associated with a story which sounds very Chinese but probably made up from the design.

The story starts with a Mandarin who had a beautiful daughter, Koong-se. She fell in love with a secretary Chang much to the anger of the Mandarin who believed the secretary was unworthy of his daughter.

Chang was banished and a fence was erected around the Mandarin's estate to prevent Chang seeing his daughter. Meanwhile Koong-se was betrothed to a warrior Duke. The Duke arrived by boat with jewels as gifts and a banquet was held. After the banquet Chang dressed in the robes of a servant came to Koong-se's room. They embraced and vowed to run away together. The couple escaped but only after Koong-se's father saw them and gave chase across a bridge.

The Mandarin continued to try and catch the couple with several near misses. The couple eventually settled on a

distant island where Chang became famous for his writings. This was his undoing because the Mandarin heard about him and sent guards to find him. The guards killed Chang and Koong-se set fire to the house while she was still inside it.*

The lovers perished and the gods immortalised them as two doves flying together in the sky.

If you look at a typical piece with the *Willow* pattern you will see most of the story. It's does sound like a nicely invented story to fit the intricacies of the pattern. A later variant of the *Willow* pattern was the *Mikado* pattern, this was a much more intricate version of the Willow pattern and was made by Carlton Ware almost throughout it's whole history. This pattern is very common as well as being very popular.

Carlton used some of the rudiments of the *Willow* pattern in many of their other Chinoiserie patterns including *New Mikado, Temple, Barge, Chinese Tea Garden, Chinese Figures, Mandarin Tree* and *Mandarins Chatting*.

New Mikado is a variant of the *Mikado* pattern. The tree designs have been changed and Storks have replaced the Kissing Doves. A photograph from the original Carlton Ware Pattern Books (see opposite page) shows a variant of the *New Mikado* pattern which is simply called Chinese Design.

Mikado - Pattern 4433
Large Ginger Jar from the Kosniowski Collection
£500 - £600

Illustration of a New Mikado Variant from an
Original Carlton Ware Pattern Book

Photograph courtesy of The Potteries Museum & Art Gallery,
Stoke-on-Trent

"4508 - Chinese on Jade Green (Enamel as 4419)"

Mikado - Pattern 2978
Medium Vase from the Margaret Jones Collection
Image courtesy of www.nicholnack.com.au
£100 - £150

Mikado - Pattern 2357
Large Vase from the Parnell Collection
Image courtesy of www.nicholnack.com.au
£150 - £200

New Mikado - Pattern 2728
Large Ginger Jar from the Kosniowski Collection
£500 - £600

Temple is a beautiful design that has an oriental scene of figures in a temple with a large circular doorway. In addition there are ornate trees and a golden sun.

A photograph from the original Carlton Ware Pattern Books (see below) shows the *Temple* design on a Crimson ground (pattern 4214). Note also the illustration of the Frieze design. The Text in the pattern book also mentions "MOP (Mother of Pearl) and Gold paint as in pattern 4204".

Temple - Pattern 3026
Bowl from the Margaret Jones Collection
Image courtesy of www.nicholnack.com.au
£150 - £200

Temple - Pattern 3129
Large Ginger Jar from the Kosniowski Collection
£600 - £700

Illustration of Temple design from an Original Carlton Ware Pattern Book
Photograph courtesy of The Potteries Museum & Art Gallery, Stoke-on-Trent
"4214 Aero Crimson"

Kang Hsi, pronounced as 'Kang she', is one of the very early depictions of the Chinoiserie design which replicates the early 17th century Chinese influence. This takes its name from the Emperor Kang Hsi who reigned during the Ching dynasty from 1662 to 1722. So quite fittingly this design features its own special back stamp.

Kang Hsi, like the *Mikado* pattern, featured a series of pagodas, temples and bridges but unlike *Mikado* included a bright golden sun.

Just to complicate matters, Carlton Ware introduced several other *Kang Hsi* designs each with the special back-stamps. These include one with cartouches of flowers and another with Fish.

Kien Lung is another Chinese design named after another of China's Emperors and was often produced on more colourful and highly glazed grounds. It has large Chinese symbols and cartouches containing birds and flowers.

Chinese Figures has an Oriental scene of figures, possibly an Emperor leaving the temple with servants in attendance. *Chinese Tea Garden*, although similar to *Chinese Figures*, depicts an oriental scene of figures enjoying refreshments in a pagoda garden. This describes the pattern accurately and you can imagine the tea being served and the Chinese enjoying it.

Mandarins Chatting has two Chinese figures chatting under a Mandarin tree. And that is exactly what the pattern is. We love the smiles on their faces, as if they are sharing some secret joke – possibly at us Carlton Ware collectors for paying so much for vases with this pattern! It is very elaborately decorated and usually appears on a high gloss finish in beautiful greens, yellows, black and rouge. This is a very desirable and sought after design for avid collectors.

Mandarin Tree is essentially the *Mandarins Chatting* design without the Mandarins! But it does have the lovely oriental and ornately enamelled trees.

Other beautiful and more rare patterns with the Chinese influence include *Chinese Bird*, which consists of a very exotic bird with attitude! It has a beautiful long curly tail; this includes some flower and cloud motifs. Similarly *Chinese Bird & Cloud* has the same exotic bird but this is set against a background of stylised cloud motifs and flowers.

New Chinese Bird has an exotic bird looking back angrily with long tail draping back but without the elaborate curly tail. Also, similarly, *New Chinese Bird and Cloud* has the same exotic bird looking back angrily whilst flying past some stylised clouds and flower heads. These patterns were introduced in the late 1920s, early 1930s.

Kang Hsi - Pattern 2021
Very Large Vase from the Kosniowski Collection
£500 - £600

Chinese Tea Garden - Pattern 2936
Medium Biscuit Barrel from the Kosniowski Collection
£150 - £200

Chinese Figures - Pattern 3199
Coffee Set from the Kosniowski Collection
£500 - £700

Chinese Bird & Cloud - Pattern 3275
Large Vase from the Kosniowski Collection
£550 - £750

Kien Lung - Pattern 2053
Large Temple Jar from the Kosniowski Collection
£300 - £400

New Mikado with Lady - Pattern 2814

Powder Bowl from the Kosniowski Collection
£100 - £150

Mandarins Chatting - Pattern 3654

Pair of Medium Ginger Jars from the Kosniowski Collection
£900 - £1,100 each

Kang Hsi - Pattern 2021

Pair of Medium Vases from the Kosniowski Collection
£500 - £600

Temple - Pattern 2971

Large Charger from the Kosniowski Collection
£400 - £500

Chinese Bird - Pattern 3197

Large Tray from the Kosniowski Collection
£400 - £500

Chinese Figures - Pattern 3199

Gondola from the Garratt-Frost Collection
£400 - £500

Mandarin Tree - Pattern 3719
Medium & Small Vase from the Kosniowski Collection
£950 - £1,250 & £400 - £600

Barge - Pattern 2519
Very Large Ginger Jar from the Kosniowski Collection
£600 - £750

Illustration of Mandarin Tree design from an Original Carlton Ware Pattern Book
Photograph courtesy of The Potteries Museum & Art Gallery, Stoke-on-Trent
"3791 as 3719 but Oven Blue in place of Green"

Finally we mustn't forget one more design with an oriental influence. This is the amazing design aptly named *Chinaland*. Many collectors consider this design very desirable, which is not surprising because of its elaborately detailed finish. The design consists of a complex and beautiful mixture of pagodas with hanging Chinese lanterns, tall trees, terraces, barges and usually a golden sun. The beautiful snow capped mountains are a particular feature of this design and are very realistic. We have seen some very small pieces without the mountains but still unmistakably *Chinaland*.

We could speculate that the mountains in the *Chinaland* pattern are based on "the roof of the world". Indeed Mount Everest (known in China as Mount Qomolangma) is on the Sino-Nepalese border and is the highest in the world. This leads to a romantic idea on why the pattern was introduced by Carlton Ware. It would have first been produced in the mid 1920s to the late 1920s. The first recorded attempts on climbing Everest, started with a reconnaissance in 1921. Seven attempts were made to climb Everest from Tibet, where a route to the summit seemed possible. All were unsuccessful. In 1953 Edmund Hillary and Tenzing Norgay reached the summit.

The *Chinaland* pattern usually has an intricate frieze in green, red and gilt. Another unique feature is a Roundel, which is circular colourful pattern consisting of oriental letters and symbols. This is found on top of some lids, on the inside of lids and in the centre of bowls and gondolas.

Chinaland is the only pattern, as far as we are aware, which has a coloured W&R logo on the base.

The ground colours that we have seen this lovely design on are orange, green, blue and red and they are all appear to have been finished with a highly lustred effect, which adds to the appearance of luscious opulence.

Chinaland - Pattern 3014
Large Ginger Jar from the Dulcie Agnes Joyce Memorial Collection
Image courtesy of www.nicholnack.com.au
£4,000 - £5,000

Chinaland - Pattern 2948
Ice Bucket from the Garratt-Frost Collection
£1,250 - £1,500

28

Chinaland - Pattern 2948

Large Ginger Jar from the Kosniowski Collection
£4,000 - £5,000

Chinaland - Patterns 2948, 3015

Tall Slender Ginger Jar (also below), Tall Vase and Two Spill vases
from the Kosniowski Collection
£1,500 - £2,000, £1,000 - £1,500, £400 - £500

Chinaland - Pattern 3014

Gondola from the Garratt-Frost Collection
£1,500 - £2,000

Chinaland Roundel and Unique Coloured Back Stamp

The Oriental Influence - Persian

The Persian influence appeared in the early 1920s and these pieces usually carry their own unique logo that includes a Star with the word Persian in it, in addition to the usual W & R Crown back stamp.

Persian is an ornate and elaborate design of very regal looking oriental figures in a temple with a tall domed roof that's reminiscent of the Taj Mahal. This is surrounded by a beautiful garden of flowers and palm trees. There are usually two white birds by the water. The lustre version of this design is really amazing with a very colourful design on a purple/blue high gloss finish. This design was made in powder blue, blue lustre, ivory with black frieze, pale cream with blue frieze and red.

Persian Garden is another really quite rare and beautiful design. This has small and large sprays of exotic enamelled flowers and foliage, some in colourful spires with star like heads. Sometimes the design has a magical tree with a variety of flower heads. This comes in three colour-ways, blue, black and green.

Babylon is, as the name suggests, reminiscent of the beautiful hanging Gardens of Babylon.

Persian Garden - Pattern 3893

Very Large Vase from the Kosniowski Collection

£2,500 - £3,000

Persian - Pattern 2884

Large Ginger Jar from the Kosniowski Collection

£650 - £800

Persian Garden - Pattern 3892

Small Vase from the Kosniowski Collection

£150 - £200

Babylon - Pattern 4125
Very Large Vase from the Kosniowski Collection
£1,600 - £2,000

Babylon - Pattern 4126
Large Vase from the Kosniowski Collection
£1,000 - £1,500

Babylon - Pattern 4125
Coffee Set from the Kosniowski Collection
£2,500 - £3,000

Another design similar to *Persian Garden* is *Persian Flowers*, also known as *Turkish*. It has a lavishly detailed enamelled flower design that comes on blue colourways. The frieze is particularly heavily gilded and enamelled and the design is very distinctive and unusual.

The Oriental Influence - Dragons

Dragons are fabulous winged animals that are usually represented as monstrous winged reptiles breathing fire. Most cultures appear to have Dragons in their mythology.

The western world usually views Dragons in a negative way and they are feared. They are loathsome beasts and evil enemies of the humans. On the other hand most of the eastern world views them as beautiful, friendly, and wise. They are treated much as the western world treats angels and instead of being hated, they are loved and worshipped.

Dragons feature in a number of Carlton Ware designs. The first patterns were produced in the 1910s. They featured ornate Oriental Dragons with a fierce expression and a long swirling body finished in gilt and colours. These were produced in a number of different colour ways with slightly different designs. The basic *Dragon* pattern was still in production towards the end of the Carlton Ware story. This was produced in the colour ways of black, yellow powder blue, orange, green armand lustre, rouge, blue lustre and white.

A later variation in the 1920s and 1930s was the introduction of a cartouche to produce the pattern *Dragon in Cartouche*. This featured a dragon in a panel together with a decorative frieze.

Also another variation at about the same time was the addition of a few clouds to the dragon to produce a pattern called *Dragon and Clouds*. The clouds were stylised and ornate. Several colour ways were produced with this pattern, deep blue, matt green, gloss red, matt blue and red.

Finally, by adding a human to the design and depicting a conflict between the dragon and human gives us a pattern called *Dragon and Traveller*. This consists of an oriental dragon confronting a Chinese traveller. Or, maybe it's an oriental seeking wisdom or worshipping the dragon. The dragon is decorated in many beautiful colours of enamel and nearby is a pretty weeping tree. A range of about five colour ways was produced, terracotta, turquoise, blue lustre, dark blue and yellow.

Persian Flowers or Turkish - Pattern 3050
Medium Vase from the Kosniowski Collection
£250 - £300

Dragon - Pattern 2064
Medium Ginger Jar from the Kosniowski Collection
£200 - £300

Dragon & Traveller - Pattern 3656
Medium Squat Vase from the Kosniowski Collection
£200 - £300

Dragon in Cartouche - Pattern 3145
Medium Vase from the Kosniowski Collection
£300 - £400

Dragon & Traveller - Pattern 3595
Large Tray from the Nicholas Pine Collection
£1,000 - £1,250

The influence of nature

It's inevitable that many non-abstract patterns produced by Carlton Ware were influenced by our surroundings, especially nature – animals, birds, trees, plants and flowers. This is not surprising as its diversity and beauty has captured the imagination and interest of most artists and designers over the centuries.

Carlton Ware were very successful at following trends and producing designs that were very evocative of the era. This began with the early Victorian Blush Ware, which mainly depicted naturalistic flower patterns with designs such as *Peony, Poppy, Violet, Azalea, Chrysanthemum* and *Camellia* to name but a few. These were and probably still are popular flowers found in the gardens and homes of Great Britain. These designs seemed to have been very desirable and popular to the Victorians. We looked at the Blush Ware and Flow Blue in earlier chapters, pages 8 to 15.

The early Black ground patterns also often depicted something from nature. These include *Chinese Quail* (a bird with a plumed tail sitting on a branch with foliage and flowers), *Stork* (depicting a White Stork and insets of colourful flowers and leaves), *Red Rose* and of course *Peach Blossom*.

It's interesting to note that producing a black ground on ceramics goes back a long way and can be achieved in a 'primitive' way by a technique known as 'Black Firing'. This involved heating a kiln to about 1,000C and then adding large amounts of sugar which volatises and impregnates the clay with carbon to give it a matt black surface.

Many of the embossed ranges from Carlton Ware were based on flora for example, *Blackberry, Raspberry, Buttercup, Apple Blossom* and *Orchid*. Other patterns included the *Crab* and *Lobster* range. We look at the embossed range in another chapter, page 160.

You can see the influence of nature on some of the Carlton China patterns. For example, *Fantail Birds on Branch* and *Birds and Trees*. More information on Carlton China may be found in a separate chapter, page 152.

Nature also had an influence on the Handcraft range. Indeed, many of the Handcraft designs were simplistic in style and often depicted floral themes but they were more abstract. Examples include *Cherry, Marigold* and *Honesty*. Further information about the Handcraft range may be found in another chapter, page 78.

Indeed nature has had an influence throughout the history of Carlton Ware.

Stork - Pattern 723
Large Vase from the Kosniowski Collection
£200 - £300

Chinese Quail - Pattern 522
Medium Tray from the Kosniowski Collection
£80 - £100

The influence of nature - Insects

Butterflies appeared in some patterns on a lesser scale with brief flitting parts and appearances. But they also featured exclusively in patterns such as the *Flies* design produced from the mid 1910s to the 1920s. The *Flies* pattern has a variety of realistic looking Moths and Butterflies in different stages of flight. Most are very intricate, colourful and detailed. About fifteen different colour-ways were produced, and most had an Armand back-stamp. The Armand back-stamp appeared on pieces with a mottled or sponged lustre effect fired under a high temperature.

Spider's Web is a beautiful design of fruiting berries at different stages of maturity with leaves and a pretty harebell and primula like flowers amongst spiky grasses. Suspended between these is a gossamer web with a spider in residence. There are also some brightly coloured dragonflies fluttering tantalisingly close by to complete the depiction of a warm summers morning. *Spider's Web* was very popular and was produced in about twenty different colour-ways.

Flies - Pattern 2134
Medium Vase from the Kosniowski Collection
£200 - £300

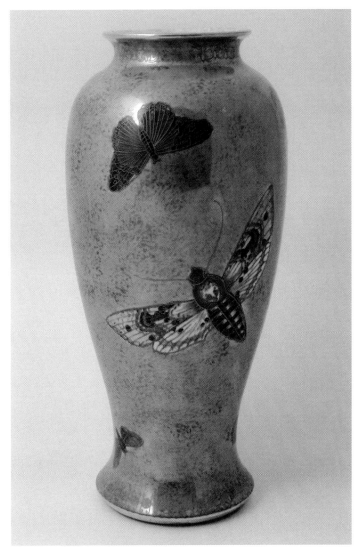

Flies - Pattern 2131
Tall Vase from the Kosniowski Collection
£200 - £300

New Flies - Pattern 3023
Small Bowl from the Kosniowski Collection
£100 - £200

Illustration of Spider's Web design from an Original Carlton Ware Pattern Book

Photograph courtesy of The Potteries Museum & Art Gallery, Stoke-on-Trent

"4244 Powder Blue Ground. Gold Paint as 4241"

Spider's Web - Pattern 4420

Coffee Set from the Kosniowski Collection

£600 - £750

Spider's Web - Pattern 4244

Pin Tray from the Kosniowski Collection
£20 - £40

Spider's Web - Pattern 4327

Tea Cup and Saucer from the Kosniowski Collection
£50 - £80

Illustration of Spider's Web design from an Original Carlton Ware Pattern Book

Photograph courtesy of The Potteries Museum & Art Gallery, Stoke-on-Trent

"4327 Yellow U/G. Gold as 4244"

Insects - Pattern 850
Cup & Saucer from the Parnell Collection
Image courtesy of www.nicholnack.com.au
£25 - £50

Butterfly - Pattern 4122
Small Vase from the Parnell Collection
Image courtesy of www.nicholnack.com.au
£40 - £70

Patterns were often "recycled". For example *Eden Canopy* is the same as *Eden* or *Tiger Tree* but without the tree. For pictures of *Eden* (*Tiger Tree*) see pages 46 and 47.

Illustration of Eden Canopy design from an Original Carlton Ware Pattern Book
Photograph courtesy of The Potteries Museum & Art Gallery, Stoke-on-Trent
"4248 as 4241 but no Tree, Ruby Ground"

The influence of nature - Plants

Many of the trees, flowers and plants loved and known by us all have appeared somewhere in the Carlton Ware designs.

Many of the plants and flowers included in the designs are stylised and more abstract than in real life. Some designs are very realistic. This includes the plants in the embossed series which are discussed in the chapter on the embossed range, page 160 onwards.

In this and the next few pages we illustrate part of the diverse range that Carlton Ware produced.

Bluebell - Pattern 3862
Large Vase from the Kosniowski Collection
£1,500 - £2,000

Primula & Leaf - Pattern 4121
Small Vase from the Kosniowski Collection
£50 - £80

Orange Blossom - Pattern 2723
Large Urn from the Kosniowski Collection
£200 - £300

Illustration of Gum Nut design from an Original Carlton Ware Pattern Book
Photograph courtesy of The Potteries Museum & Art Gallery, Stoke-on-Trent
"3789 As 3768 but Gold Traced Black in"

Gum Nut - Pattern 3794
Medium Vase (no lid) from the Kosniowski Collection
£60 - £80

Summer Flowers - Pattern 3926
Large Jug from the Kosniowski Collection
£300 - £400

Illustration of New Anemone design from an Original Carlton Ware Pattern Book
Photograph courtesy of The Potteries Museum & Art Gallery, Stoke-on-Trent
"4231, as 4219 but Pale Yellow Ground, Gold as 4108"

Illustration of 3958 Summer Flowers design from an Original Carlton Ware Pattern Book
Photograph courtesy of The Potteries Museum & Art Gallery, Stoke-on-Trent
"3958, as 3926 but no border. Aero Glaze as 3923"

41

Illustration of Lilac design from the Original Carlton Ware Pattern Book
Photograph courtesy of The Potteries Museum & Art Gallery, Stoke-on-Trent
"4279 Lilac, Grey Ground"

Illustration of Marguarite Daisy design from an Original Carlton Ware Pattern Book
Photograph courtesy of The Potteries Museum & Art Gallery, Stoke-on-Trent
"4277 Aero Yellow. Pale Green inside"

Illustration of Star Flower design from an
Original Carlton Ware Pattern Book
Photograph courtesy of The Potteries Museum &
Art Gallery, Stoke-on-Trent
"4215, Brown U/G, Aero Ruby, Stippled Stronger
Top & Bottom"

Illustration of Star Flower design from an Original Carlton Ware
Pattern Book
Photograph courtesy of The Potteries Museum & Art Gallery, Stoke-on-Trent
"4216, as 4215 Aero shaded Blue, Stippled Green & Blue Glaze"

Star Flower - Pattern 4215
Ash Tray from the Parnell Collection
Image courtesy of www.nicholnack.com.au
£50 - £75

Star Flower - Pattern 4216
Vase from the Parnell Collection
Image courtesy of www.nicholnack.com.au
£200 - £300

Parkland - Patterns 3524, 3523

Two Globular Vases from the Rodger Aitchison Collection

£600 - £750 each

Illustration of Eden (Tiger Tree) design from an Original Carlton Ware Pattern Book

Photograph courtesy of The Potteries Museum & Art Gallery, Stoke-on-Trent

"4242 Tree pattern, as 4241 but Blue & Black Ground"

Illustration of Eden (Tiger Tree) design from
an Original Carlton Ware Pattern Book
Photograph courtesy of The Potteries Museum & Art
Gallery, Stoke-on-Trent
"4241 Tree pattern, Stippled Ruby Ground"

Illustration of New Anemone design from an Original Carlton Ware Pattern Book
Photograph courtesy of The Potteries Museum & Art Gallery, Stoke-on-Trent
"4245 Turquoise & Pink Ground"

Illustration of Palm Blossom design from an Original
Carlton Ware Pattern Book
Photograph courtesy of The Potteries Museum & Art Gallery,
Stoke-on-Trent
"4278 Stippled Orange Lustre Ground"

Palm Blossom - Pattern 4297
Small Vase from the Parnell Collection
Image courtesy of www.nicholnack.com.au
£600 - £700

Bluebell - Pattern 3872
Large Vase from the Rodger Aitchison Collection
£1,500 - £2,000

Iceland Poppy - Pattern 3507
Part Tea Set from the Kosniowski Collection
£1,000 - £1,250

Iceland Poppy - Pattern 4221
Square Handled Bowl from the Kosniowski Collection
£500 - £750

Harebells - Patterns 4015, 4016
Large Jugs from the Rodger Aitchison Collection
£500 - £600 each

Harebells - Pattern 4016

Plate from the Parnell Collection
Image courtesy of www.nicholnack.com.au
£150 - £200

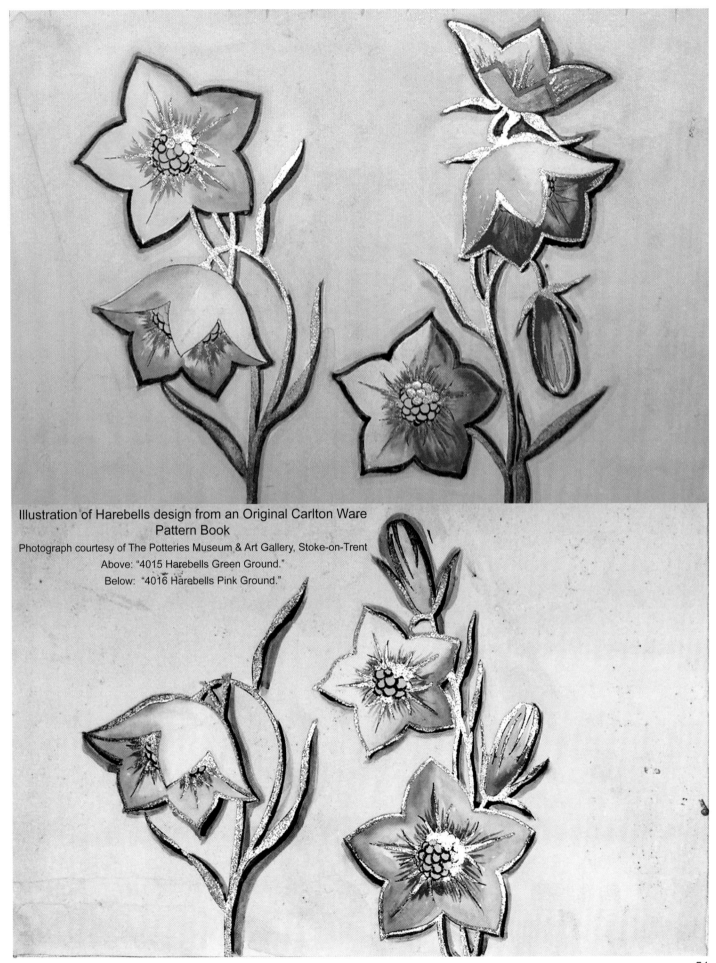

Illustration of Harebells design from an Original Carlton Ware
Pattern Book
Photograph courtesy of The Potteries Museum & Art Gallery, Stoke-on-Trent
Above: "4015 Harebells Green Ground."
Below: "4016 Harebells Pink Ground."

Victorian Garden - Pattern 3643

Vase from the Dulcie Agnes Joyce Memorial Collection
Image courtesy of www.nicholnack.com.au
£300 - £400

Prickly Pansy - Pattern 3455

Jug from the Ian & Jerome Collection
£600 - £800

Landscape Tree - Pattern 3141

Cup and Saucer from the Kosniowski Collection
£30 - £50

Sunflower - Pattern 3996

Cup and Saucer from the Kosniowski Collection
£40 - £60

Candy Flowers - Pattern 3669

Charger from the Parnell Collection
Image courtesy of www.nicholnack.com.au
£400 - £500

Norwegian Flowers - Pattern 3661

Vase from the Dulcie Agnes Joyce Memorial Collection
Image courtesy of www.nicholnack.com.au
£450 - £600

Illustration of Daydream design from an Original Carlton Ware Pattern Book

Photograph courtesy of The Potteries Museum & Art Gallery, Stoke-on-Trent

"4246 Sketching Freehand Pattern. White Matt Glaze"

Meadow - Pattern 3078

Cup and Saucer from the Kosniowski Collection

£30 - £50

Vine

Pattern 4480
Shape 1755

Ash Tray from the
Kosniowski Collection
£20 - £40

Daydream - Pattern 4246

Charger from the Dulcie Agnes Joyce Memorial Collection

Image courtesy of www.nicholnack.com.au

£400 - £600

Forest Tree - Pattern 3253
Above - Very Tall Slim Vase from the Kosniowski Collection
£400 - £600

Forest Tree - Pattern 3253
Upper Left - Large Vase from the Kosniowski Collection
£400 - £600

Forest Tree - Pattern 3240
Lower Left - Vase from the Parnell Collection
Image courtesy of www.nicholnack.com.au
£400 - £500

Forest Tree - Pattern 3244
Small Vase from the Parnell Collection
Image courtesy of www.nicholnack.com.au
£300 - £400

Forest Tree - Pattern 3244
Large Charger from the Kosniowski Collection
£700 - £900

Forest Tree - Pattern 3239
Coffee, Milk & Sugar from the Kosniowski Collection
£300 - £500

The influence of nature - Fish

Fish also featured in Carlton Ware patterns. These include *River Fish, Fish & Seaweed* and *Shabunkin. River Fish* is a beautiful design with realistic looking fish, which some people think resemble Carp. *Fish & Seaweed* depicts a more simplistic design with less elaborate fish swimming amongst long gilded seaweed. We are aware of 5 colour-ways Blue, Lemon, Pink, Powder Blue and Rouge.

Shabunkin depicts an ornamental and exotic brightly enamelled fish with flowing fins amongst exotic seabed plants. Some sources spell it as Shubunkin. The Shubunkin (Carassius auratus) is a type of goldfish. It is single-tailed and originally came from China. It differs from the wild Carp in that it has no barbells on the mouth area and has different markings at the base of the scales. The Shubunkin has a mottled pattern of white, black, and orange. It has also been called Speckled Goldfish as well as Harlequin Goldfish. The pattern is very striking. There seems to be two colour-ways of the pattern: Pale Blue and Yellow.

River Fish - Pattern 2441
Medium Bowl from the Kosniowski Collection
£100 - £130

Shabunkin - Pattern 3971
Velox Bowl from the Kosniowski Collection
£900 - £1,100

Shabunkin - Pattern 3970
Medium Ginger Jar from the Kosniowski Collection
£1,400 - £1,600

Shabunkin - Pattern 3970
Medium Charger from the Kosniowski Collection
£1,000 - £1,200

Shabunkin - Pattern 3971
Vase from the Dulcie Agnes Joyce Memorial Collection
Image courtesy of www.nicholnack.com.au
£1,000 - £1,250

River Fish - Pattern 2440
Ginger Jar (with no lid) from the Parnell Collection
Image courtesy of www.nicholnack.com.au
£300 - £350

Golden Pike
Vase from the Parnell Collection
Image courtesy of www.nicholnack.com.au
£75 - £100

Shabunkin - Pattern 3971

Large Vase from the Dulcie Agnes Joyce Memorial Collection

Image courtesy of www.nicholnack.com.au

£1,750 - £2,250

Shabunkin - Pattern 3970

Large Vase from the Kosniowski Collection

£1,500 - £2,000

Illustrations of Shabunkin design from an Original Carlton Ware Pattern Book
Photograph courtesy of The Potteries Museum & Art Gallery, Stoke-on-Trent
Above: "3970 Fish Design, Grey River Ground"
Below: "3971 Fish Design, Green & Ivory Ground"

The influence of nature - Birds

Birds feature in many Carlton Ware designs. There are over forty with pattern names that specify a bird in the title, see the Pattern List chapter for more details. Typical birds include *Stork, Worcester Birds, Love Birds, Long Tailed Bird & Tree Peony, Nightingale, New Storks, Duck, Magpies, Parrots* and *Humming Bird.*

Cock & Peony - Pattern 2250
Tall Handed Pair of Trumpet Vases from the Kosniowski Collection
£800 - £1,000

Rockery & Pheasant - Pattern 2041
Very Large Temple Jar from the Kosniowski Collection
£300 - £400

Cock & Peony - Pattern 2398
Square Dish from www.nicholnack.com.au
£200 - £300

Love Birds - Pattern 2326
Pair of Covered Vases from the Kosniowski Collection
£500 - £600

Pheasant Cartouche - Pattern 827
Covered Jars from the Parnell Collection
Image courtesy of www.nicholnack.com.au
£600 - £800

Worcester Birds - Pattern 2196
Cup & Saucer from the Kosniowski Collection
£60 - £80

Kingfisher - Pattern 2530
Handled Tray from the Parnell Collection
Image courtesy of www.nicholnack.com.au
£200 - £250

Birds & Blossom - Pattern 2089

Three Sectioned Tray from the Kosniowski Collection

£70 - £90

Nightingale - Pattern 3562

Powder Bowl from the Kosniowski Collection

£500 - £600

Nightingale - Pattern 3562

Tall Vase from the Kosniowski Collection

£900 - £1,000

Magpies

Large Vase from the Kosniowski Collection

£200 - £300

Parrots - Pattern 3018

Pair of Medium Vases from the Kosniowski Collection
£350 - £400

Malvern - Pattern 4801

Bud Vase & Bowls from the Kosniowski Collection
£75 - £90

Long Tailed Bird & Tree Peony - Pattern 2832

Powder Bowl from the Kosniowski Collection
£130 - £150

Humming Bird - Pattern 3462

Medium Ginger Jar from the Kosniowski Collection
£250 - £300

Chintzy Fat Bird

Large Ginger Jar from the Kosniowski Collection
£200 - £300

Birds on Bough - Pattern 3394

Revo Bowl from the Parnell Collection
Image courtesy of www.nicholnack.com.au
£250 - £300

Bird & Tree Peony - Pattern 2466

Plate from the Parnell Collection
Image courtesy of www.nicholnack.com.au
£30 - £50

Bird & Pine Cone - Pattern 3046

Tall Vase from the Dulcie Agnes Joyce Memorial Collection
Image courtesy of www.nicholnack.com.au
£350 - £400

Bird & Tree Peony

Biscuit Barrel from the Parnell Collection
Image courtesy of www.nicholnack.com.au
£150 - £200

Cretonne - Pattern 2913
Tall Vase from the Dulcie Agnes Joyce Memorial Collection
Image courtesy of www.nicholnack.com.au
£300 - £400

Blush Ware - Nouveau Bird & Flower
Biscuit Barrel from the Parnell Collection
Image courtesy of www.nicholnack.com.au
£150 - £200

Illustration of Wild Duck design from an Original Carlton Ware Pattern Book
Photograph courtesy of The Potteries Museum & Art Gallery, Stoke-on-Trent
"3947, as 3922 but Stippled Green Lustre Ground"

Wild Duck - Pattern 3923
Small Vase from the Kosniowski Collection
£50 - £70

Prunus & Bird - Pattern 2831
Large Dish from the Kosniowski Collection
£70 - £90

Illustration of Duck design from an Original Carlton Ware Pattern Book
Photograph courtesy of The Potteries Museum & Art Gallery, Stoke-on-Trent
"4459 Wild Duck as 4455 but Stippled Vert Ground"

Illustration of Fighting Cocks design from an Original Carlton Ware Pattern Book
Photograph courtesy of The Potteries Museum & Art Gallery, Stoke-on-Trent
"4199, as 4198 but Blue Lustre Ground"

Illustration of New Storks design from an Original Carlton Ware Pattern Book
Photograph courtesy of The Potteries Museum & Art Gallery, Stoke-on-Trent
"4304 Stork Pattern, Blown Green Ground, Blown Green Inside, Shaded at top & bottom in black."

New Storks - Pattern 4283

Small Vase from the Kosniowski Collection
£500 - £600

New Storks - Pattern 4340

Medium Dish from the Kosniowski Collection
£50 - £70

New Storks - Pattern 4339

Large Temple Jar from the Kosniowski Collection *£500 - £600*

Illustration of New Storks design

"4507 Stork & Tree on Jade Green Ground
as 4506, Enamel as 4421"

Tree & Swallow - Pattern 3384
Small Vase from the Kosniowski Collection
£200 - £300

Tree & Swallow - Pattern 3280
Medium Vase from the Kosniowski Collection
£200 - £300

Tree & Swallow - Pattern 3283
Coffee, Milk & Sugar from the Kosniowski Collection
£300 - £400

The influence of nature - Animals

Designs that feature land animals include *Rabbits at Dusk*, *Stag*, *The Hunt* and *Animal*. *Rabbits at Dusk* is a beautiful design which has rabbits playing amongst grasses, The rabbits are shown in silhouette under tall trees with green foliage. Pattern 4019 is called *Animal* and contains a decorative landscape with various woodland animals namely a Squirrel, Deer or Fox.

Rabbits at Dusk - Pattern 4247
Large Serpent Vase from the Kosniowski Collection
£800 - £1,000

Fairy Dell - Pattern 3665
Large Charger, from Kent Auction Galleries
£500 - £600

Rabbits at Dusk - Pattern 4257
Large Fruit Platter from the Parnell Collection
Image courtesy of www.nicholnack.com.au
£400 - £600

Animal - Fox - Pattern 4019
Charger from the Dulcie Agnes Joyce Memorial Collection
Image courtesy of www.nicholnack.com.au
£2,000 - £2,500

The Hunt - Pattern 2962
Cigarette Vase from the Kosniowski Collection
£20 - £30

Illustration of Rabbits at Dusk design from
an Original Carlton Ware Pattern Book
Photograph courtesy of The Potteries Museum & Art
Gallery, Stoke-on-Trent
"4247 Rabbit Tree pattern, Orange Ground, Liq Gold
Edge only"

Illustration of Rabbits at Dusk design from an Original
Carlton Ware Pattern Book
Photograph courtesy of The Potteries Museum & Art Gallery, Stoke-on-Trent
"4257, as 4256 but Aero U/G Green and Stipple Blue, Liq Gold Edge only"

Carlton Ware produced a number of Animal Figures; we have included some of those here.

Some animals were produced in the Crested Ware range – please see the chapter on Crested Ware, page 16.

Some figures of dogs were produced under the Carlton China back stamp. We have included some pictures here. They are reminiscent of the Royal Doulton style and are finished in naturalistic colours (further information about Carlton China may be found in a later chapter, page 152).

Glacielle Ware was a range that Carlton Ware introduced in 1937 presumably they wanted to create a more distinctive and luxurious design of ornaments than the usual matt glazed figures that were being produced by their competitors. This was most certainly the case with Glacielle, which soon received the royal seal of approval when it was reported to have been "greatly admired and purchased" by Queen Mary and the Duchess of Gloucester at a British Industries Fair.

The unusual texture of the glaze finish was described as "resembling melting snow and reminiscent of melting ice" hence the name which aptly describes the attributes of a glacier. This probably sums up the effect quite well.

The ranges consisted of mainly animal studies in realistic form. In addition the range included a vase (with or without a neck) which was adorned with a beautiful realistic green lizard in a raised relief style attached to the front of the vase. You can find all the known examples of Glacielle Ware by checking the list of Shapes towards the end of this book starting at page 240.

Stone Ware, as it is named, was introduced around 1934 or 1935 and had a ribbed effect with unusual varying angles. There were numerous shapes produced consisting of jugs, vases, bowls etc. There are also amusing animal designs

depicting a dog, rat, goose, penguin and a rabbit. They were generally produced in a matt glaze although some were finished in a high glaze.

The term Stone Ware appears both in the Shape Books as well as the Patterns Books. Please see the chapter on Old Stone Ware on page 202.

You can find which animal figures were produced by checking the list of Shapes towards the end of this book starting at page 240.

Stone Ware - Shapes 1181, 1180
Penguin & Goose from Zeichen Antiques
£150 - £200, £250 - £300

Stone Ware - Shape 1103
Dogs from Zeichen Antiques
£150 - £200 each

Carlton Animal - Shape 1442

Fox Terrier & Sealyham Terrier from www.carltonchina.info

£100 - £150 each

Carlton Animal - Shape 1445

Spaniels from www.carltonchina.info

£100 - £150 each

Glacielle Ware - Shape 1423

Lion Cubs from Zeichen Antiques

£400 - £450

Glacielle Ware - Shape 1475

Greyhounds from Zeichen Antiques

£450 - £500

Glacielle Ware - Shape 1469

Alsatian Dogs from Zeichen Antiques

£450 - £500

Glacielle Ware - Shape 1426

Lioness from Zeichen Antiques

£450 - £500

Tutankhamen

King Tutankhamen (1336-1327 B.C.)

Carlton Ware designers, as with most designers, were very aware of what was happening in the world. This would often influence their designs. Carlton Ware decided to celebrate the opening of the tomb of Tutankhamen by producing a range of beautifully decorated ceramics depicting symbols of the young Pharaoh. A beautiful way to commemorate this momentous occasion!

In 1922 the intrepid Egyptologist Howard Carter show cased the grand unveiling of the burial chamber and its treasures that lay with the body of the boy King. This was followed with enormous interest by the media of the time and was hailed as the event of the year.

Howard Carter was excavating on behalf of his patron Lord Carnarvon. Carter had been searching for the tomb for a number of years and Carnarvon had decided that enough time and money had been spent with no return. Fortunately Carter managed to persuade Lord Carnarvon to fund just one more season. Within days of resuming the excavation, the tomb was found in November 1922.

There was little in the way of documentation found within his tomb and we still know relatively little about Tutankhamen. He was the 12th King of the 18th Dynasty and nine years old at his succession in about 1336 BC. The boy king died in his late teens and was buried in Egypt's "Valley of the Kings" where he laid at rest for over 3,300 years until November 1922.

Carlton Ware introduced their *Tutankhamen* range soon afterwards. This is a very desirable and highly collectable design, quite rare and usually commands very high prices. The pattern contains elaborately decorated Egyptian figures, motifs and symbols that were inspired by the very artefacts unearthed from the burial chambers. They were very symbolic of the young kings life that would enable him to continue his deity in the after-world. These included enthroned figures of Tutankhamen, depicted as the Sun God RA and magnificent barges that would escort the Pharaoh on his journey to the gods. Also depicted is the beautiful winged figure of the goddess Isis. She embodied the qualities of wifely fidelity and maternal feelings. She was endowed with magical powers and was the protector goddess, guarding coffins and a divine mourner for the dead.

The most famous mask in the world, the Death Mask was made in Tutankhamen's image. Made of solid gold, it was placed directly upon the Pharaoh's mummy, and had the function of magically protecting him. The original weighed 10 kg (24 lbs) and was decorated with many semiprecious stones. This design is used as a magnificent feature for a finial or as part of the lid for certain Carlton Ware pieces in this range.

The *Tutankhamen* design was produced in many colour ways including white, orange, gloss mother of pearl, matt black, powder blue, gloss light & dark blue, and gloss light blue & yellow.

Tutankhamen - Pattern 2686
Medium Temple Jar from the Ian & Jerome Collection
£1,000 - £1,500

Tutankhamen - Pattern 2780
Medium Bowl from the Parnell Collection
Image courtesy of www.nicholnack.com.au
£600 - £800

Tutankhamen - Pattern 2711

Very large Ginger Jar with Death Mask from the Kosniowski Collection

£5,000 - £6,000

Tutankhamen - Pattern 2711
Large Footed Square Bowl from the Kosniowski Collection
£1,000 - £1,250

Tutankhamen - Pattern 3404
Floating Bowl from the Ian & Jerome Collection
£600 - £750

Tutankhamen - Pattern 2711
Powder Bowl from the Kosniowski Collection
£700 - £800

Tutankhamen - Pattern 2711

Pair of Vases and a Tall Slender Ginger Jar
from the Kosniowski Collection
£2,000 - £2,500 and £1,500 - £2,000

Tutankhamen - Pattern 2711

Large Bowl from the Kosniowski Collection
£600 - £800

Tutankhamen - Pattern 2709

Large Bowl from the Kosniowski Collection
£500 - £700

Handcraft

Carlton Ware designs were influenced by events and trends of the day. In the early 1920s Carlton Ware were producing many highly decorated pieces including Chinoiserie designs and lustre ware that were very popular at the time (and are still very popular now and collected exclusively).

By the late 1920s the advent of what we now call the Art Deco period was growing in popularity. Tastes were changing and it was not surprising to find that Carlton Ware moved with the times. By the early 1930s Carlton Ware were competing with the other Art Deco designers with their Handcraft range. It seems that they were influenced by the fact that others were producing freehand painted pottery.

The early Handcraft designs were simplistic in style and often depicted floral themes but they were more abstract. The freehand painted Handcraft range permitted more freedom of expression and design; and Carlton Ware could avoid investing in expensive lithographs or transfers. This meant that greater risks could be taken. A pattern could be quickly produced; and, if it didn't sell well then it could be discontinued. The risk was minimal. Partly because of this a large number of different Handcraft patterns were produced. Some are rare simply because they were unpopular at the time and consequently only a few copies were made.

The Handcraft pattern numbers are in the three thousand number range. The early Handcraft was generally a floral design, on a matt ground and with a blue, mauve, yellow and black colouring. This was possibly less adventurous than the bright colours and the colour bandings used by Clarice Cliff. But then at least, they couldn't be accused of merely copying! These early Handcraft patterns include the following: *Floral Scallops, Shamrock, Floribunda, Flowering Papyrus, Orchid, Marigold, Cherry, Delphinium, Honesty, Marrakesh* and *Stellata* or *Wild Cherry*. The *Cherry* patterns introduced a bit of red colour in the design, but that tended to be the exception with the early Handcraft.

The Handcraft designs were at the time described by the Pottery Gazette and Glass Trade Review as "cutting out the high lights that were associated with the brilliantly glazed and lustred pottery". The Handcraft era went on to be described as "truly decorative and impressive" and praised the elimination of details and the massing of chunks of ornament. This was in contrast to the previous highly decorated pieces including Chinoiserie designs and lustre ware.

In contrast to the very early designs of Handcraft, the next phase saw patterns with a slightly more adventurous use of contrasting colours as well as more "zig-zag" and angular shapes as well as a move away from floral designs. These designs were evolving into what we now call the Art Deco Period, and were of course very dependant upon the skills of the local painters and designers to produce eye-catching and fashionable freehand decoration with its own distinct appearance and appeal.

Flowering Papyrus - Pattern 3242
Medium Vase from the Kosniowski Collection
£300 - £400

Marigold - Pattern 3271
Medium Ginger Jar from the Kosniowski Collection
£300 - £350

The *Orchid* pattern and the *Stellata* or *Wild Cherry* pattern were reintroduced in different colour ways. Most Handcraft patterns appear to have been produced in one colour way. A few were produced in two colour ways whilst *Zig Zag* seems to have been produced in three colour ways.

The range of Handcraft extending the early Handcraft included *Farrago, Zig Zag, Carnival, Flower & Cloud, Pomona, Gentian, Stag, Scroll, Aurora, Sagitta, Arrowhead, Cherry, Holly* and *Metropolis*.

The next phase of Handcraft moves away from the restricted colour ranges and begins to sometimes incorporate a use of lustre. Many collectors believe that some of the finest art deco design is in the Handcraft range.

Some of the patterns such as *Iris, New Delphinium* and *Clematis* were very similar to the very early designs from the first phase of Handcraft. We can also see a move towards some use of transfers and an abandonment of the Matt finish with the amazingly colourful *Anemone* pattern. The *Russian* and *Hiawatha* patterns are very bold and strikingly designed.

The final phase of the Handcraft designs included *Camouflage, Peach Melba, Iris, Clematis, New Delphinium, Tree & Cottage, Geometrica, Russian, Green Trees, Mondrian, Hiawatha, Gazania, Chevrons, Carre, Summer Medley, Tiger Lily, Intersection, Lightning* and *Anemone*.

There is some confusion with the Handcraft back stamp as some pieces were probably stamped as Handcraft purely because they were finished in Matt and were of the more simplistic design. Thus some Carlton Ware had the Handcraft back-stamp when perhaps they shouldn't have. And conversely some that perhaps should have had the back-stamp didn't. It's possible that the Handcraft logo was no longer required as the transition was complete and the range had achieved the goal and led to other celebrated designs.

Shamrock - Pattern 3235
Cup & Saucer from the Kosniowski Collection
£80 - £100

Cherry - Pattern 3272
Large Vase from the Kosniowski Collection
£350 - £450

Iris - Pattern 3498
Small Vase from the Kosniowski Collection
£150 - £200

Shamrock - Pattern 3235
Medium Vase from the Kosniowski Collection
£250 - £300

Floribunda - Pattern 3236
Spill Vase from the Kosniowski Collection
£75 - £100

Honesty - Pattern 3278
Ginger Jar from the Dulcie Agnes Joyce Memorial Collection
Image courtesy of www.nicholnack.com.au
£300 - £400

Orchid - Pattern 3255

Large Candle Stick from the Kosniowski Collection
£100 - £150

Orchid - Pattern 3325

Medium Vase from the Dulcie Agnes Joyce Memorial Collection
Image courtesy of www.nicholnack.com.au
£300 - £400

Orchid - Pattern 3255

Medium Vase from the Kosniowski Collection
£250 - £350

Delphinium - Pattern 3273
Large Tray from the Kosniowski Collection
£300 - £400

Stellata - Pattern 3291
Tall Vase from the Dulcie Agnes Joyce Memorial Collection
Image courtesy of www.nicholnack.com.au
£200 - £300

Farrago - Pattern 3297
Vase from the Dulcie Agnes Joyce Memorial Collection
Image courtesy of www.nicholnack.com.au
£350 - £500

Lightning
Vase from the Dulcie Agnes Joyce Memorial Collection
Image courtesy of www.nicholnack.com.au
£200 - £250

Carnival - Pattern 3305
Vase from the Dulcie Agnes Joyce Memorial Collection
Image courtesy of www.nicholnack.com.au
£600 - £750

Lightning - Pattern 3692
Large Jug from the Kosniowski Collection
£200 - £300

Stag - Pattern 3359
Vase from the Dulcie Agnes Joyce Memorial Collection
Image courtesy of www.nicholnack.com.au
£1,000 - £1,500

Garden - Pattern 3390
Pair of Medium Vases from the Kosniowski Collection
£600 - £700

Seagulls - Pattern 3502
Vase from the Dulcie Agnes Joyce Memorial Collection
Image courtesy of www.nicholnack.com.au
£1,750 - £2,250

Garden - Pattern 3501
Pair of Small Lidded Jars from the Kosniowski Collection
£400 - £600

Camouflage - Pattern 3440
Revo Bowl from the Parnell Collection
Image courtesy of www.nicholnack.com.au
£500 - £700

Jigsaw - Pattern 3431
AshTray from the Parnell Collection
Image courtesy of www.nicholnack.com.au
£200 - £300

Holly - Pattern 3418
Jug from the Dulcie Agnes Joyce Memorial Collection
Image courtesy of www.nicholnack.com.au
£600 - £700

Green Trees - Pattern 3569
Charger from the Dulcie Agnes Joyce Memorial Collection
Image courtesy of www.nicholnack.com.au
£200 - £250

Peach Melba - Pattern 3448
Vase from the Dulcie Agnes Joyce Memorial Collection
Image courtesy of www.nicholnack.com.au
£100 - £150

Dutch - Pattern 3250
Medium Vase from the Kosniowski Collection
£250 - £350 (very rare)

Cherry - Pattern 3417
Small Vase from the Dulcie Agnes Joyce Memorial Collection
Image courtesy of www.nicholnack.com.au
£150 - £200

Geometrica - Pattern 3566
Vase from the Dulcie Agnes Joyce Memorial Collection
Image courtesy of www.nicholnack.com.au
£1,250 - £1,500

Metropolis - Pattern 3420
Small Vase from the Kosniowski Collection
£400 - £450

Rudolf's Posy - Pattern 3408
Jug from the Parnell Collection
Image courtesy of www.nicholnack.com.au
£1,000 - £1,500

Russian - Pattern 3567
Vase from the Dulcie Agnes Joyce Memorial Collection
Image courtesy of www.nicholnack.com.au
£1,500 - £2,000

New Rainbow
Charger from the Dulcie Agnes Joyce Memorial Collection
Image courtesy of www.nicholnack.com.au
£2,000 - £2,500

Hiawatha - Pattern 3590
Vase from the Dulcie Agnes Joyce Memorial Collection
Image courtesy of www.nicholnack.com.au
£400 - £500

Hiawatha - Pattern 3589
Large Bowl from the Kosniowski Collection
£200 - £300

Eclipse - Pattern 3551
Cup & Saucer from the Dulcie Agnes Joyce Memorial Collection
Image courtesy of www.nicholnack.com.au
£200 - £300

Carre - Pattern 3659
Milk Jug from the Dulcie Agnes Joyce Memorial Collection
Image courtesy of www.nicholnack.com.au
£60 - £80

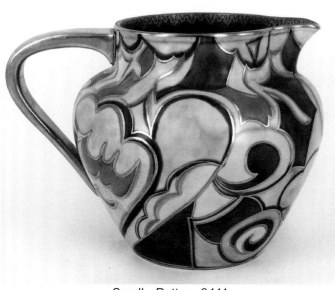

Scroll - Pattern 3411
Jug from the Parnell Collection
Image courtesy of www.nicholnack.com.au
£400 - £500

Lazy Daisy - Pattern 3414
Vase from the Dulcie Agnes Joyce Memorial Collection
Image courtesy of www.nicholnack.com.au
£400 - £500

Wind & Flower - Pattern 3508
Footed Cigarette Box from the Dulcie Agnes Joyce Memorial Collection
Image courtesy of www.nicholnack.com.au
£200 - £300

Gazania - Pattern 3592
Tray from the Dulcie Agnes Joyce Memorial Collection
Image courtesy of www.nicholnack.com.au
£300 - £400

Clematis - Pattern 3525
Vase from the Lexi James Collection
Image courtesy of www.nicholnack.com.au
£200 - £300

Sagitta - Pattern 3415
Vase from the Lexi James Collection
Image courtesy of www.nicholnack.com.au
£500 - £600

Intersection - Pattern 3690
Small Vase from the Parnell Collection
Image courtesy of www.nicholnack.com.au
£500 - £750

Summer Medley - Pattern 3663
Large Charger from the Dulcie Agnes Joyce Memorial Collection
Image courtesy of www.nicholnack.com.au
£1,250 - £1,750

Anemone - Pattern 3694
Square Bowl from the Kosniowski Collection
£500 - £750

Strata - Pattern 3553
Coffee Pot from the Parnell Collection
Image courtesy of www.nicholnack.com.au
£350 - £450

Aurora - Pattern 3412
Medium Vase from the Kosniowski Collection
£400 - £500

Anemone - Pattern 3694
Large Temple Jar from the Kosniowski Collection
£3,000 - £3,500

The *Anemone* pattern usually has a "Handcraft" back stamp but differs from the other Handcraft pieces by being produced in a Lustre rather than a Matt finish.

Anemone - Pattern 3694
Large Ginger Jar from the Kosniowski Collection
£3,000 - £3,500

The Jazz Age

The freehand painted patterns in the Handcraft range were introduced in response to the dawning of the new minimalist modern era of the late 1920s to the 1930s.

The reputation of Carlton Ware was based on its best wares, the popular and beautiful lustre and Chinoiserie designs. Carlton Ware needed to produce designs that would help them to compete with the other potteries that were moving into the new fashion for Art Deco. These were namely Clarice Cliff and Poole pottery, who had been producing the new designs since 1928.

So the priority was to produce their own range of designs but they had to have Carlton Ware's own distinct appearance. They would need to touch the imagination of the public but they needed to be fairly inexpensive to produce so they could test the market. Freehand painted wares dispensed with the need of expensive lithographs and copper plates so if patterns were unsuccessful they could be easily replaced with others.

This next phase saw Carlton Ware producing Handcraft patterns with a slightly more adventurous use of contrasting colours as well as more "zig-zag" and angular shapes and a move away from floral designs. These designs were evolving into what we now call the Art Deco Period and International Modernism. This is more obvious with the beautifully angular designs such as *Chevrons, Carre', Intersections* and *Lightning*. The pattern *Geometrica*, with its over and under glazing along with some use of transfer, is considered a classic of its time.

Thus the advent of the freehand painted Handcraft range enabled Carlton Ware to introduce its first Art Deco patterns. The success and daring of this range launched Carlton Ware into the way forward and influenced them to produce some of their most celebrated Lustre Art Deco designs. These designs include: *Sunflower Geometric, Jazz, Fan, Floral Comets, Fantasia, Explosion, Explosion & Butterfly, Awakening, Jazz Poppy, Crested Bird and Water Lily, Deco Fan, Strata, Ziggarette, Nightingale, Fairy Shadow, Kaleidoscopic, Scimitar, Bathing Belle., Egyptian Fan, Rainbow Fan* and *Bell*. The next chapter looks further into the Art Deco designs.

What had begun as an attempt to compete in the competitive market place had truly ushered Carlton Ware into the Art Deco era in style.

Zig Zag - Pattern 3299
Velox Bowl from the Ian & Jerome Collection
£2,500 - £3,000

Jazz Poppy - Pattern 3503
Small Vase from the Ian & Jerome Collection
£400 - £500

The Art Deco & Best Ware period

The Art Deco period was a popular international art design movement which affected many of the decorative arts such as interior design, visual arts, fashion and architecture this style was seen as elegant, glamorous, functional and modern.

The movement was influenced by a mixture of many different styles of the early 20th century, including Neoclassical, Constructivism, Cubism, Modernism, Art Nouveau, and Futurism. Although many design movements have political or philosophical roots or intentions, Art Deco was purely decorative. Its popularity peaked in Europe during the roaring twenties.

Various French artists strongly influenced the principles of Art Deco. The founders included Grasset, Lachenal, Bellot, Decoeur and Dufrene. They got together to form *"the society of decorative arts"* known as, *La Société des artistes décorateur*. They organized the 1925 *Exposition Internationale des Arts Décoratifs et Industriels Modernes* (International Exposition of Modern Industrial and Decorative Art) in Paris. Borne out of a desire to feature French business and decorative arts interests. The terms Style Moderne and Art Deco both derive from the exposition's title. The term Art Deco was not widely used until the art historian Bevis Hillier's book in 1968 "Art Deco of the 20s and 30s".

The structure and form of Art Deco is exhibited on aspects of abstraction based on mathematical geometric stylised shapes of chevrons, zigzags and jumbled shapes. But it also made use of many distinctive features with a dependence upon a range of ornaments and motifs with highly intensive colours. It was considered to be an elegant style of cool sophistication. The French designers showed a style that was a reaction to the fussiness of Art Nouveau with its emphasis on individual craftsman made pieces.

It was widely considered to be an eclectic form of elegant and stylish modernism being influenced by a variety of sources. Its opulence was in stark contrast to the forced austerity of World War 1 as its eclectic lavishness focused on quality and not quantity.

The purity of Art Deco, after reaching mass production slowly lost its attraction in the West when it began to be considered as garish and presenting a false image of luxury in opposition to the austerities of World War II.

Pottery from the 1920s and 1930s is now often synonymous with Art Deco. For many people, the designers that first come to mind are Clarice Cliff and Susie Cooper. Although they may be the most well known of the pottery designers, Carlton Ware also produced some stunning work

Clarice Cliff is probably the most collected of the Art Deco

Cubist Butterfly - Pattern 3190
Partial Dressing Table Set from the Kosniowski Collection
£200 - £250

Cubist Butterfly - Pattern 3194
Small Vase from the Parnell Collection
Image courtesy of www.nicholnack.com.au
£250 - £400

ceramic designers and Bizarre is her most famous range of pottery. It is characterised by its geometric shapes, bright colours and the colour bandings. As with all pottery, views about the quality of her work is divided.

Susie Cooper's work was less geometric in shape. She also experimented with decorative techniques and patterns. Her use of colour is much more subdued and autumnal than that of Clarice Cliff.

The reputation of Carlton Ware in the 1920s was based largely on its lustre products, especially the Chinoiserie designs. With the popularity of Art Deco it was not surprising to find that Carlton Ware moved with the times. Carlton Ware had to find ways of competing with the other potteries and the designs of Cliff and Cooper. One of the early Art Deco designs is *Cubist Butterfly* (bold stylised flowers, berries and butterflies). This was produced in a number of colour ways such as matt red, blue, orange, green and semi-matt blue.

Another well-known and stunning Art Deco pattern is *Jazz* (geometric design with brightly coloured lightning flashes, bands and small bubbles). This was produced in three colour ways, red lustre, orange lustre and blue lustre.

Many more designs were produced admirably with the very creative designer Violet Elmer who created many of the well known and loved designs that are collected prolifically today. Many of her designs are now considered as Art Deco such as, *Floral Comets, Fantasia, Explosion, Awakening, Fan, Scimitar, Egyptian Fan, Mandarins Chatting, Rainbow Fan, Bell, Chevrons, Wagon Wheels, Intersection, Flower & Falling Leaf* and *Tyrolean Bands* to name some.

Awakening - Pattern 3450
Part of Coffee Set from the Kosniowski Collection

Awakening - Pattern 3497

Vase from the Ian & Jerome Collection

£2,500 - £3,000

Awakening - Pattern 3450

Coffee Set from the Kosniowski Collection

£2,500 - £3,000

Floral Comets - Pattern 3422
Medium Ovoid Vase from the Kosniowski Collection
£1,000 - £1,250

Floral Comets - Pattern 3387
Small Ginger Jar from the Kosniowski Collection
£400 - £550

Floral Comets - Pattern 3405
Small Covered Vase from the Kosniowski Collection
£500 - £800

Floral Comets - Pattern 3405
Powder Bowl from the Kosniowski Collection
£600 - £800

Floral Comets - Pattern 3387
Medium Ovoid Vase from the Kosniowski Collection
£450 - £600

Floral Comets - Pattern 3387
Large Jug from the Kosniowski Collection
£500 - £600

Floral Comets - Pattern 3405

Large Charger from the Kosniowski Collection

£1,500 - £2,000

Illustration of Flower and Falling Leaf
design from an Original Carlton Ware
Pattern Book
Photograph courtesy of The Potteries Museum & Art
Gallery, Stoke-on-Trent

"3948 Green ground"

Flower and Falling Leaf - Pattern 3948
Medium Bowl from the Kosniowski Collection
£500 - £700

Flower and Falling Leaf - Pattern 3948
Medium Ginger Jar from the Ian & Jerome Collection
£750 - £900

Illustration of Flower and Falling Leaf design from the Original Carlton Ware Pattern Book
Photograph courtesy of The Potteries Museum & Art Gallery, Stoke-on-Trent
"3949 Stippled Ruby Ground"

Flower and Falling Leaf - Pattern 3949
Large Dish from the Ian & Jerome Collection
£700 - £800

Illustration of Flower and Falling Leaf design from
the Original Carlton Ware Pattern Book
Photograph courtesy of The Potteries Museum & Art Gallery,
Stoke-on-Trent
"3950 Cream and yellow Ground"

Flower and Falling Leaf - Pattern 3949
Medium Vase from the Ian & Jerome Collection
£2,500 - £3,000

Flower and Falling Leaf - Pattern 3949
Medium Vase from the Rodger Aitchison Collection
£1,500 - £2,000

Deco Fan - pattern 3552
Cup & Saucer from the Parnell Collection
Image courtesy of www.nicholnack.com.au
£200 - £300

Fan - Pattern 3558
Pair of Large Vases from the Kosniowski Collection
£1,250 - £1,500 each

Fan - Pattern 3557

Large Rocket vase from the Kosniowski Collection

£800 - £1,000

Fan - Pattern 3557

Biscuit Barrel the Kosniowski Collection

£600 - £700

Fan - Pattern 3558

Footed Conical Bowl from the Kosniowski Collection

£1,250 - £1,500

Fan - Pattern 3557

Pair of Medium Vases from the Kosniowski Collection

£500 - £600 each

Egyptian Fan - Pattern 3695
Large Bowl from the Kosniowski Collection
£750 - £1,000

Egyptian Fan - Pattern 3695
Large Tray from the Kosniowski Collection
£1,000 - £1,250

Egyptian Fan - Pattern 3696
Footed Conical Bowl from the Kosniowski Collection
£1,500 - £1,750

Egyptian Fan - Pattern 3696
Large Gondola from the Kosniowski Collection
£1,250 - £1,500

Rainbow Fan - Pattern 3700
Medium Vase from the Kosniowski Collection
£3,250 - £3,750

Rainbow Fan - Pattern 3700
Inkwell and Pen Stand from the Kosniowski Collection
£1,250 - £1,500

Bell - Pattern 3786
Large Jug from the Kosniowski Collection
£750 - £1,000

Bell - Pattern 3788
Conical Bowl from the Kosniowski Collection
£1,250 - £1,500

Illustration of Bell
design from an
Original Carlton Ware
Pattern Book
Photograph courtesy of The
Potteries Museum & Art
Gallery, Stoke-on-Trent
"3786, as 3744 but Stippled
Green Ground"

Illustration of Bell design
from an Original Carlton
Ware Pattern Book
Photograph courtesy of The
Potteries Museum & Art Gallery,
Stoke-on-Trent
"3788, as 3774 but Stippled Ruby
Ground"

Bell - Pattern 3788
Small Ginger Jar from the Kosniowski Collection
£650 - £800

Bell - Pattern 3774
Medium Squat Vase from the Ian & Jerome Collection
£1,200 - £1,500

Bell - Pattern 3855
Small Squat Vase from the Kosniowski Collection
£600 - £750

Bell - Pattern 3792
Small Vase from the Ian & Jerome Collection
£400 - £500

Illustration of Bell design from an Original Carlton Ware Pattern Book

Photograph courtesy of The Potteries Museum & Art Gallery, Stoke-on-Trent

"3774, Brown U/G"

Illustration of Bell design from an Original Carlton Ware Pattern Book

Photograph courtesy of The Potteries Museum & Art Gallery, Stoke-on-Trent

"3792, as 3788 but Powder Blue Ground and No Black Shadows"

Bell - Pattern 3786
Two Medium Vases from the
Kosniowski Collection
£600 - £750 each

Bell - Pattern 3788
Medium Ginger Jar from the Kosniowski Collection
£900 - £1,100

Illustration of Devil design from an Original Carlton Ware Pattern Book

Photograph courtesy of The Potteries Museum & Art Gallery, Stoke-on-Trent

"3767 Wedgewood Blue Ground MOP inside"

"3767A No Devil"

Illustration of Devil design from the Original Carlton Ware Pattern Book

Photograph courtesy of The Potteries Museum & Art Gallery, Stoke-on-Trent

"3769 Cream Ground"

"3769A No Devil"

Red Devil - Pattern 3765
Medium vase from the Kosniowski Collection
£2,000 - £2,500

Devil's Copse - Pattern 3767
Medium Conical Bowl from the Kosniowski Collection
£1,500 - £2000

Devil's Copse - Pattern 3767
Medium Vase from the Kosniowski Collection
£900 - £1,100

Red Devil - Pattern 3767
Large Jug from the Kosniowski Collection
£1,500 - £2,000

Red Devil - Pattern 3769
Medium Conical Bowl from the Kosniowski Collection
£2,250 - £2,750

Devil's Copse - Pattern 3787
Large Gondola from the Kosniowski Collection
£950 - £1,150

Notice that the Devil's Copse Pattern is the same as the Red Devil Pattern except that the Devil has been omitted.

Red Devil - Pattern 3765
Biscuit Barrel from the Kosniowski Collection
£2,500 - £3,000

Devil's Copse - Pattern 3787
Very large waisted Vase from the Kosniowski Collection
£1,250 - £1,500

Devil's Copse - Pattern 3787
Large Charger from the Kosniowski Collection
£1,200 - £1,500

Devil's Copse - Pattern 3787
Three large Vases from the Kosniowski Collection, *£700 - £900 each*

Towering Castle - Pattern 3458
Charger from the Kosniowski Collection
£500 - £700

Jazz - Pattern 3353
Large Vase from the Kosniowski Collection
£2,500 - £3,000

Jazz - Pattern 3352
Lidded Jar from the Kosniowski Collection
£1,350 - £1,550

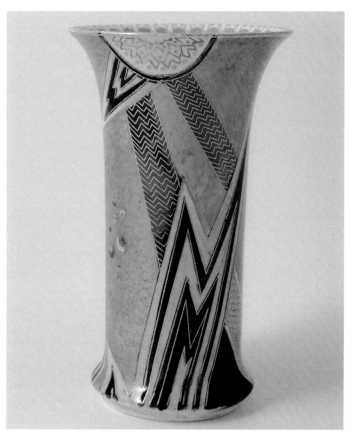

Jazz - Pattern 3353
Medium Vase from the Kosniowski Collection
£1,350 - £1,550

Jazz - Pattern 3361
Footed Powder Bowl from the Kosniowski Collection
£800 - £1,000

Scimitar - Pattern 3651
Large Vase from the Kosniowski Collection
£1,600 - £2,000

Scimitar - Pattern 3651
Large Ovoid Vase from the Kosniowski Collection
£1,600 - £2,000

Scimitar - Pattern 3651
Large Footed Bowl from the Kosniowski Collection
£1,600 - £2,000

Sun Flower Geometric - Pattern 3313
Large Bowl & Stand from the Rodger Aitchison Collection
£1,000 - £1,300

Sun Flower Geometric - Pattern 3313

Large Ginger Jar from the Kosniowski Collection

£2,000 - £2,500

Secretary Bird - Pattern 4017
Medium Vase from the Kosniowski Collection
£800 - £1,000

Secretary Bird - Pattern 4018
Very Large Vase from the Kosniowski Collection
£1,500 - £2,000

Eastern Splendour (or Sultan & Castle)
Pattern 4642
Small Tray from Gazelles of Lyndhurst
£350 - £400

Illustration of Secretary Bird design from
an Original Carlton Ware Pattern Book
Photograph courtesy of The Potteries Museum & Art Gallery,
Stoke-on-Trent
"4017 Gold Print - Garden of Paradise - Best Red Ground"

Illustration of Secretary Bird design from
an Original Carlton Ware Pattern Book
Photograph courtesy of The Potteries Museum & Art Gallery, Stoke-on-Trent
"4107 Stippled Green Lustre Ground"

Fantasia - Pattern 3421

Large Charger from the Kosniowski Collection

£1,250 - £1,500

Fantasia - Pattern 3421

Small Vase from the Kosniowski Collection

£200 - £300

Fantasia - Pattern 3388

Medium Vase from the Kosniowski Collection

£300 - £400

Fantasia - Pattern 3421

Ice Bucket from the Kosniowski Collection

£700 - £900

Fantasia - Pattern 3388
Large Charger from the Kosniowski Collection
£1,250 - £1,500

Fantasia - Pattern 3421
Large Footed Bowl from the Kosniowski Collection
£700 - £900

Feathertailed Bird & Flower - Pattern 3355

Small Vase from the Kosniowski Collection

£250 - £300

Needlepoint - Pattern 3815

Small Deco Vase from the Kosniowski Collection

£500 - £600

Explosion & Butterfly - Pattern 3452

Small Vase from the Kosniowski Collection

£300 - £400

Jaggered Bouquet - Pattern 3457

Medium Vase from Fieldings Auctioneers

£300 - £400

Wagon Wheels - Pattern 3814
Bowl from the Kosniowski Collection
£2,000 - 2,500

Wagon Wheels - Pattern 3813
Tall Vase from the Dulcie Agnes Joyce Memorial Collection
Image courtesy of www.nicholnack.com.au
£4,000 - £5,000

Wagon Wheels - Pattern 3812
Medium Vase from the Dulcie Agnes Joyce Memorial Collection
Image courtesy of www.nicholnack.com.au
£3,000 - £4,000

Illustration of Lace Cap Hydrangea design from an
Original Carlton Ware Pattern Book

Photograph courtesy of The Potteries Museum & Art Gallery,
Stoke-on-Trent

"3969 Aero Blue and Pink Ground"

Lace Cap Hydrangea - Pattern 3969

Square Handled Bowl from the Kosniowski Collection

£600 - £900

Lace Cap Hydrangea - Pattern 3966

Small Vase from the Kosniowski Collection

£400 - £600

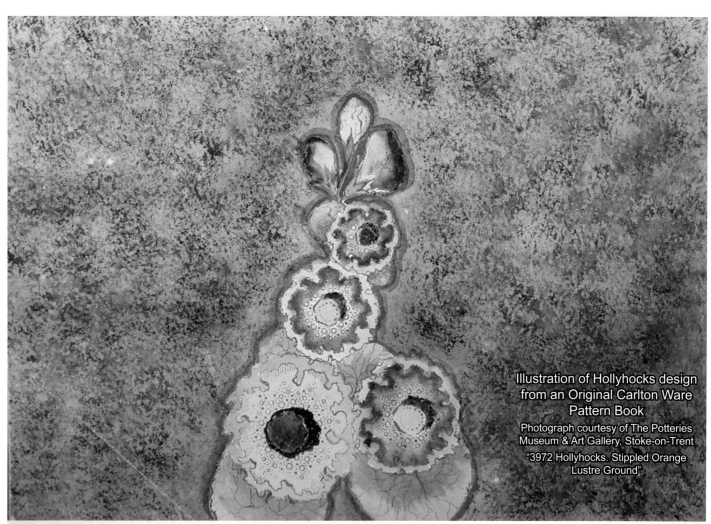

Illustration of Hollyhocks design from an Original Carlton Ware Pattern Book
Photograph courtesy of The Potteries Museum & Art Gallery, Stoke-on-Trent
"3972 Hollyhocks. Stippled Orange Lustre Ground"

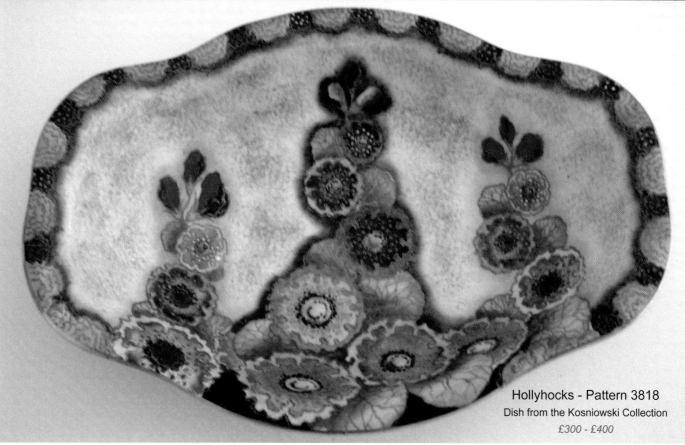

Hollyhocks - Pattern 3818
Dish from the Kosniowski Collection
£300 - £400

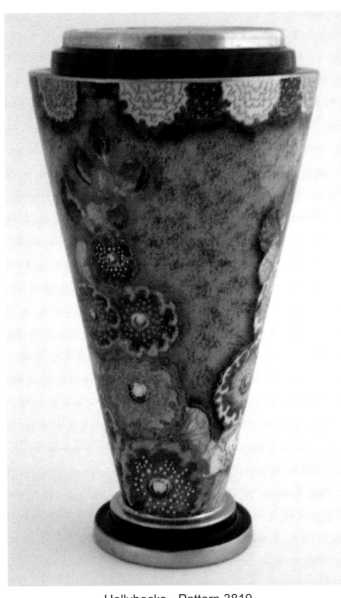

Hollyhocks - Pattern 3819
Deco Vase from the Kosniowski Collection
£400 - £600

Hollyhocks - Pattern 3820
Jug from the Kosniowski Collection
£500 - £750

Hollyhocks - Pattern 3973
Card Holder from the Ian & Jerome Collection
£150 - £200

Hollyhocks - Pattern 3818
Coffee Set from the Kosniowski Collection
£2,600 - £3,000

Illustration of Heron and Magical Tree design from an
Original Carlton Ware Pattern Book

Photograph courtesy of The Potteries Museum & Art Gallery, Stoke-on-Trent

"4160 Background Liberty Green. Shaded Oven Blue at top and under
trees. Pale Green inside"

Heron and Magical Tree - Pattern 4159
Coffee Set from the Kosniowski Collection
£1,250 - £1,500

Heron and Magical Tree

Large Jug from the Kosniowski Collection

£200 - £300

Heron and Magical Tree - Pattern 4162

Small Temple Jar from the Kosniowski Collection

£1,000 - £1,250

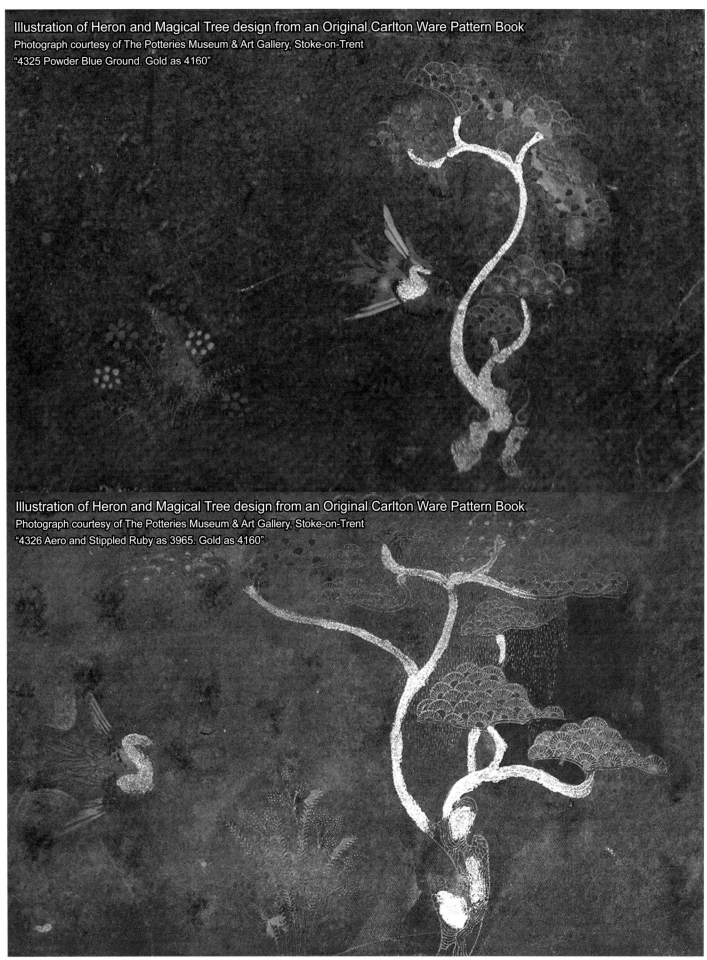

Illustration of Heron and Magical Tree design from an Original Carlton Ware Pattern Book
Photograph courtesy of The Potteries Museum & Art Gallery, Stoke-on-Trent
"4325 Powder Blue Ground. Gold as 4160"

Illustration of Heron and Magical Tree design from an Original Carlton Ware Pattern Book
Photograph courtesy of The Potteries Museum & Art Gallery, Stoke-on-Trent
"4326 Aero and Stippled Ruby as 3965. Gold as 4160"

Illustration of Sketching Bird design from an Original Carlton Ware
Pattern Book
Photograph courtesy of The Potteries Museum & Art Gallery, Stoke-on-Trent
"3890 Sketching as 3889. Matt Aero Brown and Black"

Sketching Bird - Pattern 3891

Medium Ginger Jar from the Kosniowski Collection

£600 - £900

Sketching Bird - Pattern 3891

Conical Bowl from the Kosniowski Collection

£600 - £800

Sketching Bird - Pattern 3890
Large Vase from the Kosniowski Collection
£500 - £750

Sketching Bird - Pattern 3889
Small Vase from the Kosniowski Collection
£300 - £400

Illustration of Sketching Bird design from an Original Carlton Ware
Pattern Book
Photograph courtesy of The Potteries Museum & Art Gallery, Stoke-on-Trent
"4354 Stipple Aero Ruby Lustre"

Sketching Bird - Pattern 3960
Small Globular Vase from the Kosniowski Collection
£150 - £250

Sketching Bird - Pattern 3952
Large Vase from the Kosniowski Collection
£600 - £800

Illustration of Sketching Bird design from an Original Carlton Ware Pattern Book

Photograph courtesy of The Potteries Museum & Art Gallery, Stoke-on-Trent

"3960, as 3890 but Green Ground"

Illustration of Sketching Bird design from an Original Carlton Ware Pattern Book

Photograph courtesy of The Potteries Museum & Art Gallery, Stoke-on-Trent

"4355 Aero Powder Blue"

Paradise Bird & Tree - Pattern 3151

Six Goblets from the Kosniowski Collection

£600 - £800

Paradise Bird & Tree with Cloud - Pattern 3144

Large Footed Gondola from the Kosniowski Collection

£1,000 - £1,250

Chinese Bird & Cloud - Pattern 3327

Medium Vase from the Kosniowski Collection

£300 - £450

Chinese Bird & Cloud - Pattern 3275

Large Vase from the Kosniowski Collection

£400 - £600

Paradise Bird & Tree with Cloud - Pattern 3154

Coffee Set from the Kosniowski Collection

£1,000 - £1,250

Paradise Bird & Tree with Cloud - Pattern 3144

Large Ice Bucket from the Kosniowski Collection

£800 - £1,100

New Chinese Bird & Cloud - Pattern 3322

Small Vase from the Kosniowski Collection

£200 - £250

Illustration of Bird of Paradise design from an
Original Carlton Ware Pattern Book

Photograph courtesy of The Potteries Museum & Art Gallery,
Stoke-on-Trent

"4234 Orange Lustre Ground"

Crested Bird & Water Lily - Pattern 3530

Pair of Large Goblets from the Kosniowski Collection

£600 - £800 each

Crested Bird & Water Lily - Pattern 3529

Large Vase from the Kosniowski Collection

£800 - £1,000

Chinese Bird - Pattern 3527
Large Ginger Jar from the Kosniowski Collection
£2,500 - £3,000

Fairy Carnival
Unique Large Vase from the Kosniowski Collection
£8,000 - £12,000

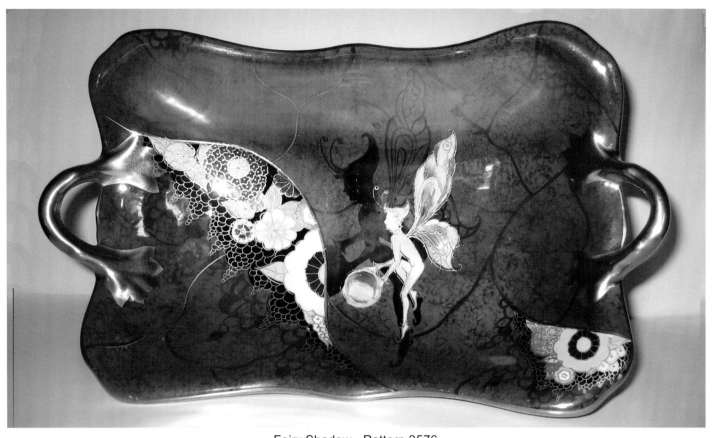

Fairy Shadow - Pattern 3576
Large Comport from the Kosniowski Collection
£3,000 - £3,500

Melange - Pattern 3601
Powder Bowl (above) & Medium Vase (right)
from the Mario & Betty Collection
£300 - £400 & £400 - £600

Tyrolean Bands - Pattern 4076
Part Tea Set from the Kosniowski Collection
£1,100 - £1,350

Banded and Crosstitch - Pattern 3976
Cup & Saucer from the Parnell Collection
Image courtesy of www.nicholnack.com.au
£100 - £150

Jacobean Figures - Pattern 3958
Small Vase, Photograph from Charterhouse Auctions
£2,000 - £2,250

Jacobean Figures was designed by Violet Elmer (1907-1988) in the late 1930s. The pattern is very rare and is rarely seen. We believe that it was produced in three colour-ways.

The two characters in the *Jacobean Figures* pattern have shadows. Violet Elmer used the idea of shadows in a number of other patterns that she designed. These include *Shabunkin, Devil, Wild Duck* and *Fairy Shadow.*

Jacobean Figures
Jug from the Peter Meyer and Gary Jessup Collection
£2,250 - £2,500

Illustration of Jacobean Figures design from an Original Carlton Ware Pattern Book
Photograph courtesy of The Potteries Museum & Art Gallery, Stoke-on-Trent
"3957 Jacobean Figure Design, Ruby Ground"

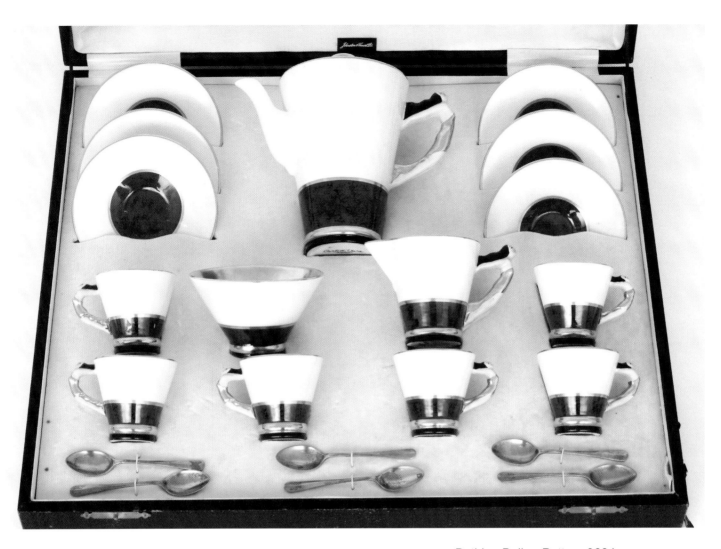

Bathing Belle - Pattern 3684
Coffee Set from the Kosniowski Collection
£2,250 - £2,500

Bathing Belle was produced in four colour-ways:
    White & Dark Blue
    White, Red, Gold & Black
    Green & Black
    Blue & Green

Carlton China

One of the back-stamps that may appear on Carlton Ware is "Carlton China". The story of this begins in 1894 with another company. Lawrence Arthur Birks was a well known ceramic artist who had trained under the famous French artist Louis Marc Emmanuel Solon of the Sevres factory in France. He had also served 22 years at the Minton factory from 1872 to 1894. Laurence and his brother in law, Charles Frederick Goodfellow, became the owners of the Vine Pottery in Stoke-on-Trent. Here they produced porcelain and fine bone china in the style of Minton. The company was known as L.A. Birks & Co. Charles Goodfellow departed in 1898 to concentrate on his business of supplying clay to his brother in law and other potteries. Meanwhile Lawrence designed a new factory and ran it for the next 28 years. In 1900 he took on two new partners, brothers Adolphus Joseph Rawlins and William Sydney Rawlins. They had been involved in the financing the original company and the pottery company was renamed Birks Rawlins & Co.

Birks Rawlins produced a large range of tea and breakfast tableware under the "Savoy China" logo. The publication "The Pottery Gazette" mentioned their pottery in 1910. The ranges extended from the more simplistic and moderately priced through to the more expensively priced and extravagantly decorated items with gilt and enamels. The pieces were advertised in a number of different shapes.

After some time the business over extended itself with the vast range of china, crested china and novelties and ran into financial difficulties. In addition the National Strike in 1926 cut supplies of essential materials and tipped the scales for the business. Wiltshaw & Robinson, the manufacturers of Carlton Ware, mounted a rescue operation and merged with Birks Rawlins. The idea behind the merger was that it would give more strength, stability and diversity in the then current market conditions. They would now be able to offer earthenware ceramics and bone china from the two different factories. Birks Rawlins became known as Birks Rawlins & Co Ltd and started producing what we now know as Carlton China. It is likely that the Savoy logo continued along side the new Carlton China logo for a while before it was eventually superseded. In 1932, unfortunately for Birks Rawlins, the downward slide could not be halted and the receivers were called in. This may have been due in part to the decline in the export market after the Wall Street crash in 1929, along with the fact that Rawlins decided to withdraw his capital.

Carlton Ware had made the most of the merger and rejuvenated the productions systems at the Vine Pottery and the emphasis was once again focused on producing quality bone china tea ware. A good variety of tea ware was produced at the Vine Pottery utilising the new portfolio of designs and shapes that had now been made available, but under the Carlton China logo.

Many beautiful designs were produced on the new Carlton China ranges and some were reputed to be by the well-known

Birds and Trees - Pattern 4998
Trio from the Kosniowski Collection
£50 - £60

Sweet Pea - Pattern 4992
Partial Set from the Kosniowski Collection
£35 - £45

artist Lawrence Arthur Birks who had previously owned the Birks Company. Many though are attributed to Violet Elmer who had joined Carlton Ware and who continued to produce some of the best designs that Carlton ware ever produced. Some of the better known designs in the Carlton China range are probably *Bluebells, Tulip, Wisteria, Butterfly, Sunshine, Delphinium, Lilac Posy, Springtime, Enamelled Berries, Starburst Tree & Birds, Chinese Lanterns, Orange Tree, Poppy, Clematis, Sweet Pea, Dahlia, Aster* and *Bright Daisy*. These are just a selection of the beautiful patterns that can be found on Carlton China and they are still collected avidly for their quality of finish, design and just their sheer attractiveness.

Gilt Festoon - Pattern 4727
Trio from the Kosniowski Collection
£40 - £50

Sunshine - Pattern 4693
Coffee Set from the Kosniowski Collection
£200 - £250

Fantail Birds on Branch - Pattern 4864
Trio from the Kosniowski Collection
£55 - £65

153

Swags of Flowers - Pattern 4758

Trio from the Kosniowski Archives

£40 - £50

Honeysuckle - Pattern 4648

Tea Cup from the Kosniowski Collection

£15 - £25

Sylvan Tree - Pattern 4903

Trio from www.carltonchina.info

£40 - £50

Summer Posy - Pattern 4923

Trio from the Kosniowski Collection

£30 - £35

Susan also called Scarlet - Pattern 4988

Trio from www.carltonchina.info

£25 - £35

Starburst Tree & Birds also called Firecracker Tree
Pattern 4907

Plate from www.carltonchina.info

£20 - £30

Orange Tree - Pattern 4979

Cup and Saucer from the Kosniowski Collection

£30 - £35

Orchard Walk - Pattern 4609

Trio from www.carltonchina.info

£30 - £50

Imari - Pattern 4658

Part Coffee Set from www.carltonchina.info

Coffee Pot £40 - £60, Sugar & Cream £25 - £40,
Cup & Saucer £25 - £40

Savoy China - Pattern 4544

Cup & Saucer from www.carltonchina.info

£10 - £20

Powder Puff - Pattern 4990
Cup & Saucer from www.carltonchina.info
£30 - £45

Spider Flower also called Cornflower
Cup & Saucer from www.carltonchina.info
£30 - £50

Moon House - Pattern 5001
Trio from www.carltonchina.info
£30 - £50

Springtime - Pattern 4754
Set from www.carltonchina.info
*Tea Pot £60 - £100, Milk & Sugar £30 - £40,
Mug £80 - £100 (rare!)*

River Fish - Pattern 4801
Trio from www.carltonchina.info
£80 - £100

Butterfly - Pattern 4683

Cup & Saucer from www.carltonchina.info

£40 - £50

"MONICA"

Illustration of China Figures from an Original
Carlton Ware Pattern Book
Photograph courtesy of The Potteries Museum & Art Gallery,
Stoke-on-Trent
"4260 Monica"
"4261 Monica Pink"

Illustration of China Figures from an Original
Carlton Ware Pattern Book
Photograph courtesy of The Potteries Museum & Art
Gallery, Stoke-on-Trent
"4301 Joan"   "4302 Grandma"

Carlton China Figure
3 examples of Peggy from www.carltonchina.info
£100 - £200 each

Carlton China Figure
2 examples of Verona from www.carltonchina.info
£80 - £150 each

Embossed Ware

In 1925 Carlton Ware began production of the embossed ware ranges. Such was their popularity and the public's love affair that production continued (albeit not in such great detail as the earlier pieces) throughout the 1960s and well into the 1970s. In the main, embossed ware was created in a specific design with the pattern embedded into the mould. This meant that each piece was a specific pattern which unlike many other shapes, such as vases, which once produced, could be decorated with any pattern or design. One embossed design which is the exception to this is the *Blackberry* and *Raspberry* designs which are the same design but painted in different colours accordingly.

The first of the embossed wares that were produced were Salad Wares. These were realistic pieces that resembled lettuce leaves adorned with vivid red tomatoes, crayfish and lobsters etc. The *Lobster* design was very popular and remained in production until the 1970s.

Many other embossed ranges were introduced and this included Floral Embossed, Fruit Embossed as well as Salad Ware. The popularity of these wares is testament to the quality of the finished piece. The designs are naturalistic interpretations with clever use of each fruit, stems and flowers. All pieces were modelled expertly and hand painted.

The Embossed Ware Ranges were very popular and indeed remain so today. Although they were produced at the same time as other extravagant pieces, such as the Best Wares, they were cheaper and quicker to produce. This meant that vast quantities could be made and sold to the public at large, which helped Carlton Ware survive through difficult times.

A full list of the various designs produced may be found within the chapter about Dating Carlton Ware, page 193, and in the chapter containing the list of shapes, page 240.

Lettuce & Tomato - Shape 2131

Cruet Set from the Kosniowski Collection

£40 - £60

LETTUCE & TOMATO DESIGN   *CarltonWare*   GREEN

LETTUCE & TOMATO DESIGN

Prices—each   Green

Pepper & Salt l/s 4/–		Cruet Set 5/5	Salad Set 13/9	Butter 1/6		Sauce Boat & Stand 3/3
{ Pepper 2/– { Salt 2/–		Pepper & Salt s/s boxed 2/10 Pepper 1/2 Salt 1/2	{ Bowl 9/3 { Servers 4/6			{ Sauce Boat 2/2 { Stand 1/1
Tray l/s 5/11		Tray m/s 4/8		Tray s/s 2/11		Cucumber Tray 3/8
Triangular Plate 6″ 2/9		Triangular Plate 8″ 4/5		Triangular Plate 9″ 5/5		

Cottage
Sugar Sifter from the Kosniowski Collection
£80 - £100

Fruit Basket
Vase, Image courtesy of www.nicholnack.com.au
£30 - £40

Rock Garden - Shape 1239
Vase, Image courtesy of www.nicholnack.com.au
£40 - £60

Anemone - Shapes 1753, 1761

Jam & Spoon from the Kosniowski Collection

£45 - £70

Buttercup - Shapes 1395, 1402

Butter & Knife from the Kosniowski Collection

£45 - £70

Blackberry - Shapes 1473, 1477

Jam & Spoon from the Kosniowski Collection

£45 - £70

Cherry - Shape 2134

Butter & Knife from the Kosniowski Collection

£40 - £70

Apple Blossom - Shapes 1621, 1655

Butter & Knife from the Kosniowski Collection

£50 - £80

Daisy - Shape 1472

Butter & Knife from the Kosniowski Collection

£45 - £70

Forget-me-not - Shape 1769
Jam & Spoon from the Kosniowski Collection
£45 - £60

Red Currant - Shapes 1603, 1605
Butter & Knife from the Kosniowski Collection
£30 - £50

Primula - Shapes 1982, 2052
Jam & Spoon from the Kosniowski Collection
£30 - £50

Wallflower - Shapes 1752, 1763
Jam & Spoon from the Kosniowski Collection
£45 - £60

Pyrethrum - Shapes 1751, 1757
Jam & Spoon from the Kosniowski Collection
£45 - £80

Hazel Nut - Pattern 4505, Shape 2316
Small Oval Bowl from the Kosniowski Collection
£25 - £35

Anemone - Shape 975
Tall Pitcher from the Kosniowski Collection
£350 - £450

Anemone
- Shapes 932, 975, 975, 928, 925, 979, 1174,1033
Collection from the Kosniowski Collection
Plate £40 - £60, Pitcher (medium) £200 - £300
Pitcher (tall) £300 - £400, Tray £75 - £110
Preserve with cover and base £120 - £175
Sugar Sifters £90 - £125 each

Buttercup
3 Bar Toast Rack from the Kosniowski Collection
£70 - £100

Apple Blossom - AW - Shape 3183
Preserve from the Kosniowski Collection
£40 - £60

Water Lily - Shape 1588
Open Jam (or Grapefruit) from the Kosniowski Collection
£100 - £120

Lobster & Langouste - Shape 2125
Plate from the Kosniowski Collection
£20 - £30

Foxglove - Pattern 4286, Shape 1881
Preserve with Spoon from the Kosniowski Collection
£60 - £80

FOXGLOVE DESIGN *CarltonWare*

FOXGLOVE DESIGN

Prices—each

4285 Yellow
4286 Green
4621 Peach/Chartreuse

Beaker 3/7	Toastrack 4/1	Sugar 3/–	Preserve & Spoon boxed 5/7 {Preserve 3/7 {Spoon 1/3	Cup & Saucer 3/3	Teapot 2 cup 5/8
Covered 4/9				
Pepper & Salt l/s 4/– {Pepper 2/– {Salt 2/–	Sauce Boat & Stand 3/2 {Sauce Boat 2/1 {Stand 1/1	Cream Jug 2/9	Jug ½ pint 3/7	Jug 1 pint 4/9	Jug 1½ pint 6/–
Handled Basket 11/8	Bon Bon 3/11	Oval Bowl s/s 3/11	Oval Bowl m/s 5/5	Oval Bowl l/s 6/10
Leaf Tray 4/5	Dish 4″ 2/1	Dish 6″ 2/9	Dish 9″ 5/5	Salad Set 15/2 {Bowl 10/10 {Servers 4/4
Cruet Set 5/5 {Pepper & Salt s/s boxed 2/10 {Pepper 1/2 {Salt 1/2	Butter & Knife boxed 3/3 {Butter 1/5 {Knife 1/3	Combined Butter & Knife and Jam & Spoon boxed 6/2	Jam & Spoon boxed 3/3 {Jam 1/5 {Spoon 1/3	Individual Boxed Butter 2/–

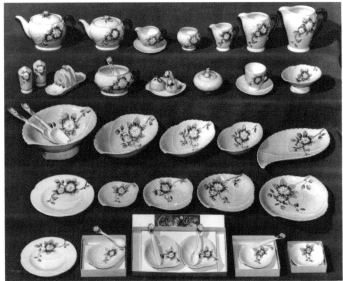

WILD ROSE DESIGN   *Carlton Ware*   4427 YELLOW   4428 GREEN

WILD ROSE DESIGN   4427 Yellow   4428 Green

Prices—each

| Teapot 4 cup 7/9 | Teapot 2 cup 5/11 | Sauce Boat & Stand 3/7 | Sugar 2/9 | Cream 3/- | Jug s/s ½ pint 4/6 | Jug l/s 1 pint 5/8 |

{ Sauce Boat 2/5
{ Stand 1/2

| Pepper & Salt l/s 4/- | Combined Toastrack 4/11 | Mayonnaise Bowl & Ladle 6/11 | Cruet Set 5/5 | Preserve 3/7 | Cup & Saucer 3/8 | Bon Bon 3/11 |

{ Pepper 2/-
{ Salt 2/-

{ Bowl 4/8
{ Ladle 2/3

{ Pepper & Salt s/s boxed 2/10
{ Pepper & Salt s/s not boxed 2/4 pr.

{ Preserve & Stand 4/7
{ Preserve & Spoon 4/9
{ Preserve, Spoon & Stand 5/9
{ Preserve & Spoon boxed 5/7

| Salad Bowl & Servers 15/2 | Oval Bowl l/s 6/10 | Oval Bowl m/s 5/5 | Oval Bowl s/s 3/11 | Supper Tray 5/8 |

{ Bowl 10/10
{ Servers 4/4

| Plate 8" 4/5 | Dish 4" 2/1 | Dish 6" 2/9 | Dish 8" 4/5 | Dish 9" 5/5 |

| Plate 5" 2/4 | Boxed Jam & Spoon 3/3 | Comb. Butter & Knife and Jam & Spoon Boxed 6/2 | Boxed Butter & Knife 3/3 | Individual Butter Boxed 2/- |

{ Jam 1/6
{ Spoon 1/2

{ Butter 1/6
{ Knife 1/2

Leaf - Shape 2367
Medium Tray from the Kosniowski Collection
£15 - £25

Water Lily - Shape 1783
Plate from the Kosniowski Collection
£30 - £55

Oak Tree - Pattern 3810, Shape 1144
Large Charger from the Kosniowski Collection
£130 - £150

Orchid - Shape 2576
Trinket Box from the Kosniowski Collection
£45 - £70

HAZEL NUT DESIGN

Carlton Ware

4504 MATT CREAM
4505 GREEN
4620 BLUE

HAZELNUT DESIGN

4504 Matt Cream
4505 Green
4620 Blue

Prices—each

2-way Tray l/s 16/11	2-way Tray s/s 12/6	Oval Serving Dish s/s 12/6	Oval Serving Dish l/s 16/11

Oval Bowl l/s 6/10	Oval Bowl m/s 5/5	Oval Bowl s/s 3/11

Cruet Set 5/5	Pepper & Salt l/s 4/-	Butter & Knife or Jam & Spoon 2/9	Sauce Boat & Stand 3/9
{ Pepper & Salt s/s boxed } 2/10	{ Pepper } 2/- { Salt } 2/-	{ Butter & Knife or Jam & Spoon boxed } 3/3	{ Sauce Boat } 2/6 { Stand } 1/3
{ Pepper & Salt s/s not boxed } 2/4	{ Pepper & Salt l/s boxed } 5/6	{ Individual Butter or Jam in cellophane box } 2/-	
{ Cruet Set boxed } 7/2		{ Butter or Jam } 1/6 { Knife or Spoon } 1/2	

HAZEL NUT DESIGN

Carlton Ware

4504 MATT CREAM
4620 BLUE **4505** GREEN

HAZELNUT DESIGN

4504 Matt Cream
4505 Green
4620 Blue

Prices—each

Salad Set 15/2	Jug s/s ½ pint 4/6	Jug m/s 1 pint 5/8	Jug l/s 6/10
{ Bowl 10/10 { Servers 4/4			

Teapot 2 cup 5/11	Teapot 4 cup 7/9	Television Set 6/10	Tray 4/5

Plate 5" 2/4	Bon Bon 3/11	Cup & Saucer 3/9	Sugar 2/9	Cream 2/11

168

Presenting "CONVOLVULUS" by *Carlton*

Convolvulus by Carlton combines the best of modern shapes with traditional design and is available in three background colourings: Lavender, Blue or Chartreuse. A very full range of tableware items is available, including Trays, Bowls, Salad Sets, Early Morning Sets, Twenty-one piece Teasets, Coffee Sets, together with a small range of Vases.

Buy *Carlton* —first with the latest and best

CARLTON WARE LTD · COPELAND STREET · STOKE-ON-TRENT

Hydrangea Shape 2161
Tray, Image courtesy of www.nicholnack.com.au
£60 - £120

Magnolia - Shape 2607
Medium Bowl from the Kosniowski Collection
£30 - £40

Convolvulus - Shape 2500

Covered Cheese from the Margaret Jones Collection
Image courtesy of www.nicholnack.com.au
£40 - £60

Convolvulus - Shape 2511

Coffee Pot from the Margaret Jones Collection
Image courtesy of www.nicholnack.com.au
£40 - £70

Poppy & Daisy - Shape 2042

Large Bowl from the Kosniowski Collection
£100 - £140

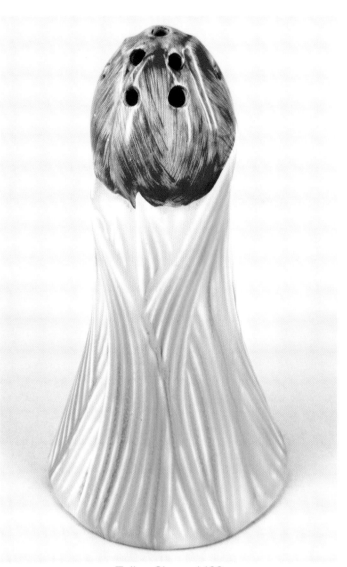

Tulip - Shape 1422

Sugar Sifter, Image courtesy of www.nicholnack.com.au
£60 - £95

Grape - Shape 2254

Three Way Tray, Image courtesy of www.nicholnack.com.au
£60 - £80

Novelty Ware

Wiltshaw & Robinson were producing Novelty wares as far back as the 1920s. They were supposed to be "novelties", that is, a bit of fun and tongue in cheek. The early ones could probably be better described as Novel Wares as they were often very colourful but were still created with the usual quality of finish that was the trademark of Carlton Ware. The early items were along the tableware lines with serviette holders in the form of a *Deer, Crinoline Lady, Scotchman, Sailor, Cat, Dog, Guardsman* and *Jester*, etc. These are amusing little characters. Others that were popular were small figures that were actually bells such as *Clergyman Bell, Maid Bell, Dandy Bell, Page Bell* and *Crinoline Lady Bell*. There was also an array of cruets sets including a soldier set called *Toy Drum Major* which was two cute little guardsman with a drum. Carlton Ware were very ingenious at creating humorous novelties that were in great demand and appealing to ladies to brighten up their tableware.

The early 1920s is also the time when the production of the early salad and lobster wares were introduced. These were designed to replicate a salad leaf with bright tomatoes or the fabulous *Langouste (Lobster)* range that were cleverly designed with claws used as dish feet. Carlton Ware continued to produce prolific amounts of novelties through the years and there are as many as the imagination could dream up and much too many to list here individually. Further to the ranges mentioned are preserve pots, cigarette holders, egg timers, bottle stoppers, ashtrays, lighter holders and mugs including musical mugs. Please see the section on Shapes which lists most shapes produced and includes many of the Novelty items.

After the take over of Birks Rawlins in 1928 alongside the production of Carlton China a collection of figurines and dogs were available. From as early as 1902 Carlton Ware moved into the then lucrative market of producing Heraldic China which they proudly advertised as their latest speciality and once again they were very keen to maintain some semblance of quality and integrity with Coats of Arms etc. Some of these early examples of Carlton Ware mentioned above are still very desirable to collectors today.

The novelty ranges were continued throughout the life of the company and often took on the diversity of popular demand. Advertising wares such as *Guinness* were in production in the early to mid fifties and items were created also for *Pick Flowers Keg Bitter, Martell Brandy, Beefeater Gin* and *Babycham*. In the mid 1960s saw a series named *Carlton Village* which were buildings that realistically resembled centuries old buildings named as *Inn, Smithy, Water Mill, Windmill, Church, Cottage, Butter Market, Shop* and *Hall*.

In 1958 Wiltshaw & Robinson Limited changed their name to Carlton Ware Limited and in 1966 the firm was sold to Arthur Wood & Sons. Because of its reputation for fine quality products, Arthur Wood & Sons operated Carlton Ware independently, although it was part of the Arthur Wood

170

Novelty Bell - Shape 1004
Clergyman from the Kosniowski Archives
£60 - £80

Novelty Napkin Ring
Clown from the Kosniowski Archives
£50 - £60

Coronation Street - Shape 3516
Ena Sharples from the Kosniowski Archives
£30 - £50

Group. Under the direction of the Arthur Wood Group, sales rose dramatically in the 1970s due to designs for the Walking Ware range introduced and designed by Roger Michell and Danka Napiorkowska. The *Walking Ware* gained immediate popularity, and it was probably this range that kept the company afloat during the 1970s. Anthony Wood (the Managing Director and son of Arthur Wood) tried to re-introduce some of the earlier pieces of Carlton Ware, but nothing caught the public's imagination. So, it was left to the *Walking Ware* range of Carlton Ware to keep the company prosperous.

Roger Michell and Danka Napiorkowska owned a small pottery in Yorkshire called Lustre Pottery. They were studio potters and exhibited a Walking Ware Dinner and Tea service at an exhibition in London. This received rave reviews and orders poured in from all over the world. But, Lustre Pottery could not cope with the demand and had to consider sub-contracting to a larger manufacturer. After a few rejections from some Staffordshire potteries, Anthony Wood from Carlton Ware expressed an interest. This resulted in a working relationship for about eight years.

The initial range of *Walking Ware* included various sizes of teapots, sitting sugar bowls, mugs, cups, eggcups etc. This was followed by *RJS* tea service (Running, Jumping and Standing Still), which had plaid, socks and sandals.

The moulds from the first series were used to produce the *Caribbean* series. These had a palm tree and sunset scene with yellow shoes and blue line for socks. The fourth series was *Big Feet,* which had oversized feet with coloured polka dots. Other items produced included Birthday Mugs and Royal Commemorative Ware such as the Queen's Silver Jubilee mug of 1977, which had bended knees.

In the later years Carlton Ware produced quite a number of what is now known as Novelty Items! These usually consisted of copies of everyday items and gimmicky pieces for fun. As mentioned the most famous are the Walking Ware series but there are some less known novelty items. These were probably produced quite cheaply in abundance for a mass market. These ranges include the usual cruet sets, butter dishes, milk jugs, teapots etc, as well as preserve pots that replicated vegetables.

Another novelty design is the *Alligator Range, Bird & Worm, Flat Back Money Boxes, Bug Eye Money Boxes* and *Cow* etc.

The *Flat Money Boxes* were mainly designed by Vivienne Brennan in the early 1970s. They were produced over a period of about eight years. The flat surfaces were ideal for decorating and each shape was produced in a number of different decoration. Four *Bug Eye Money Boxes* were made in the 1970s, these had protruding eyes.

Other later Novelty Wares that were produced for the mass market were Advertising Ware such as *Hovis, Robertson*

Coronation Street - Shapes 3514 to 3519

£30 - £50 each

Golly, Harrods, Kit Kat. Further information may be found in the next chapter on page 179.

Let's not forget the well known old favourites of *Coronation Street* fame namely Stan, Hilda Ogden, Albert Tatlock, Mike Baldwin, Bet Lynch and the unforgettable Ena Sharples. This is good example of Carlton Ware taking advantage of public appeal to their distinct advantage.

A highly prized range of Novelty Ware is the *Circus Series* produced in the 1980s. These pieces are rare and highly sought after, in particular shape 3341 *Woman Covered Butter* which is often described as Women Wrestlers! A price list from the late 1980s indicates that the *Circus Series* was discontinued - that may be why they are so rare!

This is just a brief glimpse of what is probably a few of the several hundreds made. Not to everyone's taste but some are very unusual and still bear the marks of our beloved Carlton Ware.

Some of them are coming in to their own and are being considered very "Retro" which has many fans. Perhaps the "antiques" or collectables of the future! Good fun anyway!

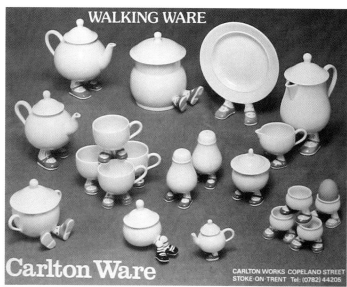
First Walking Ware Range

Running Jumping & Standing Still Walking Ware Range

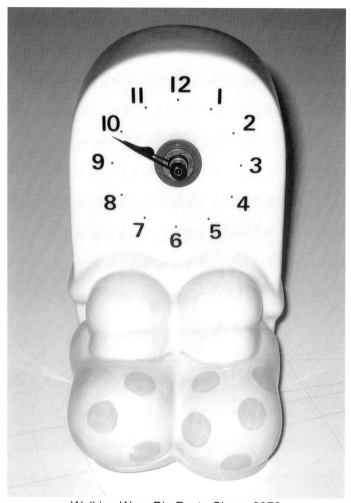
Walking Ware Big Feet - Shape 3373
Clock from the Kosniowski Archives
£70 - £110

Caribbean Walking Ware Range

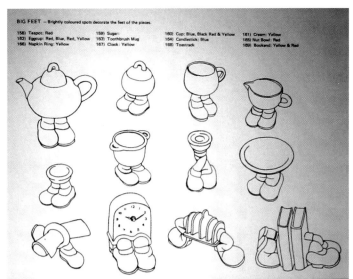

BIG FEET — Brightly coloured spots decorate the feet of the pieces.

158) Teapot: Red
162) Eggcup: Red, Blue, Red, Yellow
166) Napkin Ring: Yellow

159) Sugar:
163) Toothbrush Mug
167) Clock: Yellow

160) Cup: Blue, Black Red & Yellow
164) Candlestick: Blue
168) Toastrack

161) Cream: Yellow
165) Nut Bowl: Red
169) Bookend: Yellow & Red

Big Feet Walking Ware Range

Wellington & Other Walking Ware Range

Walking Ware
Collection from the Kosniowski Collection
£40 - £60

HOVIS BREAKFAST SET

Carlton Ware

CAT CHEESE

CARLTON WORKS
COPELAND STREET STOKE-ON-TRENT Tel: (0782) 44205

MILKSHAKE PRESERVES

WAFER BUTTER

Carlton Ware

COPELAND WORKS COPELAND STREET
STOKE-ON-TRENT Tel: (0782) 44205

Circus Series — Decorated

3338 CLOWN PRESERVE
3339 STRONG MAN DISH
3341 WOMAN COV BUTTER (Sept '81)
3342 CLOWN CREAM (ON DUCK) (Sept '81)
3343 CLOWN CREAM (PANTOMIME HORSE)
3351 CLOWN TEAPOT
3355 DOUBLE EGG CUP

Carlton Ware   DRAGON TEAPOTS

PARCEL CREAM

CUPID MUG

SANTA CLAUS MUG

CHICKEN EGGCUP

CARLTON WORKS
COPELAND STREET
STOKE-ON-TRENT
Tel: (0782) 44205

BIRTHDAY CUPS

Musical Mug - Shape 1284
Hangsman from the Kosniowski Collection
£150 - £250

Mug - Shape 1972
Hangsman from the Kosniowski Collection
£40 - £80

Red Devil
Large Figure from the Kosniowski Collection
£100 - £200

Money Box - Shape 3150
Carousel from the Kosniowski Collection
£30 - £40

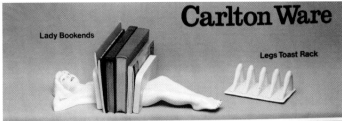

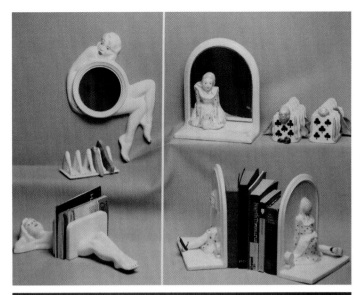

Dovecote - Shape 3262
Cream, Coffee & Sugar from the Kosniowski Archives
£20 - £30, £40 - £60, £30 - £50

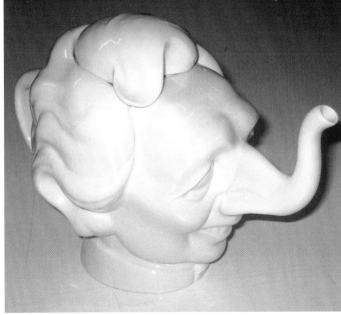

Spitting Image - Shape 3531
Thatcher from the Kosniowski Archives
£50 - £80

Money Box - Flat Back - Shape 3086
Pig from the Kosniowski Collection
£35 - £50

(51)	Round Tray Dia 4.1/2"	(52)	Oblong Tray
	Oxford £3.00		Oxford £4.25
	Peking £6.35		Peking £8.40

(53) Covered Vase Ht. 4.1/2"
Oxford £9.30
Peking £20.20

(54) Bud Vase Ht. 7.1/2"
Oxford £4.25
Peking £10.75

(55) Urn Ht. 5.1/4"
Oxford £7.65
Peking £15.85

(56) I/s Covered Box
Oxford £6.35
Peking £15.85

(57) s/s Covered Box
Oxford £3.00
Peking £5.80

(58)	Mushroom Cruet	£5.05
(59)	Shell Cruet	£3.60
(60)	Shell P & S/Stand	£2.20
(61)	Fruit Cruet	£3.40
(62)	Fruit P & S/Stand	£2.05
(63)	Vegetable Cruet	£4.00
(64)	Vegetable P & S/Stand	£2.65
(65)	Split Apple P & S	£2.75
(66)	Split Pear P & S	£2.75
(67)	Pear Preserve/Stand	£2.65
(68)	Apple Preserve/Stand	£2.65
(69)	Jaffa Preserve/Stand	£3.00
(70)	Pear Individual Butter	£0.82
(71)	Banana Split Lth. 10"	£1.40
(72)	Lemon Individual Butter	
(73)	Apple Individual Butter	
	Loose	£0.82
	Boxed	£1.05

Leaf — 74-84 inc. - Discontinued

Functional Fun Items

(85)	Hovis Store Jar	£3.25
(86)	Hovis Plate Lth. 7.1/2"	£1.80
(87)	Hovis Butter Lth. 5.1/2"	£3.15
(88)	Hovis Toastrack	£2.20
(88A)	Hovis Mug	£1.65
(89)	Fried Egg Eggcup	£1.75
(90)	Discontinued	
(91)	Discontinued	
(92)	Discontinued	
(93)	Wing Nut Vase Ht. 6.3/4"	£4.25
(94)	Nail/Screw P & S	£3.40
(95)	Plug Ashtray Dia 7"	£5.65
(96)	Tap Teapot	£7.05
(97)	Milk Shake Preserve	£3.25
(98)	Wafer Butter	£3.15

Animal Range

(108)	Lamb Store Jar Lth. 10.1/2"	£6.75
(109)	Lamb Mint Sauceboat/Stand	£3.20
(110)	Lamb Toastrack	£2.70
(111)	Discontinued	
(112)	Owl P & S Bxd.	£2.45
(113)	Duck Eggcup	£3.95
(114)	Cat Cheese Lth. 12"	£13.30
(115)	Robin P & S	£1.95
(116)	Penguin P & S Bxd.	£2.45
(117)	Chicken Eggcup	£4.25
(119)	Camel Teapot	
	Litho	Disc.
	No Litho	£7.85
(120)	Pig Jug	
	l/s	£8.00
	s/s	£6.75

Circus Range — 121-126 inc. - Discontinued

(135)	Can Can Mug Ht. 4"	£1.85
(136)	Corset Mug Ht. 4"	£1.85
(137)	Discontinued	
(138)	Legs Toastrack Lth. 6"	£3.45
(139)	Lady Bookend	£6.75

Walking Ware

(140)	I/s Teapot	£7.95
(140A)	Walking Cup	£2.60
(141)	s/s Teapot Ht. 7"	£6.70
(142)	Mini Teapot Ht. 3.1/4"	£3.45
(143)	Sugar	£3.65
(144)	Cream Ht. 3.1/2"	£3.10
(145)	Plate Dia. 8.1/4"	£5.75
(146)	Eggcup	£1.75
(147)	Cross Legged Sugar	£4.55
(148)	P & S	£6.35
(149)	Biscuit Barrel Ht. 7.1/2"	£7.95
(150)	Soup Ht. 5"	£4.70
(151)	Coffee Pot Ht. 9"	£6.70

R.J.S & Caribbean

		R.J.S.	Caribbean
(152)	Teapot	£7.40	£8.45
(153)	Sugar	£3.95	£4.80
(154)	Cream	£3.40	£3.80
(155)	Standing Cup	£2.75	£3.55
(156)	Running Cup	£3.15	£3.80
(157)	Eggcup	£2.00	£2.45

Early Bird

(170)	Mug Ht. 4.1/2"	£2.35
(171)	Toastrack Lth. 6"	£4.20
(172)	Egg P & S	£1.20
(173)	Eggcup Ht. 2.2/3"	£1.50

Potts

(174)	Eggcup Bxd. Ht. 2.1/4"	£1.05
(175)	Plate Bxd. Dia. 6.1/4"	£1.80
(176)	Bowl Dia. 5.1/2" Bxd	£1.80
(177)	Mug Bxd. Ht. 3"	£1.80
(178)	Discontinued	
(179)	Birthday Mug	£3.65
(180)	Discontinued	
(181)	Santa Claus Mug	£6.05
(182)	Adam Mug Ht. 5"	£3.60
(183)	Eve Mug Ht. 4.3/4"	£3.10
(184)	Waitress Mug Ht. 5"	£4.55
(185)	Wellington Eggcup Ht. 3.1/2"	£1.90
(186)	Discontinued	
(187)	Beach Towel Soap Dish	£1.55
(188)	Shark Tidy Safe	£1.75
(190)	Hamburger Tidy Safe	£1.75
(191)	Pelican Tidy Safe	£1.75
(192)	Cushion Spoon Rest	£1.13
(194)	Half Pint Tankard	£1.60
(195)	Carrier Bag	£1.50

Alice Range

(198)	Cheshire Cat Butter	£3.95
(199)	Queen Hearts Preserve Ht. 6.1/2"	£3.95
(200)	Gardener Toastrack	£3.80
(201)	Doormouse Eggcup	£2.10
(202)	Caterpillar Sugar Ht. 7"	£4.25
(203)	Mad Hatter Eggcup	£2.50
(204)	Playing Card P & S	£1.85
(205)	Duck Teapot Ht. 5"	£5.35
(206)	Cow Cream	£5.05
(207)	Bath Soap Dish	
	l/s Decorated	£6.05
	s/s Plain	£3.10
(208)	Elephant Teapot	£5.35
(210)	Loving Mug	£3.15
(211)	Cow in Butter Dish Lth. 7.1/2"	£9.20
(212)	Cat/Mouse Toastrack	£3.10

Dovecote & House & Garden

		Dovecote	House & Garden
	Teaset (exc. plates)	£37.75	£37.75
	Coffee Set (exc. plates)	£39.45	£39.15
(213)	Teapot 9"	£10.75	£10.75
(214)	Coffee Pot Ht. 11.3/4"	£12.45	£12.45
(215)	Plate Dia. 6"	£1.70	£1.00
(216)	Cup/Scr. Ht. 3.1/4"	£3.45	£3.40
(217)	Sugar	£3.30	£3.30
(218)	Cream	£3.00	£3.00
(219)	Store Jar Ht. 8"	£3.80	£6.95
	(also available in Lovebird)		
(221)	Double Egg Holder Ht. 6.1/2" Dovecote/Finch/Parrot		£5.35

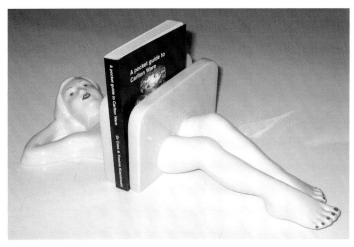

Lady - Shape 3318
Book Ends from the Kosniowski Archives
£20 - £40

A list of the Novelty items may be found in the Shapes chapter within this book, page 248 onwards. This also includes a price guide.

An old price list from the late 1980s appears on the opposite page and shows the original prices of some of the Novelty Ware.

CARLTON WARE LTD
468 King Street, Fenton, Stoke-on-Trent ST4 3DH Tel: 0782 599544, Fax: 0782 599382, Telex: 367144

CARLTON WARE LTD
468 King Street, Fenton, Stoke-on-Trent ST4 3DH Tel: 0782 599544, Fax: 0782 599382, Telex: 367144

CARLTON WARE LTD
468 King Street, Fenton, Stoke-on-Trent ST4 3DH Tel: 0782 599544, Fax: 0782 599382, Telex: 367144

Cow in Bath - Shape 3219
Butter from the Kosniowski Archives
£40 - £60

Musical Mug - Shape 1213
Humpty Dumpty from the Kosniowski Collection
£100 - £200

Village - Shapes 2646, 2647
Smithy & Water Mill from the Kosniowski Collection
£40 - £60 each

Advertising Ware

Most collectors are aware that Carlton Ware produced ceramic pieces for many high profile companies. Many collectors specialise in these pieces to the exclusion of everything else. Carlton Ware were commissioned by numerous companies to produce advertising ware. The range produced for Arthur Guinness is probably the most well known. The *Guinness* range has a huge following is still collected prolifically in the UK and internationally.

The success of this particular range and the high prices it commands has resulted in many fakes being produced. This along with the fact that when Carlton Ware was liquidated in 1989 some of the original moulds ended up in the hands of disreputable people and many fakes were made. These fakes often appear for sale – so buyer beware! Although to the seasoned collector the fakes are more obvious by the vastly inferior standard of the finish. Carlton Ware was renowned for its fine quality of paint work and for the attention to detail that was lavished on the pieces. Where in contrast this is not in evidence on the fakes, which are often crudely finished and not as subtly defined and blended as the originals. This is easier to see when making a direct comparison, which is not always easy for new collectors.

The first piece to be produced for Guinness was the *Toucan* in 1955. The beak of the *Toucan* is orange changing to deep yellow at the top. In 1956 the Zoo collection was introduced. This consisted of a *Zoo Keeper, Ostrich, Tortoise, Kangaroo*, small *Toucan* and *Sea Lion*. The *Toucan Lamp*, the *Flying Toucans* and the *Drayman* were introduced in 1957. The *Toucan Lamp* is like the *Toucan* but has a hole in the Toucan's head for the electrical fitting. Other pieces such as the *Toucan Jug* and *Penguin* were introduced in later years.

Listed here are some of the other advertising ware produced by Carlton Ware, together with an approximate date for the first item produced (other pieces may have been produced at a later date). Further details may be found in the chapter with the Shapes list, page 240.

1934 - 1935	Dimple
1935	Abbotts, Haig, Craven A
1935 - 1936	White & Mackey
1936 - 1937	Bovril
1950 - 1953	Dewars
1955 - 1958	Schweppes, Kensitas, Brandyman, Gilbey, Tio Pepe, Guinness Figures
1958 - 1959	Dunhill, Gordons Gin, Noilly Prat, Haig, Babycham, Boothe. Morris
1959 - 1964	Martell, Carreras, Flowers
1964 - 1968	Guinness Penguin Lamp, Williams & Humbert, Berhard & Mays
1968	Guinness, Makeson
1968 - 1969	Colibri
1969 - 1970	Heinekin
1970 - 1971	Carlsburg, Ballantyne
1976 - 1980	Hovis, Brown & Poulson

1980 - 1985	Cadbury, Tetley Tea
1985 - 1986	Robertson Golly, Singapore Airlines, Castlemaine, Bisto, BHS, Harrods, Bovril, Russell Hobbs, Sainsbury
1986+	Whitbread

TEAPOT SETS		£ p
TEAPOT	BLACK PRESTIGE	7.60
TEAPOT	WHITE PRESTIGE	7.00
CREAM JUG	BLACK PRESTIGE	2.57
CREAM JUG	WHITE PRESTIGE	2.36
COV SUGAR BOX	BLACK PRESTIGE	5.04
COV SUGAR BOX	WHITE PRESTIGE	4.67

Hovis Tableware

CARLTON WARE LTD
468 King Street, Fenton, Stoke-on-Trent ST4 3DH Tel: 0782 599544, Fax: 0782 599382, Telex: 367144

Guinness

Shapes 2320, 2308, 2317, 2331, 2319

Seal, Kangaroo, Ostrich, Zookeeper, Tortoise

from Fieldings Auctioneers

£100 - £150 each

Flowers - Shape 2614
Shakespeare Figure from Fieldings Auctioneers
£50 - £75

Flowers - Shape 2583
Brewmaster Figure from Fieldings Auctioneers
£50 - £75

Guinness - Shape 2325
Toucan Lamp with Shade
from Fieldings Auctioneers
£300 - £400

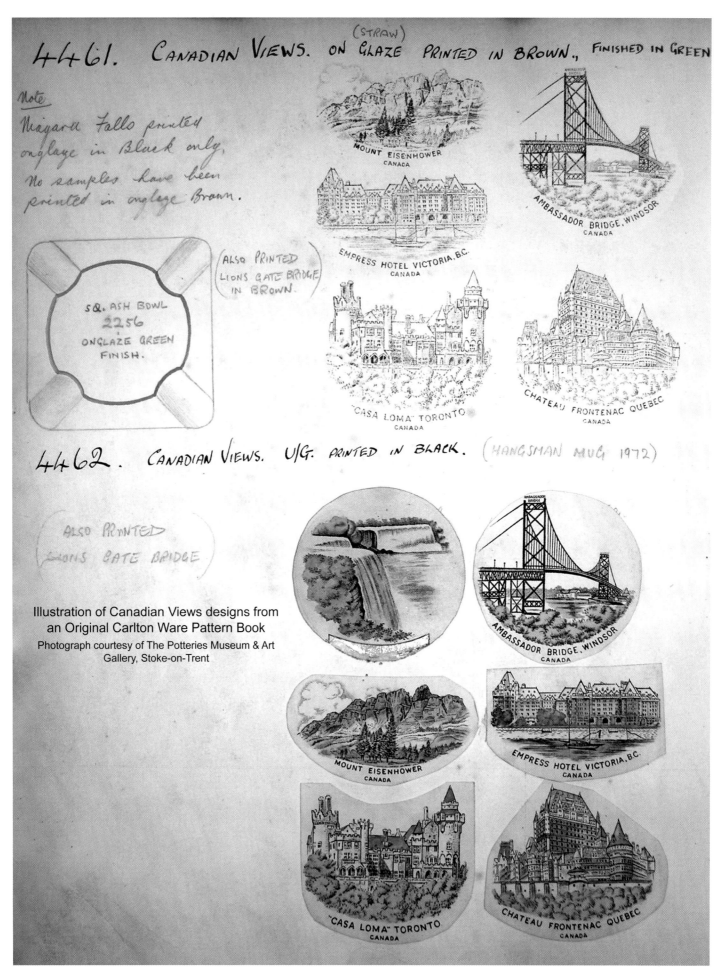

4461. CANADIAN VIEWS. ON GLAZE PRINTED IN BROWN., (STRAW) FINISHED IN GREEN

Note

Niagara Falls printed onglaze in Black only. No samples have been printed in onglaze Brown.

SQ. ASH BOWL 2256 + ONGLAZE GREEN FINISH.

(ALSO PRINTED LIONS GATE BRIDGE IN BROWN.)

MOUNT EISENHOWER
CANADA

AMBASSADOR BRIDGE, WINDSOR
CANADA

EMPRESS HOTEL VICTORIA. B.C.
CANADA

"CASA LOMA" TORONTO
CANADA

CHATEAU FRONTENAC QUEBEC
CANADA

4462. CANADIAN VIEWS. U/G. PRINTED IN BLACK. (HANGSMAN MUG 1972)

(ALSO PRINTED LIONS GATE BRIDGE)

Illustration of Canadian Views designs from an Original Carlton Ware Pattern Book

Photograph courtesy of The Potteries Museum & Art Gallery, Stoke-on-Trent

AMBASSADOR BRIDGE, WINDSOR
CANADA

MOUNT EISENHOWER
CANADA

EMPRESS HOTEL VICTORIA. B.C.
CANADA

"CASA LOMA" TORONTO
CANADA

CHATEAU FRONTENAC QUEBEC
CANADA

Utility Ware

Carlton Ovenware was introduced in 1929. It was a fire-resisting white ware in semi-matt glaze decorations. Carlton Ware marketed it as both utilitarian and ornamental. It could be used for cooking and then taken straight to the dining table. This was quite novel for the period.

Because the concept of oven to table was quite new, Carlton Ware guaranteed the ware for twelve months against breakage in oven use. This guarantee statement was included in the back-stamp. To verify any possible claims against the guarantee each piece was date stamped with the month and year, for example 5/30 would be May 1930. This means that you can date *Carlton Ovenware* pieces quite accurately. Carlton Ware Ovenware is not considered to be particularly collectable.

In 1958 Carlton Ware introduce a new range of Utilitarian Ware called *Windswept*. The decoration is simple but effective. It consists of three long grass-like leaves blowing in the wind. The shapes of the range reflect this decoration to great effect.

Windswept was produced in twin-tone colours. These colours were matt cream with brown, glossy pale blue with glossy bottle green and dusky pink with pale blue. Another colour, matt cream with sage green was abandoned. The dusky pink with pale blue is quite rare compared to the other colours, perhaps it was less popular back in the 1950s and 1960s.

Other patterns and shapes of Utilitarian Ware followed.

1929	Ovenware
1935	Moderne
1958 - 1959	Windswept, Pinstripe, Linen
1959 - 1964	Shelf
1964 - 1968	Orbit, Floral Spray
1968	Tapestry, Daisy Chain
1968 - 1969	Athena, Skye, Canterbury, Oslo, Java
1969 - 1970	Wellington, Sunflower
1971 - 1976	Gourmet
1985 - 1986	Utility, Cook

Sometimes the same shape was used with different designs. For example *Orbit* and *Floral Spray*. *Orbit* has a "retro" design which appears to depict the orbit of electrons or the orbit of satellites around the Earth. *Floral Spray* depicts some yellow flowers on a wooden branch.

Skye has a textured embossing with criss-cross lines. It was produced in three colours Roman Green, Sunglow (yellow) and Thistle (purple). The Sunglow was the most popular and this vibrant colour also led *Skye* to being called Sunburst.

The list of shapes towards the end of this book, page 240 onwards, contains information about the items produced in the various ranges.

PRESENTING... *Carlton* WINDSWEPT WARE

Carlton

EDINBURGH COFFEE SET "WINDSWEPT"

Carlton Ware
4581 MATT CREAM & BROWN
4582 MATT CREAM & SAGE GREEN
4583 GLOSSY PALE BLUE & BOTTLE GREEN
4622 DUSKY PINK & PALE BLUE

EDINBURGH COFFEEWARE "WINDSWEPT" DESIGN

4581 Matt Cream & Brown
4583 Glossy Pale Blue & Bottle Green
4622 Dusky Pink & Pale Blue

	Each	Each
Coffeeset	40/-	Boxed 42/6
Coffeepot	8/9	
Sugar	3/4	
Cream	3/11	
Cup & Saucer	4/-	

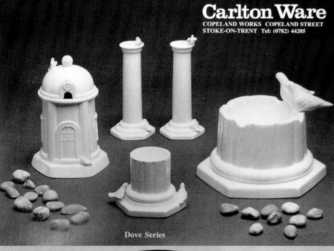

Dove Series

Windswept - Pattern 4583, Shape 2404

Plate from the Kosniowski Collection

£10 - £20

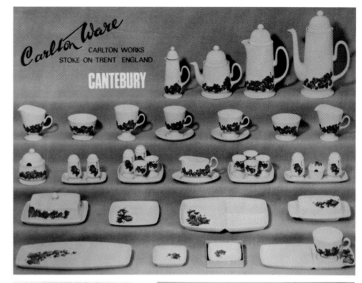

The *Oslo* range was produced in a number of colours. It was introduced in the late 1960s. The *Oslo* range is the same as the *Canterbury* (or *Vine*) range but without the embellishments that *Canterbury* has. Note that the *Oslo* range and *Canterbury* range have different shape numbers. Carlton Ware took the *Oslo* shape and added a matt Black Floral design on the white *Oslo* shape and called it *Java*.

Fruit - Apple - Shapes 3296, 3340
Bachelor Tea Set from Fieldings Auctioneers
£80 - £120

Wellington & Sunflower - Shape 2983
Coffee Pot from the Kosniowski Archives
£10 - £20 (for Sunflower), £20 - £30 (Wellington - plain vibrant colours)

Linen - Shape 2448

Wall Vases from the Ian & Jerome Collection

£20 - £40 each

Jugs

Toby Jugs from the Kosniowski Collection

£30 - £40 each

Gallant - Pattern 2867

Coffee & Tea Pot from the Kosniowski Collection

£25 - £40 each

Vertical Stripes - Pattern 4077
Coffee Set from the Kosniowski Collection
£250 - £300

Orbit - Shape 2654
Cruet Set from W & H Peacock Auctioneers
£50 - £80

Enchantment Medallion - Pattern 4908
Ginger Jar and vases from the Kosniowski Collection
£20 - £30 (Vases each), £175 - £225 (Jar)

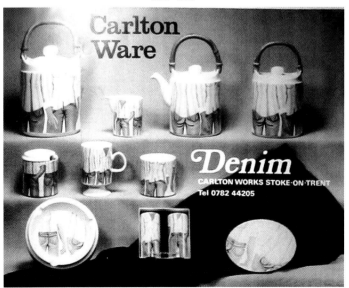

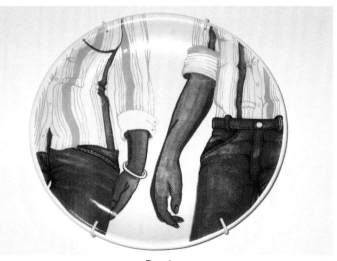

Denim
Plate from the Kosniowski Collection
£10 - £20

CarltonWare
Gourmet Range

Carlton Works Copeland Street Stoke-on-Trent Telephone: (0782) 44205

VENICE:
A range of tableware in white and primary: red, yellow or green.
The Plates are white edged with colour. The holloware white inside solid colour outside.

222) Cheese	223) Teapot Capacity 2 pints	224) Butter	225) Preserve
226) Cup 1/3rd pint	227) Cream ½ pint	228) Mug ½ pint	229) Plate Dia. 5"	230) P & S
231) Sandwich Plate	232) Sugar	233) Individual Butter	

Pattern Numbers and Impressed Numbers

There are two numbers that are important when looking at Carlton Ware; these are the Pattern and Impressed Numbers. Broadly speaking the Impressed (or Shape) number, which is applied before the firing process, indicates the "shape" of the item. On the other hand the Pattern number is usually hand painted on the base or on to a Carlton Ware sticker. This number represents the "pattern" and "colour" of the piece and is applied when the decorating takes place.

Sometimes the pattern numbers and the impressed numbers are not present or are very difficult to read. In the later years the pattern number was written on a paper sticker attached to the base of the piece and often this has been removed!

In this picture the pattern number is 2929 - hand painted towards the top. The shape or impressed number is 130 - on the left hand side. The hand painted marking towards the bottom o/2919 is an order number.

The pattern number 4217 is shown on a paper sticker. The shape number 1232 and size E appears on the paper sticker as well as being impressed.

Impressed numbers indicate the shape of a piece. For example the impressed number 217 is a vase. This shape has been used over a large number of years and came with many different patterns. Furthermore the vase was produced in different sizes.

Dutch, Jazz, New Chinese Bird & Cloud, Heinz
Shape 217 Vases from the Kosniowski Collection
£250 - £350, £1,250 - £1,500, £200 - £250, £50 - £80

Often an impressed number is followed by a space or "/" followed by further numbers. These further numbers refer to the "size" of the Carlton Ware piece. For example the conical shape 777 usually came with an additional number 10, 8 or 6 which represents the size in inches. Be aware that the size number isn't always a size in inches.

In principle if you know the correct Pattern number, the Impressed number and the size then you should then be able to determine what the item looks like including its colour.

With the embossed range of Carlton Ware the Impressed number also characterises the pattern. For instance, Shape 2311 is a Jug with the *Hazelnut* pattern. It came in three sizes: large, medium and small. It was also available in three colours Matt Cream, Green and Blue. Each would have its own pattern number (in the 4000 number range). Thus, although the impressed number in this case would also identify the pattern, the pattern number would also tell you the pattern and the colour.

Of course life with Carlton Ware is not always that simple. Pattern numbers sometimes had an additional letter added and that produced a slightly different pattern. For example

3765 Red Devil
3765 Devil's Copse

Both are on a gloss turquoise ground. The second pattern is the same as the first but without the Red Devil on it.

Sometimes the same pattern numbers were produced with different colourways such as:

2907 Magpies on red ground
2907 Magpies on blue ground

Finally we have examples where the patterns are different and the colourways are different. For example:

3965 Heron and Magical Tree on cream ground.
3965 Plain Rouge Royale

We have received many examples of this particular pair from several different people. It is therefore unlikely to be just the case of one person misreading a number

In summary you can characterise Carlton Ware, almost uniquely, by the pattern number (with additional suffixes) and impressed number (with additional suffixes for size).

Both of these numbers may be used to help date a piece of Carlton Ware.

Dating Carlton Ware by Back-Stamps

To help date Carlton Ware you can look at the back-stamp or logo. We have included a comprehensive range of Carlton Ware back-stamps. These provide an approximate indication of the date that a piece might have been made. Some fake pieces of Carlton Ware have a back-stamp from the wrong date period!

Kang He Cock & Peony
Early 1910s
- Early 1920s
(also Kosniowski Collection sticker)

Kang Hsi
Early 1910s
- Early 1920s

Kien Lung
Early 1910s
- Early 1920s

Crown Variation
1906 - 1927

Carlton China
1925 - 1957

Tutankhamun
1920s

Chinaland
Mid 1920s
A coloured back-stamp.

Ribbon or Blue Bird
1890 - 1894
The earliest back-stamp, usually in blue, brown or maroon.

Crown
1894 - 1927
The green colour is very rare

Round the World
1895 - 1915
The centre depicts the World.

Handcraft
1929 - 1939

Orchard
Mid 1920s

Ovenware
1929 - 1942

Carlton China Crown
1906 - 1927

Persian
Mid 1920s

Glacielle Ware
1929 - 1940

Script
1925 - 1970
One of the most common back-stamps

Kang He Rockery & Pheasant
Early 1910s
- Early 1920s

Cloisonne Ware
Early 1910s
- Early 1920s

Armand Lustre,
Early 1910s
- Early 1920s

Australian
1935 - 1961
The one on the right was used during the later years.

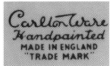
Rouge Royale (Red)
1940+

Bleu Royale (Blue)
1940+

Vert Royale (Green)
1940+

Noire Royale
(Black)
1940+

Handpainted
1952 - 1962

These Royale lustre colours were introduced in the 1940s, the colours of the wares were much more uniform and were easily distinguishable from the pre-war versions.

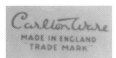
Curved
1967 - 1989

Plain
1968 - 1990

Yellow Script
1967-1987

Reproduction of another pottery.

Lustre Pottery
1973 - 1989

Walking Lustre
used on
Walking Ware
1973 - 1989

E F Paul
Signed by the
Designer

from the Kosniowski
Collection

Retailers Mark
Various Dates
Retailers with special orders often had a special back-stamp.

Recent
Francis Joseph
Back Stamps
1997 -

The current owner of Carlton Ware, Francis Joseph, does have some of the original moulds. In addition he has introduced some new pieces of Carlton Ware. These more recent pieces have a distinctive back stamp. The Swallow Device back stamp is used but with amendments to distinguish it from the early Swallow back stamp it has "Est 1890" within it. Also there is no use of "W & R" and it is often accompanied by the prefix "Genuine" Carlton Ware to set it apart from fakes.

British Registered Design Number

An identification mark that has often caused confusion to many is the Rd number that appears on the base of some Carlton Ware. Registered Design numbers are a consecutive numbering system which was first introduced in Britain in 1884. This is similar in principal to a Patent. Designs that have been registered by companies are held at the Public Record Office, Ruskin Avenue, Kew, Surrey.

The definition of Registered Designs is summed up in the current act, which refers to Design, Complex Product and Product, is as follows:

"Design" means the appearance of the whole or a part of a product resulting from the features of, in particular, the lines, contours, colours, shape, texture or materials of the product or its ornamentation. Examples of designs include floral or other decorative patterns, graphic symbols, including computer icons and works of art such as sculptures.

"Complex Product" means a product which is composed of at least two replaceable component parts permitting disassembly and reassembly of the product; and
"Product" means any industrial or handicraft item other than a computer program; and, in particular, includes packaging, get-up, graphic symbols, typographic type-faces and parts intended to be assembled into a complex product.

Not all designs are registerable. Broadly speaking a design has to be new with regard to anything which is previously known anywhere before the date of filing of an application to register the design. Features of appearance of a product which are solely dictated by the product's function are not registerable

The Registered Design number, usually written as Rd followed by the number gives the date when that design was registered. Original designs were usually registered to help prevent copying. The number was shown on the base of some pieces of Carlton Ware, particularly the older W & R pieces. Note that a particular design may have been in continuous production for many years after being registered, so dates should not be taken as the exact date of manufacture.

Something like a coffee set would probably come under the Complex Product definition, which would explain why a coffee pot and creamer might have the same Rd number. Carlton Ware would have registered such a design based on its shape. It is therefore not surprising that sets with different patterns would have the same Rd number.

Sometimes a piece of Carlton Ware will have two Registration Numbers on the base. This is because one of the numbers would be a Rd number for the shape and one for the pattern.

Dating Carlton Ware by RD number

Carlton Ware designs were often registered and the British Registered Number sometimes appears on the bottom of some pieces of Carlton Ware, particularly the older W & R pieces.

Registered Number 187328, registered in 1892

The following list of Registered Design numbers and approximate dates may be of help in identifying the date of manufacture.

Note that a design might have been in continuous production for many years after being registered, so dates should not be taken as dates of manufacture. Note also that for simplicity we have rounded off the Registered numbers to the nearest hundred.

Year	Rd No	Year	Rd No	Year	Rd No
1884	1 -	1917	659000 -	1950	860900 -
1885	19700 -	1918	662900 -	1951	863100 -
1886	40500 -	1919	666100 -	1952	866300 -
1887	64500 -	1920	673700 -	1953	869300 -
1888	90500 -	1921	680100 -	1954	872500 -
1889	116600 -	1922	687100 -	1955	876100 -
1890	141300 -	1923	695000 -	1956	879300 -
1891	163800 -	1924	702700 -	1957	882900 -
1892	185700 -	1925	710200 -	1958	887100 -
1893	205200 -	1926	718100 -	1959	891700 -
1894	224700 -	1927	726300 -	1960	895000 -
1895	247000 -	1928	734400 -	1961	899900 -
1896	268400 -	1929	742700 -	1962	904600 -
1897	291200 -	1930	751200 -	1963	909400 -
1898	311700 -	1931	760600 -	1964	914500 -
1899	331700 -	1932	769700 -	1965	919600 -
1900	351200 -	1933	779300 -	1966	924500 -
1901	368200 -	1934	789000 -	1967	929300 -
1902	385200 -	1935	799100 -	1968	934500 -
1903	402200 -	1936	808800 -	1969	939900 -
1904	424400 -	1937	817300 -	1970	944900 -
1905	447800 -	1938	825200 -	1971	950000 -
1906	471800 -	1939	832600 -	1972	955300 -
1907	494000 -	1940	837500 -	1973	960700 -
1908	518600 -	1941	838600 -	1974	965200 -
1909	535200 -	1942	839200 -	1975	969200 -
1910	552000 -	1943	840000 -	1976	973800 -
1911	574800 -	1944	841000 -	1977	978400 -
1912	594200 -	1945	842700 -	1978	982800 -
1913	612400 -	1946	845500 -	1979	987900 -
1914	630200 -	1947	849700 -	1980	993000 -
1915	644900 -	1948	853300 -	1981	998300 -
1916	653500 -	1949	857000 -	1982	1004500 -

Anemone - Shapes 925, 979, 1174
Preserve from the Kosniowski Collection
£120 - £175
Rd No 786475
Registered in 1933

Dating Carlton Ware by Pattern number

Pattern numbers provide an approximate date of manufacture. At least - they indicate approximately when the first piece with that pattern was produced. The list below gives an approximate date range for various pattern number ranges.

Pattern Number	Approximate Dates
up to 2000	up to 1916
2001 to 2700	1916 to 1923
2701 to 4000	1923 to 1936
4001 to 4500	1936 to 1940
4501 onwards	1940 onwards

There is a simple calculation (for pattern numbers above 1500) that provides a crude approximation to the date of the first production of a pattern. Simply ignore the last two digits of the pattern number and subtract 4 from the first two digits. The resulting number is an approximate date in the 1900s when the pattern would have been introduced. For example, with the pattern number 3025, we would first of all ignore 25, then we would subtract 4 from 30 to give 26 and this would give us an approximate date of 1926. We reiterate that this is a crude approximation and not an actual date of manufacture!

Dating Carlton Ware by Shape number

The impressed or shape numbers are not always useful for dating an item. For example the impressed number 1582 was first introduced in the late 1930s. It was used for coffee sets for several years. This picture shows three coffee pots, all with the same impressed number 1582 but with different patterns and different pattern numbers.

impressed number. The picture here contains a selection of items from coffee sets including coffee pots, milk jugs, sugar bowls, cups and saucers. All have the same impressed number 1582.

Spiders Web, Spots, New Mikado (Back & Centre)
Spiders Web, New Storks, Spots, Spiders Web (Front)
Shape 1582 - Coffee Sets from the Kosniowski Collection

Spiders Web, Spots, New Mikado
Shape 1582 - Coffee Pots from the Kosniowski Collection

The impressed number 1582 was used for coffee sets and as such sets were sold in sets, all items in the set had the same

The following table indicates approximately when a shape was first introduced. These dates will only indicate how old the item might be but cannot be a guarantee of its age. Some shapes were produced for many years after being introduced.

Shape Number	Date when first introduced	
Upto 1000	upto 1934	Crab and Lobster Salad Ware, Fruit Basket, Cottage
1000 - 1100	1934	Gum nut, Anemone, Bluebell, Crinoline Lady
1100 - 1200	1934 - 1935	Oak Tree, Lemon
1200 - 1300	1935	Rock Garden, Moderne, Crab, Musical Mugs & Jugs
1300 - 1400	1935 - 1936	Curled Lettuce, Buttercup
1400 - 1500	1936 - 1937	Tulip, Daisy, Blackberry, Raspberry, Pear
1500 - 1600	1937 - 1938	Water Lily, Wild Rose, Crocus, Musical Mugs & Jugs, Thistle
1600 - 1700	1938 - 1939	Red Currant, Apple Blossom
1700 - 1800	1939	Water Lily, Crocus, Pyrethrum, Clover, Shamrock, Narcissus, Begonia, Campion, Crinoline Lady, Bell, Daffodil, Arum Lily, Gladioli, Forget me not
1800 - 1900	1939 - 1940	Lily, Margarite, Foxglove
1900 - 2000	1940 - 1945	Basket, Chestnut, Clematis, Primula, Cherry, Wallflower, Dogshead
2000 - 2100	1945 - 1950	Delphinium, Apple Blossom, Poppy, Late Buttercup or Buttercup Garland, New Daisy, Poppy and Daisy, Hydrangea, Salad Ware
2100 - 2200	1950 - 1953	Wild Rose, Card Series, Langouste
2200 - 2300	1953 - 1955	Grape
2300 - 2400	1955 - 1958	Guinness figures, Hazel Nut, Leaf Salad
2400 - 2500	1958 - 1959	Windswept, Pinstripe, Langouste, Convolvulus, Fruit Ware, Novelty Cruet, Linen
2500 - 2600	1959 - 1964	Magnolia, Orchid, Aladdin's Lamp
2600 - 2700	1964 - 1968	Guinness Penguin Lamp, Carlton Village, Orbit, Floral Spray
2700 - 2800	1968	Guinness, Tapestry, Onion, Daisy Chain
2800 - 2900	1968 - 1969	Military, Athena, Skye, Vine
2900 - 3000	1969 - 1970	Wellington, Sunflower, Money Box - Flat
3000 - 3100	1970 - 1971	New Buttercup, Somerset, Money Box, Money Box - Bug Eyes
3100 - 3200	1971 - 1976	Early Walking Ware, Apple Blossom, Later Walking Ware, Flow Blue
3200 - 3300	1976 - 1980	Dovecote, Hovis, Pig
3300 - 3400	1980 - 1985	Charles & Di, Walking Ware Big Feet
3400 - 3500	1985 - 1986	Robertson Golly
3500+	1986+	Coronation Street

How Carlton Ware was made

Pottery has been made all over the world for thousands of years but it was in about 1680 that the area of Staffordshire became especially noted for pottery. Indeed, by the 1800s it was the national centre of the industry. This was probably because of the proximity of the River Trent and the fact that in 1767 a canal was cut which linked the River Mersey to the Trent. This enabled raw materials to be moved into the area easily. The railways probably superseded this mode of transport in 1848, along with tramways that linked the factories, railways and collieries.

The pottery area originally consisted of six small towns called Tunstall, Burslem, Hanley, Stoke, Fenton and Longton. In 1910 the six towns were united, albeit unwillingly, to be known as Stoke on Trent, or The Potteries.

China Clay, Ball Clays, Flint and Stone were the basic ingredients of the earthenware produced by Carlton Ware. The mixture was approximately 25% Ball Clay from Dorset, 25% China Clay from Cornwall, 15% China Stone also from Cornwall, and 35% Flint from the South East and East Anglia. The local clay was deemed unsuitable as it would have been too red when fired, but it was usually used to make the saggars. The flint had to be ground to a fine white powder by a flint mill prior to being sent to the factory.

All these ingredients were transported to the factory where they would all be mixed and put through a process of sieving and filtering. Magnets were used to remove any iron filings in the mix; otherwise this could leave red marks on the fired pottery.

A pug mill was used to ensure that the resultant clay had no lumps in it or pockets of air that could have made it burst when fired. It would eventually be ready for the potters to work with. Plates and saucers were made by pressing and what was known as jolleying, which shaped the wares by hand. Other pieces were cast in moulds; this would be pieces such as vases or other 'hollow ware'.

Initially a designer would have prepared a picture of the item. A master of the design would then have been produced. From this master a mould would have been made. The mould was made from plaster of paris and consisted of two or more pieces which when assembled would have a interior which was the shape of the item being produced. Each mould would have been used many times.

Once a mould was ready the clay was mixed with water. The resultant creamy liquid was called slip. This was poured into the plaster of paris moulds and left for a certain amount of time to start drying depending on the thickness of the piece required. The slip would dry closest to the mould and after the desired time the surplus slip would be poured off (and reused). The mould would be taken apart and the resulting item, called green ware, would be left overnight for initial drying in what was known as the Green House.

The Slip

Pouring slip into a Mould

Green Ware being removed from Mould

The green ware would then be stacked into the saggers, which were clay containers that were used to protect the pottery during the firing process. Workers called placers would carefully position several thousand saggers in the bottle kiln. This could take several weeks, but when full the kiln door would be bricked up and coal fires were lit. The firing could last up to five days and temperatures inside would reach above 1000° C. About 15 tons of coal would be required for each firing. Modern electric ovens replaced the bottle kilns at the Carlton Ware factory in the late 1940s. This enabled wares to be fired when they were required, rather than the long drawn out process using bottle kilns.

After this firing, the door would be broken down and the saggers removed. The ware now was called biscuit ware and would be taken into the factory where any joints and protrusions would be filed off. This filing with a metal file was called fettling. The Carlton Ware would then have an under glaze coat of colour applied by hand although in the 1920s and 30s this was applied by the newer airbrush method.

The piece would then be dipped in a barrel of lead glaze after which it would go back into the kiln to be fired again; this was called glost firing. After the second firing the decoration would be applied by means of a transfer, this process is explained over the page. In the 1930s and 40s multicolour lithographic transfers would be printed and then applied. The wares would then be fired again in a glost kiln, normally at the slightly lower temperature.

Saggars

The next task was to apply the decoration, up to twelve colours, all carried out by paintresses in the factory.

After the third firing, gilding would be applied, this consisted of a mixture of gold and mercury which would be brushed on to the rim and or foot of the piece. After a further firing to fix the gold this would then be burnished to leave the finished shining effect.

One of Carlton Ware's specialities was lustre ware and the firm developed a highly prized range of twelve glazes.

In the 1950s the clean air acts came in and bottle ovens were outlawed and replaced by electric ovens. Lead glaze was banned, as was flint which was replaced with ground bones from abattoirs.

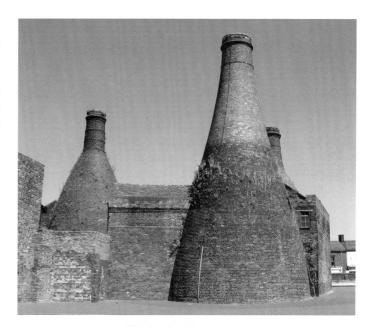

Old Bottle Kiln - today!

Transfer Printing

Many designs of Carlton Ware patterns were produced by "transfer printing". Transfer printing was started in England in the 1750s. It was a new way of illustrating a design within pottery manufacture.

Basically, transfer printing was a mass production method of placing a design or image onto a curved or uneven surface. Even though classed as a mass production method it was still a skilful process. Firstly, a designer would need to create the image or design for the wares. Carlton Ware had a number of celebrated designers. They produced some fantastic patterns that are highly desired today. The next stage in the process was for an engraver to reproduce the pattern onto a copper plate. This required a great deal of skill and it is a shame that the engravers are often overlooked in the history of Carlton Ware. The outline of the pattern on the copper plate is a "V" shaped groove, any shading would be dots or lines. The deeper the cutting, the deeper the print will appear on the pottery. Transfer printing is also known as lithography or decal.

Preparing a Transfer from a Copper Plate

The next stage was for the copper plate to be taken to the colour department. The colour or pigment was added to the plate. The colour was made from a mixture of metallic oxides and was usually mixed with oil. The copper plate was heated to allow the colour to run deeper into the engravings. The mixture was spread over the whole plate to ensure it was completely covered. The plate was then wiped and any surplus colour removed so that only the dots, lines and grooves were filled. The plate was now ready for the next stage.

The image from the plate was transferred to a piece of paper or strong tissue paper which could be easily cut and shaped to fit around the curved pottery. The paper was usually coated with a mixture of soft soap and water to prevent it sticking to the copper plate. After the paper had been laid on the plate a roller was used ensure that the paper was pressed into every crevice in the copper plate. The reverse rolling of the roller allows the paper to peel away from the copper plate. The paper now had picked up the colour from the grooves in the plate so that it had a printed picture of the image.

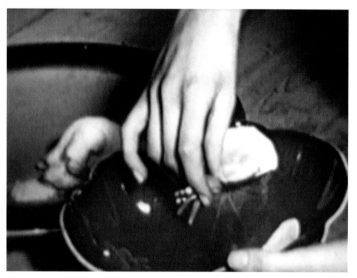

Using a Transfer

From here the paper was passed to the transfer section. A cutter removed any surplus paper and placed the paper in the correct area on the pottery. The oil was sticky and kept the paper in place on the pottery. The paper needed to be rubbed to ensure that the pattern was transferred to the pottery. Using strong tissue paper meant that the pot with the paper could be dipped into water to soften it so that it could be easily removed. The colours were unaffected because they were in oil! After the paper was removed you were left with the pattern on the pot.

Painting

Enamelling

Additional decoration, colours, enamel, etc could be applied in different stages to enhance the piece and produce a finished item.

A beautiful effect was achieved by using enamels. Highly skilled paintresses would paint powdered metal oxides mixed with turpentine and fat oil to add the final touches of colour to the pottery. For example, Iron oxides would provide a red or brown colour, Copper oxides would provide either green or red depending on the atmosphere in the kiln. The exact recipe of metal oxides used was kept secret from competitors!

The last firing would have been in what was known as the enamel or muffle kiln. Thus the final piece would now have made several trips to the kiln before being considered as a finished item.

We have illustrated some beautifully enamelled Carlton Ware on this and the next two pages.

Some finishing touches

C Wiltshaw and W G Purser admiring Carlton Ware

A beautifully enamelled jug
Kingfisher
Large Jug from the Kosniowski Collection
£200 - £300

Pomander Pendant - Pattern 2843
Cup & Saucer from the Kosniowski Collection
£150 - £200

Kaleidoscopic - Pattern 3565
Jug from the Peter Meyer and Gary Jessup Collection
£4,000 - £5,000

Spots
Coffee Set from the Kosniowski Collection
£450 - £550

Spots
Cup & Saucer from the Kosniowski Collection
£25 - £40

Gypsy - Pattern 3506
Footed Bowl from the Kosniowski Collection
£250 - £300

"4232"
"Aero Pale Green with Red spots"

"4322"
"Black with White spots"

"4323"
"Aero Pink with White spots"

"4324"
"Aero French Green with White spots"

Illustrations of Spots design from an Original Carlton Ware Pattern Book
Photograph courtesy of The Potteries Museum & Art Gallery, Stoke-on-Trent

Entangled Droplets - Pattern 3555
Coffee Set from the Kosniowski Collection
£500 - £600

Crazing

Crazing is the fine crackling you often see on glazed pottery. Crazing is in the glaze and is not detectable when you rub you fingernail over crazing. Crazing usually occurs during the pottery production when the clay body and glaze cool at different rates. This can also happen afterwards if the item is subjected to extreme temperature or humidity changes as the body expands and contracts at a different rate to the glaze, and hence little cracks appear. Crazing is also part of the natural ageing process of ceramics.

Crazing is a very common condition. These cobweb-like lines are NOT hairlines! They only run through the surface glaze and not the body of the piece itself.

Although not a fault like a chip, hairline or restoration, heavy crazing can detract from the appearance of a piece, and therefore should be noted in the condition statement by any reputable dealer.

Crazing

Tube Lining

Tube-lining is a technique where the decorator uses thin lines of coloured slip to outline and highlight the coloured glazed areas of the pattern. Carlton ware produced a number of different patterns using tube-lining. These include the following as well as some with unknown pattern numbers:

3943, 3944 Tube Lined Tree
3945 Tube Lined Flower
3974 Tube Lined Poppy & Bell
3975 Persian Rose
4012 Tube Lined Marigold
4138 Tube Lined Fields & Trees
4162 Tube Lined Tulip

Persian Rose
Bowl from the Kosniowski Collection
£250 - £300

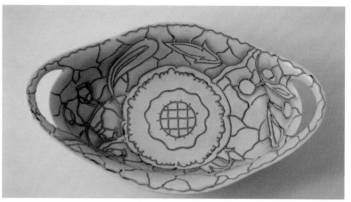

Persian Rose - Pattern 3975
Unfinished Bowl from the Kosniowski Collection
£40 - £60

Illustration of Tube Lined Tulip design from an Original Carlton Ware Pattern Book
Photograph courtesy of The Potteries Museum & Art Gallery, Stoke-on-Trent
"4162 Tulip Pattern. Tube Lined. Aero Green in and out."

Illustration of Tube Lined Flower design from an Original Carlton Ware Pattern Book
Photograph courtesy of The Potteries Museum & Art Gallery, Stoke-on-Trent
"3945 Tube Lined Flower Pattern. Stone Ground"

Tube Lined Flower - Pattern 3945
Pair of Vases from the Kosniowski Collection, £250 - £300

Engine Turned, Old Stone Ware, Incised Ware and Drip Ware

In this chapter we have included some of the Carlton Ware that may be described as less intricate than much of the so called "Best Ware" that Carlton Ware produced.

The Engine Turned range is a very uniformly produced style with the groves evenly spaced as if they were done by machine. Old Stone Ware (also called Ribbed Stone Ware) by comparison has the appearance of being hand thrown with the grooving much more random. Much of the Old Stone Ware comes with a simple pattern, often a plain colour. Stone Ware also includes some of the Animals produced by Carlton Ware, for example Dogs, which was discussed in an earlier chapter about the influence of Nature - Animals, page 72.

You can find a list of colourways for the Engine Turned range in the Patterns List chapter of this book. The shapes produced may be found in the Shapes List chapter, page 240 onwards.

Incised Ware is almost the opposite of Tube Lined Ware and has incisions made to produce a pattern.

The name Drip Ware is very descriptive of the range, appearing as if the colours have been allowed to run randomly down the piece. Drip Ware is often Old Stone Ware.

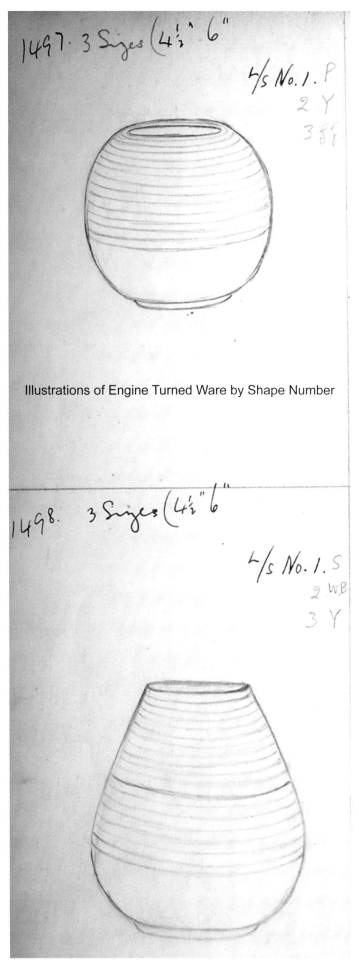

Illustrations of Engine Turned Ware by Shape Number

Engine Turned Ware - Pattern 3980, Shape 1487

Plate from the Ian & Jerome Collection

£30 - £50

Engine Turned Ware - Patterns 3981, 3977, 3978, 3980, Shapes 1500, 1498, 1492, 1497

Collection from the Ian & Jerome Collection

Cruet *£60 - £80*, Pink Vase *£30 - £60*, Green Vase *£60 - £80*, Yellow Vase *£40 - £60*

Engine Turned Ware - Pattern 3980, Shape 1491

Bowl from the Ian & Jerome Collection

£30 - £50

Incised Diamond - Pattern 3901

Tray from the Dulcie Agnes Joyce Memorial Collection

Image courtesy of www.nicholnack.com.au

£80 - £120

3770	Old Stone Ware. Aero in u/g. Dark Green (Pale at top to Dark) Stippled pale Green Blue (Matt Glaze
3771	" " " Freehand at Top u/g Matt Blue, Stone & Claret Brown. Stone in. " " O
3772	" " " " " " Stone Colour, u/g Golden Brown & Claret Brown. Stone in. " " O
3773	" " " " " " u/g Yellow, Liberty Green, dark Green & mixed Grey. Special Matt Glaze. (Aero Liberty Green in & painted dark Green). O
3775	Old Stone Ware. Aero in u/g. Turquoise (Matt Glaze.)
3776	— — — — — — Matt Blue. Matt Glaze
3777	— — — — — — Stone. Matt Glaze. Stippled.
3778	— — — — — Mixed Grey & Green. Special Matt Glaze. ×
3779	— — — Matt Blue & Mauve. Matt Glaze.
3780	— Pale u/g Mauve, Stippled Matt Blue. Matt Glaze.
3781	— — — Turquoise & Dark Green Rings. Matt Glaze.
3782	— — — — Mixed Matt Blue & Mauve & Green Blue Rings. Matt Glaze.
3783	— — Stone & Matt Blue Rings. Shaded Base Claret Brown. Matt
3784	— — at Top in u/g Pale Turquoise. Base in Claret Brown. (Hardly any colour in centre of ware) (Thin u/g Black on Base) Matt. Colour is split.

Old Stone Ware

Some Details from a Carlton Ware Pattern Book

Incised Diamond - Pattern 3901

Very Tall Vase from the Dulcie Agnes Joyce Memorial Collection
Image courtesy of www.nicholnack.com.au
£300 - £400

Engine Turned Ware - Pattern 3981, Shape 1497

Vase from the Ian & Jerome Collection
£40 - £60

Incised Square - Pattern 3900
Jug from the Dulcie Agnes Joyce Memorial Collection, Image courtesy of www.nicholnack.com.au
£100 - £150

Heinz
Vase from the Kosniowski Collection
£50 - £80

Drip Ware - Pattern 3917
Medium Vase from the Ian & Jerome Collection
£50 - £75

Some Carlton Ware Designers

Designers were a very important cog in the wheel of a pottery companies business. They could be in fact considered as vital and crucial for the well being and future of the company. This was indeed the case for Carlton Ware, and its many competitors, as their wares were sold on the merits of designs that appealed to the discerning and the masses. Potteries did produce designs that were the trend at that time but each company tried to add their own slant or interpretation on a variety of different shapes and sizes. This is obvious in the early days of Carlton Ware when they emulated the very popular Blush Ware designs produced by Royal Worcester. This is also in evidence with the *Grecian* and *Dancing Figures* known as Sprigged Ware or Jasper Ware. This has raised relief motifs in the style made famous by Josiah Wedgwood. Other popular designs include Flow Blue, *Imari* and *Reproduction Swansea China*.

The importance of designers to the pottery companies that employed them is undoubted. But, it's interesting that although many had immense talent and that they may have received some notoriety in their field of expertise not that many are well known outside of their circle. This is probably due to the fact that Wiltshaw & Robinson, and other potteries, did not wish to glorify the designer. They probably, along with many other potteries including Wedgwood, may have discouraged identifying the artist as they wished the focus to be on the expertise of the companies brands and not necessarily the designer who could quite easily leave a company. This is in contrast to the Shorter Group pottery with Clarice Cliff and the A E Gray pottery with Susie Cooper fame.

Sometimes this makes the task of identifying and attributing a design to a particular designer an inexact science. This is obvious when you consider that even when the artists put a master copy within the pattern book it was not annotated personally in any way. This in some way is probably in the interest of the company, as they then owned the design. It's probably fair to say that most of Carlton's designs were attributed to the chief designer employed by them during the relevant period of their employment and with the style in which they worked. This is in addition to the fact that the workforce of painters and paintresses who were very talented were often shared among a number of companies and paid on a piecework basis. This was considered more prudent as the work was very labour intensive.

Wiltshaw & Robinson, as the company was known at its conception, consisted of the three directors and in 1911 after disagreements James Wiltshaw split with the Robinson brothers and proudly announced that he was now the sole proprietor. He employed Horace Wain as the company's designer to lift the company out of the dated Victorian wares. He successfully introduced many popular designs and is accredited with introducing the very popular Oriental themes. This included the Chinoiserie designs of pagodas, barges, dragons, exotic birds of paradise as well as the Cloisonne ranges and other oriental designs such as *Persian, Kien*

Lung, Kang Hsi and Armand Lustre, which all have their own back stamp. Horace left Carlton Ware in the mid 1920s and eventually took up a position with A.G.Harley-Jones & Co, the manufacturers of Wilton Ware. You can see the similarities and styles of some designs produced by Carlton Ware and Wilton Ware. Indeed, one can get confused with some designs, particularly if the back stamp is unclear.

Persian (left) designed by Horace Wain

Tutankhamen (right) designed by Enoch Boulton

Enoch Boulton joined Wiltshaw & Robinson in 1908 whilst Horace Wain was in control as the chief designer. This was after his apprenticeship at Grimwades where he was reported to have studied at the reputable Burslem School of Art, which produced some of our most famous ceramic designers accredited with the Art deco movement, Susie Cooper and Clarice Cliff. Over the next 13 to 14 years at Carlton Ware he worked his way up to senior designer and then replaced Horace as the Design Manager.

This period was very productive time for Carlton Ware as Frederick Cuthbert Wiltshaw had taken over the reigns of the company after the tragic death of his father James Wiltshaw in 1918. New designs were abundant and Boulton proved to be a very successful designer and artist, which was good for the company. Howard Carter's discovery of the tomb of Tutankhamen heralded the way forward with some magnificent designs. Enoch obviously utilised the momentous and historical occasion to commercially commemorate it with style. Pieces were adorned with Egyptian hieroglyphics finished in overglaze with ornate finials replicating the death mask of the boy king. These Egyptian designs were produced on many different shapes. Boulton was probably the force behind the change of back stamp from the old traditional Crown W & R back stamp to a new and more modern design, which is known as the Script Mark which, would remain for more than 60 years. He did the same thing when he moved to Crown Devon and updated their back stamp.

Boulton as an artist was influenced, like many at that time, by the 1925 Exposition Internationale des Arts Décoratifs et Industriels Modernes (International Exposition of Modern Industrial and Decorative Art) in Paris. The movement was widely considered to be an eclectic form of elegant and stylish modernism being influenced by a variety of sources. Amongst his other notable contributions were the opulent *Chinaland* design, the new freehand painted handcraft designs, *Paradise Bird and Tree* and the amazing Art Deco *Jazz*. In 1929 he was head hunted by Fieldings of Crown Devon fame and became their Chief Designer for them and lifted them out of the doldrums with beautiful designs, some which bear a cunning similarity to some Carlton Ware designs.

Violet Elmer was another very talented artist and designer. Her work was noticed by F C Wiltshaw after she had entered some of her art work into an Arts Exhibition in the potteries. She was invited to join Carlton Ware as a designer in 1928 at the age of 21 and would have worked with Enoch Boulton until his departure for Crown Devon. Initially she would have designed for the Carlton China ranges, which would have been as a consequence of the Birks Rawlins takeover. She is well known for her beautiful, colourful designs. She would have continued to take the initial handcraft designs to new dimensions with *Floral Comet, Anemone, Hollyhocks, Scroll* and *Iceland Poppy*. Along with producing many other highly respected and very popular Best Wares such as *Awakening, Fantasia, Fairy Shadow, Mandarins Chatting, Bell, Sketching Bird, Red Devil* and *Shabunkin* etc. And, of course some of the fabulous Art Deco designs attributed to her are *Scimitar, Egyptian Fan, Rainbow Fan, Chevrons, Intersection, Tyrolean Bands, Explosion* and *Fan*.

In June 1937 she was married to Arthur Joseph Longton and so discontinued her career, as it was then the custom for the wife to care for the home and husband. Violet Elmer had left behind a great legacy, a tribute to her talent, her work was richly colourful, stylistic and creative.

The best wares produced between the wars are considered to be the most influential and prolific time in the history of Carlton Ware. The 1920s and 30s saw the production of amazingly colourful designs that were very evocative of the period of decadence. These extravagant excesses were curtailed with the onset of the Second World War when materials were scarce and ceramic companies were banned from such practices.

It is only possible to attribute certain designs to designers by the periods of their time with Carlton Ware and so we may not be 100% accurate by all accounts. Some designs may have been started by one designer and then taken to another dimension by others. But it's true to say that collectively these three influential designers shaped the fine quality and heady designs produced between the 1920s and 30s.

Olive Kew followed by Irene Pemberton, who had also trained at the famous Burslem School of Art, succeeded Violet Elmer. But once again marriage and childbirth interrupted a great talent in the early forties. Some of Pemberton's designs were *Spider's Web, Heron & Magical Tree* and *Rabbits at Dusk*.

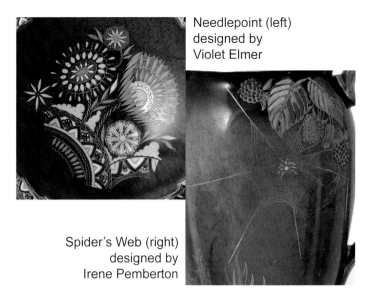

Needlepoint (left) designed by Violet Elmer

Spider's Web (right) designed by Irene Pemberton

John Gilroy (1898-1985) was an illustrator and artist who produced lots of advertising material. In 1930 he produced his first Guinness poster whilst a designer at the advertising agency S H Benson Ltd. he produced more than 100 press advertisements and 50 poster designs for Guinness over 35 years. The Guinness animals including the toucan and kangaroo as well as the zookeeper appeared on posters, press advertisements, show cards and waiter trays from the 1930s to the 1960s. And, of course, as Carlton Ware ceramics in the 1950s and 1960s.

The *Orbit* range of Carlton Ware was introduced in the mid 1960s. Peter Forster is accredited with this design.

Other designers included, John Hassall (Novelties), Ken Coxon, Chris Boulton, Angela Fox and Vivian Brennan. We have already mentioned, elsewhere, Roger Mitchell and Dana Napiorkowska as designers of *Walking Ware*. Kathleen Parsons is accredited with designing the *Coronation Street* Figures.

Sometimes designs were commissioned and one that we are aware of is *Fairy Carnival*. Our research shows that this was commissioned for the wife of one of the Carlton Ware Directors. The vase was signed E F Paul and it is believed to have been a very talented student, which is obvious by the quality of the finished piece. Only two examples of this design are known to exist, one of which was a small demonstration piece made for approval by the Directors. The other is in the Kosniowski Collection.

Why Restore?

We are often asked if it is worthwhile restoring damaged pieces of Carlton Ware. Hopefully these notes will help answer this and some related questions.

The restoration of ceramics is not a new phenomena, it has been going on for ages. There may be several reasons to get a piece restored. Collectors may be looking for a particular piece and only a damaged one may be available; restoration of that piece is the answer. Or, a collector may have damaged a favourite piece by accident. Dealers usually want to maximize their income and may not be able to sell a damaged piece for a reasonable price. Of course, a good dealer will always point out any restorations and price accordingly.

Restoration does affect the value of a piece. A restored item may appear "perfect" after restoration but its value will be less than a similar piece in "perfect" condition. Usually a restored piece is more valuable than the piece with the damage.

Whether it is worth restoring a piece depends on its sentimental value or real value and the cost of restoration. Usually only the more expensive pieces of Carlton Ware are worth restoring. These include many of the "best-ware" pieces. It's often not worth while restoring many of the embossed range of Carlton Ware. However, it's not uncommon to find amateur repair work.

Amateur repairers often end up causing further damage by scratching the surface or rubbing the gilding. Sometimes the glue used may be impossible to remove and so a professional restoration may not be possible.

Professional restoration work usually follows a few basic procedures. Firstly any cracks or breaks are glued (not just with any old glue). This is then followed by using some special filler to smooth over the break. Then paint is applied to match the original colour and glaze. This may require several coats to get an accurate match. Between the application of each coat the piece is heated gently to harden the paint. A good restoration may be "invisible" to see.

A professional restoration may take some time and you should be prepared to wait for quality work. Remember that restoration is a fine craft.

Detecting restoration is not always easy. There are some basic things you can do, otherwise there are more elaborate methods.

The first thing is to look at the piece to see if the colouring is consistent. If there is crazing (and most pieces have some crazing) then there shouldn't be any patches without crazing. Run your fingers over the piece to see if you feel any lumps or bumps. The places that damage occurs is often on rims, handles and lids.

Many people advocate the "Ping" test. Lightly tap your fingernail on the side of the piece. If a clear ringing sound is heard then that is good. A "clunk" may indicate restoration or a hairline. But, some perfect pieces don't "ping". And, many good restorers can regain a "ping" back into a repaired piece! This test is useful on an initial inspection

Other people advocate using their "teeth" to feel any restoration work which is often "softer". Others suggest trying to detect any difference in temperature around a piece of Carlton Ware. The restored part is usually warmer than the original piece. Mind you, we're not sure if dealers would be happy with you sticking the item in your mouth!

There are more accurate tests for restoration which include Ultraviolet Light, Fluorescent Light or X-rays.

A good way to find a qualified restorer is to contact a museum in your area and ask them where and who does work for them.

On a final note: - be careful with your Carlton Ware, you don't want to cause any damage, never pick up a piece of Carlton Ware by its handle or knob, remove lids carefully.

Damaged in the post!

Amateur Repair!

Collecting Carlton Ware

How did you start your Carlton Ware collection? Many of us started by accident! We may have been given a piece or acquired a piece from a relative. Or, it might have been love at first sight. Whatever the reason for starting, once the love affair has begun it can become an obsession as we can testify. One of the sad aspects of Carlton Ware was the lack of accurate and comprehensive written material. This to us became a mission to right the wrong and get publishing. We wanted to raise the profile of Carlton Ware and make people aware of its beauty and intricacies and to show that it wasn't a poor relation to some of the other well-documented ceramics companies.

One of the wonders of Carlton Ware is the diverse range that was made so there is something to suit all tastes and pockets. This is an accolade to the company's quest to always produce items of great quality even though this was probably partly the cause of their downfall because to create the intricate designs was very labour intensive and expensive. Many collectors select a theme and stick to it but we may be the exception because in our collection we have tried to include the complete range of Carlton Ware although only part of our collection is on display at any time. Space is often a problem when a collection gets too large! The excuse for our large collection was that we needed it to do the research for our web site and for the books we have written, as it was important for us to verify patterns numbers, shapes and colours.

In the not too distant past, building up a collection was quite time consuming. You had to visit antique shops, antique fairs or auctions, time consuming but fun. Nowadays, with the Internet, you could build up a collection quite quickly. Indeed there are many internet sites where many pieces of Carlton Ware are on offer. Auction houses are still a good place for Carlton Ware, particularly as the auctioneer will provide an honest condition report. Whichever way you shop, finding that exquisite piece of Carlton Ware is a wonderful experience.

The thrill of finding that elusive piece is amazing and even more so if you manage to get it for a good price. Sometimes or perhaps always when you are a collector it's hard to apply the brakes and you frequently let your heart rule. We are perhaps all guilty of sometimes paying more than we would have wished to just to get that desired piece.

We often feel that the joy of building a collection is compounded when you receive your new addition, which is then lovingly held and devoured. This is followed by the euphoria of deciding how to rearrange things so to accommodate your new treasure and show it to its best advantage. Once it's settled in you get used to having it but often smile to yourself when you pass it by. The other enormous enjoyment that you can get from your collection is showing it to others who have an appreciation of its beauty. We have loved exhibiting our collection to our VIP club members at club meetings, at the NEC Antiques Fair and of course on our web site and in our books.

Most of the Carlton Ware pieces shown in this book are from our own collection but many have been supplied by other people. A large number were supplied by Bruce Nichol from Australia. Bruce runs an internet site www.nicholnack.com.au. He writes: *the story of Nicholnack's conception and birth is akin to the story you will hear from many business owners. I had been collecting some embossed Carlton Ware items for some time - nothing compulsive, just the occasional piece - when I found eBay during 2000 and collecting became a lot easier. At the time I was doing a sales job that I loathed. So early in 2001 I decided that I should try dealing on eBay. I put aside A$2,000 as a seed fund and off I went to a local estate auction. I bought some items and listed them on eBay under the name of Nicholnack, most of these items quickly sold to the US. So I reinvested my money and went around again. I soon decided I could not afford to be both a collector and a dealer. So I decided that while I could not keep the items I purchased I could collect the images and the data I amassed along the way. This led to www.nicholnack.com.au which serves two purposes; it is a sales gallery for my stock and a forum to host the data and images that I had been amassing.*

Many of the pictures supplied by Bruce are from two large Carlton Ware collections; "The Parnell Collection" and the "Dulcie Agnes Joyce Memorial Collection".

The curator of "The Parnell Collection" came to Carlton Ware over 30 years ago. Her interests in Carlton Ware are right across the full range of their production. Her collection is vast; it is in reality many collections in one. It encompasses magnificent collections of Handcraft and Best Ware including W&R and Blush Ware patterns. It also includes many Embossed patterns, novelty items and figurines. The curator of this collection comes from humble origins, with a large and closely held family. She runs a successful catering business in rural Australia from which she funds her collecting.

The "Dulcie Agnes Joyce Memorial Collection" began with the items that Dulcie was given as gifts from her husband which he had purchased for her, brand new, in the 1950s. The present curator of this collection houses it in an apartment in an inner Melbourne Bayside suburb. This collection is really limited by space, when a large new item is purchased another item has to be sold. For this reason many of their later purchases are small to medium sized objects. The collection encompasses magnificent examples of Best Ware, including lustre and hand painted patterns from the W&R and Carlton Ware eras. This collection also has many items from Carlton Ware's Handcraft range; it also holds a large selection of Figurines and Napkin rings. The curator is a single man with multiple collections and many and varied passions.

1997 – A New Beginning

In 1997 Frank Salmon (Francis Joseph) purchased the rights to Carlton Ware, the trade name and a good number of original moulds. So, once again the Carlton Ware name was resurrected from its demise.

Frank commissioned a set of female figures, which are set in flowers; the inspiration for this was to represent earlier Carlton Ware flower designs. These were followed by the Carlton Kids series, which consists of children dressed in war uniforms. These were made from original moulds that had been shelved during the war and had never before been used. The Red Baron teapot quickly followed which featured celebrities in the cockpit such as Elvis Presley and Winston Churchill. Many other figurines were featured that included Enid Blyton's Golly and The Snowman. The range was extended with further hand painted designs by Marie Graves.

Frank has now re-registered the Carlton Ware back stamp to prevent it being taken up by anyone else. So he has the warrant to use the Swallow back stamp along with the name "Royale". To save any confusion some amendments have been made to the pre 1928 back stamp in that it doesn't contain the initials "W & R" but still retains "Est 1890" and is usually accompanied by the prefix "Genuine Carlton Ware". The intention was always to continue the good name of Carlton Ware with quality collectables made at British potteries, and this has fortunately been the case.

Carlton Girl
Hollyhocks & Butterfly Girl from the Kosniowski Collection
£100 - £150 each

Red Devil
Lidded Vase (painted by Marie Graves) from carltonware.co.uk
£1,500 - £1,750

Churchill
Mug from carltonware.co.uk
£30 - £40

Fido Dog
Mabel Lucie Attwell inspired from carltonware.co.uk

£25 - £40

Tree & Swallow
Pair of Small Ginger Jars from the Kosniowski Collection

£80 - £100 each

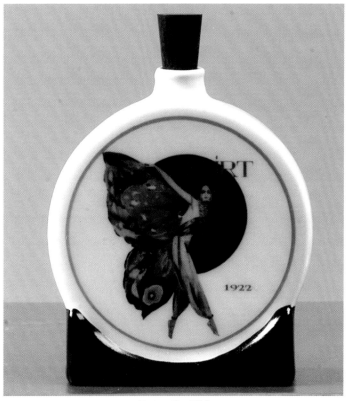

Butterfly Girl
Deco Flirt Flask from carltonware.co.uk

£25 - £40

Koi Carp
Vase (design by Peter Graves) from carltonware.co.uk

£200 - £250

Patterns

Carlton Ware designed several thousands of different patterns; and these were produced in many different shapes and colours. Each design and associated colour was normally designated a pattern number. This number was usually either painted on the base or written on a paper sticker stuck to the bottom.

We have, over many years, been collating a list of patterns together with their associated pattern numbers. The list has been compiled from a number of sources – from our research, our own collection and from other collectors. We would like to thank everyone that has sent us pictures of their Carlton Ware.

Sometimes hand painted numbers are difficult to read and therefore we may attribute two different patterns to the same number. Sometimes Carlton Ware used the same number for different patterns which they distinguished by the addition of an extra letter. Please see the chapter on Pattern Numbers and Impressed Numbers on page 189 for more information.

The following is a list of the patterns that we are aware of. This list is not perfect and we apologise for any errors.

52 Blush Ware - Cistus *Colourful flowers.*
74 Blush Ware - Cistus *Colourful flowers.*
110 Blush Ware *Flowers.*
128 Chequered Border *Border design on Red ground.*
142 Blush Ware - Sweet Violet *Violet like flowers on pale pink and cream ground.*
184 Blush Ware - Camellia *Camelia flowers on pale cream ground.*
186 Blush Ware - Peony *Peony flowers.*
194 Blush Ware - Peony *Peony flowers.*
206 Blush Ware - Poppy *Flowers*
220 Flow Blue - Florida *Flow blue, flowers and leaves in blue and gilt with gilt background.*
230 Flow Blue *Flow Blue*
237 Blush Ware - Violet *Violet like flowers.*
253 Blush Ware *Flowers.*
303 Blush Ware - Poppy *Poppies on White/ Cream.*
305 Blush Ware - Poppy *Poppies on pale Blue.*
306 Blush Ware - Poppy *Poppies on Pink.*
307 Blush Ware - Poppy *Poppies on Pink.*
347 Blush Ware - Azalea *Flowers.*
348 Blush Ware - Rose Garland *Flowers*
376 Blush Ware - Convolvulous *Pinkish Convolvulous flowers.*
401 Blush Ware - Chrysanthemum *Chrysanthemum flowers, pale cream ground.*
403 Blush Ware - Rose Bud *Flowers.*
405 Blush Ware - Chrysanthemum *Chrysanthemum flowers on pale Pink.*
406 Blush Ware - Chrysanthemum *Chrysanthemum flowers on pale Pink.*
407 Blush Ware - Chrysanthemum *Chrysanthemum flowers, pale cream ground.*
409 Blush Ware - Chrysanthemum *Chrysanthemum flowers.*
418 Blush Ware - Heather *Flowers*
421 Bird *A bit like lovebirds*
425 Blush Ware - Camellia *Flowers on pale cream ground.*
428 Blush Ware - Arvista *Flowers.*
438 Blush Ware - Dianthus *Carnation like flowers.*
438 Blush Ware - Rose Garland *Flowers*
439 Blush Ware - Roses *Roses on pale cream ground.*
458 Blush Ware - Dianthus *Flowers.*
476 Blush Ware - Arvista *Flowers.*
483 Blush Ware - Carnation *Flowers.*

491 Blush Ware - Petunia *Colourful flowers.*
504 Blush Ware - Chrysanthemum *Flowers.*
508 Blush Ware - Royal May *Flowers.*
509 Blush Ware - Royal May *Flowers*
522 Chinese Quail *Bird with plumed tail sitting on branch with foliage and flowers. Black ground.*
523 no name *Long tailed bird.*
524 Blush Ware *Flowers.*
528 Red Rose *Red roses and leaves on matt black ground.*
534 Flow Blue - Petunia *Flowers*
538 Blush Ware - Peony *Flowers*
547 Flow Blue - Catalpa *Flowers*
561 Blush Ware - Arvista *Colourful poppy like flowers on pale cream ground.*
561 Flow Blue - Arvista *Poppy like flowers.*
566 Flow Blue *Flowers on Flow Blue*
578 Blush Ware - Tulips *Flowers.*
585 Blush Ware *Flowers.*
586 Flow Blue - Flower Garland *Flowers in blue.*
595 Bird & Tree Peony *Small bird on Peony like blossoms. Matt black ground.*
596 Kang Hsi *Variety of flowerheads, blossom and leaves on white ground within blue bordered cartouches.*
597 Kang Hsi Fish *Beautiful realistic looking orange fish swimming amongst gilt seaweed. Blue ground with Kang Hsi backstamp.*
599 Kang Hsi *Variety of flowerheads, blossom and leaves on white ground.*
601 Grecian Figures *Frieze of white foliage and white Grecian style figures raised as in Wedgewood. Pink ground.*
601 Plain *Plain pink with gilt.*
602 Grecian Figures *Frieze of white foliage and white Grecian style figures raised as in Wedgewood. Grey ground.*
602 Blush Ware - Royal May *Flowers.*
602 Grecian Figures with no Figures *Normally with a frieze of white foliage and white Grecian style figures raised as in Wedgewood. Grey ground.*
603 no name *Pale green ground with white perimctcr band.*
604 Grecian Figures *Frieze of white foliage and white Grecian style figures raised as in Wedgewood. Pale green ground.*
614 Dancing Figures *Frieze of white foliage and white Grecian style dancing figures raised as in Wedgewood. Dark green matt ground.*

616 Flow Blue *Flow Blue*
621 Blush Ware - Carnation Spray *Carnation flowers*
624 Reproduction Swansea China *Colourful posies of flowers in gilt cartouches with decorative gilt leaves and bands on black ground.*
624 Blush Ware - Picotees *Carnation like flowers*
628 Pheasant Cartouche *Cartouche of multi-coloured exotic birds, flowers and butterflies. Often has Kang Hsi back stamp.*
634 Blush Ware - Hibiscus *Flowers.*
637 Blush Ware - Cornucopia *Multi-coloured flowers.*
638 Blush Ware - Hibiscus *Hibiscus floral cluster, rim edged in gold. Pale ground.*
639 Blush Ware - Hibiscus *Flowers.*
641 Blush Ware - Daffodil *Daffodil like flowers*
642 no name *Flowers and foliage on cream ground.*
649 Blush Ware *Flowers.*
653 Blush Ware - Cornucopia *Multi-coloured flowers.*
659 Blush Ware - Wild Rose *Flowers.*
661 Blush Ware - Catalpa *Flowers.*
666 Blush Ware - Honfleur *Flowers.*
670 Blush Ware *Flowers.*
682 Blush Ware - Dahlia *Flowers.*
683 Blush Ware - Dahlia *Flowers.*
686 Blush Ware - Daisy *Flowers*
694 Blush Ware - Petunia *Flowers.*
695 Blush Ware - Petunia *Flowers.*
698 Blush Ware - Petunia *Flowers.*
708 Blush Ware *Flowers.*
709 Blush Ware - Cornflower *Flowers*
722 Stork *White Stork bird with insets of colourful flowers and leaves. Cloisonne Ware on matt green ground.*
723 Stork *White Stork bird with insets of colourful flowers and leaves. Cloisonne Ware on matt black ground.*
732 Blush Ware *Flowers.*
735 Blush Ware - Dahlia *Flowers.*
739 Blush Ware - Cornucopia *Blossom on pale cream ground.*
751 Flow Blue - Poppy *Blue lined design of poppies on white gloss ground.*
752 Flow Blue - Poppy *Blue lined design of poppies on white gloss ground.*
777 Flow Blue - Diadem *Blue flowers on white ground.*

821 Blush Ware - Clematis *Flowers.*
826 Blush Ware - Clematis *Flowers.*
827 Pheasant Cartouche *Cartouche of multi-coloured exotic birds, flowers and butterflies.*
832 Blush Ware - Cornucopia *Multi-coloured flowers design.*
838 Blush Ware - Nouveau Poppies *Poppies on pale cream ground.*
839 Blush Ware - Hibiscus *Flowers.*
843 Blush Ware - Camellia *Flowers and leaves*
848 Blush Ware - Camellia *Flowers and leaves*
849 Blush Ware - Camellia *Flowers and leaves*
850 Insects *Insects and foliage on white ground.*
852 Plain *Plain white with gilt on handles.*
856 Blush Ware - Queen Victoria *Flowers with Queen Victoria.*
860 Blush Ware - Camellia *Flowers and leaves*
876 Flow Blue - May *Flowers*
878 Blush Ware - Dahlia *Dahlia like flowers*
886 Blush Ware - Nouveau Poppies *Poppies on white ground.*
888 Blush Ware - Nouveau Poppies *Poppies on pale cream ground.*
913 Blush Ware - Roses *Flowers.*
914 Blush Ware - Pansy *Flowers*
921 Blush Ware - Honfleur *Flowers.*
945 Blush Ware - Peony *Peony flowers*
949 Blush Ware - Peony *Peony flowers*
975 Blush Ware *Flowers.*
1002 Blush Ware - Honfleur *Flowers.*
1006 Flow Blue - Poppy *Blue lined design of poppies on white gloss ground.*
1015 Blush Ware - Poppy *Poppies*
1031 Blush Ware - Arvista *Flowers on pale cream ground.*
1031 Flow Blue - Poppy *Blue lined design of poppies on white gloss ground.*
1034 Blush Ware - Peony *Peonies*
1038 Blush Ware - Carnation *Carnation like flowers*
1041 Blush Ware - Carnation *Carnation like flowers*
1041 Flow Blue - Poppy *Blue lined design of poppies on white gloss ground.*
1042 Blush Ware - Poppy Spray *Flowers*
1057 Blush Ware - Arvista *Flowers on pale cream ground.*
1075 Blush Ware *Flowers.*
1089 Blush Ware - Chrysanthemum *White to light cream ground with orange and beige chrysanthemums.*
1091 Blush Ware - Chrysanthemum *White to light cream ground with pink and mauve chrysanthemums.*
1123 Blush Ware - Wild Rose *Flowers.*
1125 Blush Ware - Wild Rose *Flowers.*
1153 Blush Ware - Camellia *Flowers on creamy background.*
1162 Blush Ware - Cornucopia *Brownish ground, deep blue border, multi-coloured flowers.*
1166 Blush Ware - Heather *Flowers.*
1172 Rose Bud *Flowers*
1186 Blush Ware - Rose Garland *Flowers*
1219 Blush Ware *Flowers.*
1220 First Blush of Day *Intricate design which appear to depict a bird and sun.*
1221 Blush Ware - Roses *Flowers.*
1225 Flow Blue *Flow Blue*
1229 Blush Ware - Royal May *Flowers.*
1230 Blush Ware *White ground with figures of grey and brown.*
1242 Blush Ware - Carnation Spray *Flowers on pale ground.*

1246 Blush Ware *Apple blossom & butterfly.*
1274 Flow Blue *Flowers in blue and colours edged in gilt on pale cream ground.*
1283 Blush Ware - Violet *Violets*
1304 no name *Patterned flowers on green and red ground.*
1315 Blush Ware - Violet *Violets*
1332 Blush Ware - Violet *Violets*
1340 Blush Ware *Flowers.*
1358 Blush Ware *Flowers.*
1372 Blush Ware - Chrysanthemum *Orange and beige chrysanthemums on white to light cream ground.*
1400 Blush Ware - Dog Rose *Flowers.*
1406 Flow Blue *Flowers in blue and gilt.*
1414 Blush Ware *Flowers.*
1422 Flow Blue - Iris *Iris like flowers.*
1451 Blush Ware - Petunia *Flowers*
1453 Blush Ware - Petunia *Flowers.*
1467 Blush Ware - Petunia *Flowers*
1474 Blush Ware - Cistus *Colourful flowers.*
1509 Blush Ware *Brownish ground, gilt feet and rim. Sprays of Flowers.*
1518 Blush Ware *Flowers.*
1524 Blush Ware - Dog Rose *Flowers.*
1572 Blush Ware *Flowers.*
1573 no name *Blue transfer flowers, raised gilding.*
1582 Blush Ware - Carnation *Flowers*
1601 Blush Ware - Honeysuckle *Honeysuckle flowers*
1609 Blush Ware - Wild Rose *Flowers.*
1619 Flow Blue *Multi-flowered panels*
1621 Blush Ware *Flowers.*
1624 Blush Ware *Flowers.*
1630 Blush Ware - Arvista *Flowers.*
1631 Flow Blue *Flowers on pale ground.*
1635 Flow Blue - Chrysanthemum *Blue Chrysanthemums edged in gilt and with heavy gold surrounding.*
1635 Blush Ware - Hibiscus *Flowers.*
1639 Flow Blue - Honfleur *Flowers.*
1646 Flow Blue - Daffodil *Daffodil flowers on Flow Blue*
1650 Blush Ware - Diadem *Thistle like flowers*
1652 Blush Ware - Arvista *Flowers on pale cream ground.*
1653 Blush Ware - Dahlia *Flowers*
1653 Blush Ware *Flowers*
1655 Blush Ware - Marguerite *Patterns of flowers in cobalt blue outlined in gilt. Gold floral design on cream ground.*
1658 Blush Ware - Peony *Peony flowers*
1661 Blush Ware - Peony *Peony flowers on pale cream ground.*
1664 Blush Ware *Flowers.*
1681 Blush Ware *Deep blue like Doulton.*
1682 Blush Ware - Peony *Peony flowers*
1683 Blush Ware - Peony *Peony flowers*
1685 Blush Ware - Peony *Peony flowers*
1693 Blush Ware - Carnation *Carnations on pale cream ground with some blue.*
1713 Blush Ware - Heather *Flowers.*
1728 no name *Chinoiserie design, light blue ground and enamels.*
1732 Blush Ware - Carnation *Floral sprays printed in colours.*
1733 Blush Ware - Carnation *Carnations on pale cream ground.*
1739 Blush Ware *Flowers.*
1741 Blush Ware - Dahlia *Chrysanthemum flowers on pale cream ground.*
1742 Blush Ware - Heather *Flowers.*
1747 Blush Ware *Flowers.*

1749 Blush Ware *Flowers.*
1750 Blush Ware - Gladioli *Flowers.*
1752 Blush Ware *Flowers.*
1757 no name *Figures in garden, blue ground.*
1769 Blush Ware - Cistus *Colourful flowers*
1770 Blush Ware - Poppy *Multi-coloured poppies*
1775 Chrysanthemum *Blue Chrysanthemum type flowers.*
1786 Blush Ware *Flowers.*
1795 Blush Ware - Mixed Cottage *Pansy like flowers.*
1799 Blush Ware *Flowers.*
1804 Blush Ware - Cistus *Colourful flowers*
1810 Blush Ware - Petunia *Flowers.*
1832 Blush Ware - Peony *Peony flowers*
1839 Blush Ware - Peony *Peony flowers on pale cream ground.*
1846 Chorisia
1848 Blush Ware *Flowers on pale cream ground.*
1853 Blush Ware - Peony *Flowers.*
1863 Blush Ware *Flowers.*
1865 Blush Ware - Peony *Flowers.*
1869 Blush Ware - Peony *Flowers.*
1878 Blush Ware - Dahlia *Flowers.*
1879 Blush Ware - Arvista *Flowers.*
1883 Mikado *Chinoiserie design of pagodas, bridges, oriental ladies and usually a pair of kissing birds. Coral and black ground.*
1886 Mikado *Chinoiserie design of pagodas, bridges, oriental ladies and usually a pair of kissing birds. Coral and black ground.*
1902 Blush Ware *Flowers.*
1905 Almond Blossom *White blossom on blue ground.*
1911 Flow Blue - Catalpa *Flowers*
1918 Blush Ware - Wild Rose *Sprays of flowers on pale cream ground.*
1919 Blush Ware - Wild Rose *Sprays of flowers on pale cream ground.*
1928 Blush Ware *Flowers.*
1935 Blush Ware *Flowers.*
1939 Blush Ware - Wild Rose *Flowers.*
1941 Flow Blue - Multi- Flowers *Gilt outline of flowers with blue banding*
1942 Blush Ware *Flowers with frieze.*
1946 Blush Ware - Arvista *Flowers.*
1947 Blush Ware - Wild Rose *Sprays of flowers with blue border.*
1950 Flow Blue *Blue flowers and leaves on white ground.*
1960 Flow Blue - Poppy *Poppy flowers.*
1966 Blush Ware - Petunia *Flowers*
1974 Blush Ware - Wild Rose *Flowers.*
1981 Carnation *Sprays of carnations, enamels and gilt. Blue ground.*
1982 Blush Ware - Dahlia *Flowers.*
1986 Blush Ware - Wild Rose *Sprays of flowers on pale cream ground.*
1987 Blush Ware - Petunia *Blue flowers on white ground.*
1990 Blush Ware - Arvista *Flowers on pale cream ground.*
1996 Blush Ware - Peony *Peony flowers*
2006 Dragon *Oriental dragons in gilt and colours. Black ground.*
2007 Blush Ware - Petunia *Petunia flowers on pale cream ground.*
2021 Kang Hsi Chinoiserie *Chinese design of Foliage and Pagodas, one has an ornamental wall and one has a post fence. A gold sun and a frieze of oriental motifs. Blue ground.*

2021 Blush Ware - Hibiscus *Flowers.*

2030 Peach Blossom *Pink and green blossom sprays on matt black ground.*

2031 Kien Lung *Birds on prunus blossom and flowers within cartouches of good luck symbols. Pink ground.*

2033 Cartouche of Flowers *Cartouche with flowers. Blue lustre ground.*

2040 Blush Ware *Flowers.*

2041 Rockery & Pheasant *Pheasant on a rockery of ornate flowers and foliage. Blue ground.*

2041 Willow *Chinoiserie design of willow trees, pagodas, bridge and a fence. Also a pair of kissing birds in flight. Similar to Mikado. White ground with blue frieze.*

2044 Swansea Flowers *Flowers on white ground with yellow border.*

2046 Chintz *Vividly decorated with intensely packed (usually) multi-coloured flowers.*

2047 Chintz *Vividly decorated with intensely packed multi-coloured flowers.*

2053 Kien Lung *Small flowers on black good luck symbols. Terracotta and black ground.*

2053 Dragon *Chinese Dragon on a yellow ground.*

2062 Dragon *Chinese Dragon on a powder blue ground.*

2064 Dragon *Chinese Dragon on a yellow ground.*

2066 Dragon *Chinese Dragon in red on matt black ground.*

2067 Dragon *Chinese Dragon on red ground.*

2069 Chintz *Vividly decorated with intensely packed flowers in greens, yellow, blue, purple and orange.*

2071 Rockery & Pheasant *Pheasant on a rockery of flowers and foliage, highly enamelled design. Blue ground.*

2080 Rose Trellis *Realistic Roses on a white ground amidst black lines.*

2083 Blush Ware - Cornucopia *Multi-coloured flowers.*

2086 Blush Ware - Cornucopia *Flowers on pale cream ground.*

2089 Birds and Blossom *Variety of birds, including swallows, and blossom on a white ground.*

2091 New Mikado *Chinese Figures, Pagodas, Bridges and sometimes two crane like birds. Gloss olive green ground.*

2093 Flies *Large and small butterflies or moths on deep red lustre ground.*

2095 Flies *Large and small butterflies or moths on a pinky red lustre ground. Armand back stamp.*

2099 Flies *Large or small butterflies or moths on pinky red lustre ground. Armand back stamp.*

2102 Dragon *Chinese Dragon. Armand Lustre Ware.*

2103 Dragon *Chinese Dragon. Armand Lustre Ware.*

2105 Flies *Large and small butterflies or moths on green ground. Armand back stamp.*

2109 Flies *Large and small butterflies or moths on blue ground. Armand back stamp.*

2112 Flies *Large and small butterflies or moths on dark green lustre ground. Armand back stamp.*

2115 no name *Five yellow cartouches of birds of paradise. Matt black ground.*

2121 Lovebirds *Birds in tree, Armand backstamp. Pale Blue ground.*

2124 Basket of Flowers *Ornate formal basket of flowers. Light blue ground.*

2126 no name *Bird in flowers and foliage on a white ground.*

2131 Flies *Large and small butterflies or moths on orange lustre ground.*

2133 Flies *Large and small butterflies or moths on a pale pink ground.*

2134 Flies *Large and small butterflies or moths on pale blue lustre. Armand backstamp.*

2143 Pink Carnation *Pink Carnation like blossom on matt black ground.*

2145 Worcester Birds *Enamelled bird design set in black decorative panels. Matt coral ground.*

2151 Basket of Flowers *Ornate formal basket of flowers. Blue ground.*

2154 Blush Ware - Nasturtium *Flowers*

2166 Blush Ware - Hibiscus *Flowers.*

2174 Flies *Butterflies or Moths on pale blue. Armand backstamp.*

2175 Worcester Birds *Enamelled bird design set in black decorative panels. Matt coral ground.*

2175 Worcester Birds without Birds *Enamelled design set in black decorative panels. Matt coral ground.*

2178 Dancing Figures *Grecian style dancing figures. Dark green ground.*

2179 Blush Ware - Petunia *Petunia flowers on pale cream ground.*

2184 Basket of Flowers *Ornate formal basket of flowers. Blue ground.*

2185 Basket of Flowers *Ornate formal basket of flowers. Black ground.*

2186 Rockery & Pheasant *Pheasant on a rockery of flowers and foliage, highly enamelled design. White ground.*

2189 Basket of Flowers *Ornate formal basket of flowers. Blue ground and white panels.*

2191 Old Wisteria *Trailing wisteria design on matt black ground.*

2192 no name *Peony flowers on Matt black ground.*

2193 no name *Armand backstamp?*

2195 Worcester Birds *Enamelled bird design set in black decorative panels. Blue lustre ground.*

2196 Worcester Birds *Enamelled bird design set in black decorative panels. Yellow ground.*

2197 no name *Plain matt black with orange interior.*

2199 Mikado *Chinoiserie pagodas, bridges, oriental ladies and usually a pair of kissing birds. Blue ground.*

2212 Geometric Clouds *Pale blue ground.*

2215 Blush Ware - Wild Rose *Flowers*

2216 Cartouche of Flowers *Cartouche with flowers with butterfly. Terracotta ground.*

2218 Bird & Chequered Border *Cartouche with bird design. Yellow ground*

2221 Bird & Chequered Border *Cartouche with bird design. Matt black ground.*

2224 Blush Ware - Daisies *Flowers on pale cream ground.*

2227 Blush Ware - Daisies *Flowers on pale cream ground.*

2234 no name *Yellow ground with black pattern border.*

2238 Old Wisteria *Vertical panels, decorated stripes, sprays of wisteria. Black ground.*

2240 Mikado *Chinoiserie pagodas, bridges, oriental ladies and usually a pair of kissing birds. Matt black ground.*

2244 Rockery & Pheasant *Pheasant on a rockery of flowers and foliage, highly enamelled design. Blue ground.*

2250 Cock & Peony *Two cockerels standing amongst foliage. Also has a variety of beautifully enamelled flowers including peonies. Sometimes has a Cock & Peony backstamp. Powder Blue ground.*

2264 Mikado *Chinoiserie pagodas, bridges, oriental ladies and usually a pair of kissing birds. Blue ground.*

2270 Mikado *Chinoiserie pagodas, bridges, oriental ladies and usually a pair of kissing birds. Coloured enamels and Matt black ground.*

2280 Cock & Peony *Two cockerels standing amongst foliage. Also has a variety of beautifully enamelled flowers including peonies. White ground.*

2281 Cock & Peony *Two cockerels standing amongst foliage. Also has a variety of beautifully enamelled flowers including peonies. Sometimes has a Cock & Peony backstamp. Matt black ground.*

2282 Cock & Peony *Two cockerels standing amongst foliage. Also has a variety of beautifully enamelled flowers including peonies. Sometimes has a Cock & Peony backstamp. White ground.*

2284 Dancing Figures *Green jasper finish with white Grecian style dancing ladies, similar to Wedgewood.*

2285 Cock & Peony *Two cockerell standing amongst foliage. Also has a variety of beautifully enamelled flowers including peonies. Sometimes has a Cock & Peony backstamp.*

2286 Roses *Roses on a black ground.*

2287 Cock & Peony *Two cockerels standing amongst foliage. Also has a variety of beautifully enamelled flowers including peonies. Sometimes has a Cock & Peony backstamp. Yellow ground.*

2288 Cock & Peony *Two cockerels standing amongst foliage. Also has a variety of beautifully enamelled flowers including peonies. Sometimes has a Cock & Peony backstamp. Bright Blue ground.*

2300 Blush Ware - Camellia *Flowers.*

2301 Blush Ware - Marguerite *Patterns of flowers in cobalt blue outlined in gilt. Gold floral design on cream ground.*

2308 Cock & Peony *Two cockerels standing amongst foliage. Also has a variety of beautifully enamelled flowers including peonies. Sometimes has a Cock & Peony backstamp. Pale blue ground.*

2309 Blush Ware - Primula *Flowers.*

2314 Mikado *Chinoiserie pagodas, bridges, oriental ladies and usually a pair of kissing birds. Powder blue ground.*

2319 Flow Blue *Flow Blue. Flower heads and petals.*

2326 Lovebirds *Birds in tree, Armand backstamp. Pale Blue ground.*

2328 Lovebirds *Birds in tree, Armand backstamp. Orange ground.*

2332 no name *Pheasant on pale blue ground.*

2333 Lovebirds *Birds in tree, Armand backstamp. Green ground.*

2334 Rose Medallion *Roses and a chain of bells.*

2339 Blush Ware *Flowers*

2340 Mikado *Chinoiserie pagodas, bridges,*

oriental ladies and usually a pair of kissing birds. Black ground.

2341 Willow *Parts of Willow pattern in checkered border. Mauve ground.*

2351 Willow *Chinoiserie pagodas, Willow tree, bridge, and a fence. Usually a pair of kissing birds in flight. Orange lustre ground.*

2352 Willow *Chinoiserie pagodas, Willow tree, bridge, and a fence. Usually a pair of kissing birds in flight. Pale blue lustre ground.*

2355 Mikado *Chinoiserie pagodas, bridges, oriental ladies and usually a pair of kissing birds. White mother of pearl lustre ground.*

2356 Mikado *Chinoiserie pagodas, bridges, oriental ladies and usually a pair of kissing birds. Pale blue ground.*

2357 Mikado *Chinoiserie pagodas, bridges, oriental ladies and usually a pair of kissing birds. Matt blue ground.*

2359 Chinoiserie design *Figures, Pagodas, Bridges. Powder blue ground.*

2361 Mikado *Chinoiserie pagodas, bridges, oriental ladies and usually a pair of kissing birds. Red ground.*

2363 Mikado *Chinoiserie pagodas, bridges, oriental ladies and usually a pair of kissing birds. Black ground and colourful frieze.*

2364 Mikado *Chinoiserie pagodas, bridges, oriental ladies and usually a pair of kissing birds. Powder blue ground.*

2366 Blush Ware *Flowers.*

2367 Mikado in Cartouche *Chinoiserie pagodas, bridges, oriental ladies and usually a pair of kissing birds. Orange ground.*

2368 Mikado in Cartouche *Chinoiserie pagodas, bridges, oriental ladies and usually a pair of kissing birds. Yellow ground.*

2369 Fairy and Sunflower *Fairies, sunflowers and butterflies on a pale blue ground. Armand backstamp.*

2370 Mikado *Chinoiserie pagodas, bridges, oriental ladies and usually a pair of kissing birds. Matt black ground.*

2371 Peach Blossom *Pink and green blossom sprays on matt black ground.*

2377 Blush Ware - Floral *Flowers*

2385 Cornflower *Cornflower like flowers on pale ground (see also 2392).*

2392 Cornflower *Cornflower like flowers on pale ground (see also 2385).*

2393 no name *Flowers on cream ground.*

2398 Cock & Peony *Two cockerels standing amongst foliage. Also has a variety of beautifully enamelled flowers including peonies. Sometimes has a Cock & Peony backstamp. Light blue ground.*

2399 Mikado *Chinoiserie pagodas, bridges, oriental ladies and usually a pair of kissing birds. Blue ground and gilt outlines.*

2405 Cock & Peony Spray

2406 Blush Ware - Cherry Blossom *Flowers*

2407 Blush Ware - Chrysanthemum *Flowers.*

2410 Mikado *Chinoiserie pagodas, bridges, oriental ladies and usually a pair of kissing birds. Black ground with green frieze.*

2410 Blush Ware - Chrysanthemum *Flowers.*

2412 Quince *Blossom spray on matt black ground.*

2412 Prunus and Bird *Bird on prunus blossom spray. Pale yellow ground.*

2413 Prunus and Bird *Bird on prunus blossom spray. Blue ground.*

2420 Flies *Butterflies on powder blue ground - Armand backstamp.*

2421 Prunus and Bird *Bird on prunus blossom spray. Lemon ground.*

2422 Mikado *Chinoiserie pagodas, bridges, oriental ladies and usually a pair of kissing birds. Orange and red ground.*

2424 no name *Flowers and foliage on peach ground.*

2428 New Mikado *Chinese Figures, Pagodas, Bridges and two crane like birds. Blue lustre ground.*

2428 New Mikado without Mikado *Normally with Chinese Figures, Pagodas, Bridges and two crane like birds. Blue lustre ground.*

2431 Prunus and Bird *Bird on prunus blossom spray. Bright yellow ground.*

2436 Peach Blossom *Pink and green blossom sprays on matt black ground.*

2437 River Fish *Beautiful realistic looking fish swimming amongst gilt seaweed. Blue ground.*

2440 River Fish *Beautiful realistic looking fish swimming amongst gilt seaweed. Lemon ground.*

2441 River Fish *Beautiful realistic looking fish swimming amongst gilt seaweed. Pink ground.*

2442 Mikado *Chinoiserie pagodas, bridges, oriental ladies and usually a pair of kissing birds. Red ground with greyish blue frieze.*

2445 Almond Blossom *White flowers on dark pink ground.*

2446 Berries and Bands *Multicoloured berries on multicoloured bands. Yellow ground.*

2454 Berries and Bands *Multicoloured berries on multicoloured bands. Light purple ground.*

2455 Blush Ware - Heather *Flowers.*

2456 Flies *Butterflies or Moths on orange interior, blue exterior.*

2458 Blush Ware - Dahlia *Flowers.*

2460 Berries and Bands *Multicoloured berries on multicoloured bands. Purple ground - see 2446, 2454, 2931 for different colourways.*

2461 Berries and Bands *Multicoloured berries on multicoloured bands. Yellow ground.*

2463 New Prunus Spray *Sprays of white and pink prunus blossom on yellow ground.*

2466 Bird & Tree Peony *Small bird on Peony like blossoms. White ground.*

2469 Flies *Large and small butterflies or moths on a pink ground.*

2470 Mikado *Chinoiserie pagodas, bridges, oriental ladies and usually a pair of kissing birds. Matt black ground.*

2473 Flies *Butterflies or Moths on cream.*

2474 Blush Ware - Cornucopia *Multi-coloured flowers.*

2477 Oriental Water Garden *Oriental lady on bridge in garden.*

2480 Peach Blossom *Pink and green blossom sprays on matt black ground.*

2481 Temple *Oriental scene of figures in temple with large circular doorway. Ornate trees and a golden sun. Blue ground with coloured enamels.*

2482 Temple *Oriental scene of figures in temple with large circular doorway. Ornate trees and a golden sun. Blue ground (as 2481 but in gilt only).*

2486 Blush Ware - Carnation *Flowers*

2494 Blush Ware - Cistus *Colourful flowers.*

2497 Rainbow Portal *Bird sitting on a bough and a cameo with multicoloured stripes. Yellow ground.*

2500 Rainbow Portal *Bird sitting on a bough and a cameo with multicoloured stripes. Red/Purple ground.*

Rainbow Portal - Pattern 2500

Pair of Medium vases from the Kosniowski Collection

£400 - £500 each

2510 Blush Ware - Hibiscus *Flowers.*

2517 Kingfisher *Kingfisher sitting or flying. Pale blue lustre ground.*

2518 no name *Nursery Ware.*

2519 Barge *Chinoiserie design with punt like boat. Blue ground.*

2530 Kingfisher *Kingfisher sitting or flying. Cream lustre ground.*

2537 Kingfisher *Kingfisher sitting or flying. Pale yellow lustre ground.*

2539 Basket of Fruit *Colourful basket full of fruit including grapes, bananas, pineapple, etc. White ground with yellow band and black.*

2552 Temple *Oriental scene of figures in temple with large circular doorway. Ornate trees and a golden sun. Pale blue ground with coloured enamels.*

2556 Basket of Fruit *Colourful basket full of fruit including grapes, bananas, pineapple, etc. White ground with yellow band and black.*

2560 Fruit *Fruit (pears, grapes etc) on pale blue ground.*

2560 Blush Ware - Impatiens *Flowers*

2561 Blush Ware - Arvista *Flowers.*

2562 Blush Ware - Arvista *Flowers.*

2564 Fruit *Fruit (pears, grapes etc) on lemon, orange ground.*

2565 Fruit *Fruit (pears, grapes etc) on blue ground.*

2567 Fruit *Fruit (pears, grapes etc) on black ground.*

2586 Brodsworth *Odd looking colourful bird amongst flowers.*

2591 Italian Scenes *Market scene in Italy (Genoa) in gilt. Powder blue ground.*

2621 Kingfisher *Kingfisher sitting or flying. Pal blue ground.*

2630 Eighteenth Tee *Playing Golf on the 18th tee on a lemon ground.*

2633 Eighteenth Tee *Playing Golf on the 18th tee on a lemon ground.*

2634 Long Tailed Bird and Tree Peony *A long tailed exotic bird sitting on a branch with Peony like flowers. White ground.*

2636 Eighteenth Tee *Playing Golf on the 18th tee on a blue ground.*

2642 Flies Border *Plain red with Butterflies and Moths on a black border.*

2644 no name *Geometric pattern in colours.*

2654 Moderne Lady *Moderne Lady in 18th/19th century dress.*

2659 Blush Ware *Flowers.*

2662 Blush Ware - Convolvulous *Flowers.*

2669 Blush Ware - Convolvulous *Pink and blue Convolvulous flowers.*

2681 Temple *Oriental scene of figures in temple with large circular doorway. Ornate trees and a golden sun. Blue ground with coloured enamels.*

2686 Tutankhamen *Egyptian figures and motifs in colours and gilt on pale blue ground.*

2687 Blush Ware - Hibiscus *Flowers.*

2689 Tutankhamen *Egyptian figures and motifs in colours and gilt on orange ground.*

2691 Blush Ware - Peony *Flowers.*

2700 Blush Ware - Camellia *Flowers.*

2706 Tutankhamen *Egyptian figures and motifs in colours and gilt. Gloss mother of pearl ground.*

2708 Tutankhamen *Egyptian figures, motifs and symbols in gilt. Matt black ground.*

2709 Tutankhamen *Egyptian figures, motifs and symbols in colours and gilt. Matt black ground, colours and gilt detail.*

2710 Tutankhamen *Egyptian figures, motifs and symbols in gilt. Powder blue ground.*

2711 Tutankhamen *Egyptian figures, motifs and symbols in colours and gilt. Blue lustre ground.*

2711 Tutankhamen *Egyptian figures, motifs and symbols. Orange or brown ground.*

2713 Blush Ware - Heather *Flowers.*

2718 Blush Ware - Heather *Flowers.*

2721 Orange Blossom *Bird, butterflies and white Orange blossom tree. Pale lemon ground.*

2722 Orange Blossom *Bird, butterflies and white Orange blossom tree. Orange ground.*

2723 Orange Blossom *Bird, butterflies and white Orange blossom tree. Blue ground.*

2723 Pomander Pendant *Enamelled design representing balloons with strings. Mauve ground.*

2724 Orange Blossom *Bird, butterflies and white Orange blossom tree. Pale purple ground.*

2725 Orange Blossom *Bird, butterflies and white Orange blossom tree. Red ground.*

2727 New Mikado *Chinese figures, pagoda, bridge and trees. Sometimes has two cranes and punt like boat. Red ground.*

2728 New Mikado *Chinese figures, pagoda, bridge and trees. Sometimes has two cranes and punt like boat. Blue ground.*

2729 New Mikado *Chinese figures, pagoda, bridge and trees. Sometimes has two cranes and punt like boat. Blue ground with gilt only (no enamels).*

2731 no name *Delicate border design on plain yellow.*

2740 New Mikado *Chinese figures, pagoda, bridge and trees. Sometimes has two cranes and punt like boat. Pearl lustre ground.*

2749 Blush Ware - Nasturtium *Flowers*

2752 Chinoiserie *Chinese figures, pagoda, bridge and trees. Mother of Pearl ground, blue rim.*

2755 Chinoiserie *Figures, Pagodas, Bridges (possibly Mikado). Pale blue ground.*

2757 Blush Ware - Heather *Flowers.*

2779 Spray of Flowers *Spray of flowers with yellow borders on pale ground.*

2780 Tutankhamen *Egyptian figures and motifs in colours and gilt. White ground.*

2782 Lovebirds *Birds in tree, Armand backstamp. Pale blue ground.*

2787 Flow Blue - Dragons & Unicorn *Dragons and Unicorn in blue.*

2788 New Mikado *Chinese figures, pagoda, bridge and trees. Sometimes has two cranes and punt like boat. Rouge ground.*

2794 Birds on Bough *Yellow birds with long feathery tails in tree with blue foliage. Pale ground.*

2798 Blush Ware - Cistus *Pansies*

2804 Gallant *Lady and Dandy with gazebo in garden. Orange ground.*

2810 Chinoiserie *Figures, Pagodas, Bridges. Matt black ground with green frieze with motifs.*

2814 New Mikado *Chinese figures, pagoda, bridge and trees. Sometimes has two cranes and punt like boat. Blue lustre ground.*

2814 New Mikado with Lady *Chinese figures, pagoda, bridge and trees. Sometimes has two cranes and punt like boat. Blue lustre ground. Also with a moderne Lady.*

2814 New Mikado without Mikado *No Chinese figures, pagoda or bridge. Cranes, two flying and two wading. Blue lustre ground.*

2815 New Mikado *Chinese figures, pagoda, bridge and trees. Sometimes has two cranes and punt like boat. Red lustre ground.*

2816 Cock & Peony *Two cockerels standing amongst foliage. Also has a variety of beautifully enamelled flowers including peonies. White ground.*

2818 Dragon *Chinese Dragons and symbols in gilt. Rouge ground.*

2820 Temple *Oriental scene of figures in temple with large circular doorway. Ornate trees with black stems. Coral ground with black frieze.*

2822 Stork and Bamboo *Two storks (one drinking) in pool next to bamboo. Deep blue ground.*

2822 no name *Pheasant and blossom on pale blue ground.*

2825 New Mikado *Chinese figures, pagoda, bridge and trees. Sometimes has two cranes and punt like boat. Orange, red ground with gilt.*

2830 New Mikado *Chinese figures, pagoda, bridge and trees. Sometimes has two cranes and punt like boat. Orange, red ground with gilt.*

2831 Prunus and Bird *Bird on prunus blossom spray with white background.*

2832 Long Tailed Bird and Tree Peony *A long tailed exotic bird sitting on a branch with Peony like flowers. Pale blue ground.*

2833 Blush Ware - Iris *Flowers*

2834 Long Tailed Bird and Tree Peony *A long tailed exotic bird sitting on a branch with Peony like flowers. Ice blue ground.*

2837 New Flies *Spiders web and butterfly. Dark blue ground.*

2839 Gallant *Lady and Dandy with gazebo in garden. Red, orange ground.*

2841 Willow *Chinoiserie pagodas, Willow tree, bridge, and a fence. Usually a pair of kissing birds in flight. Orange lustre ground.*

2843 Pomander Pendant *Enamelled design representing balloons with strings. Blue lustre ground.*

2845 Pomander Pendant *Enamelled design representing balloons with strings. Blue ground.*

2851 Willow *Chinoiserie pagodas, Willow tree, bridge, and a fence. Usually a pair of kissing birds in flight. Red ground.*

2851 Willow *Chinoiserie pagodas, Willow tree, bridge, and a fence. Usually a pair of kissing birds in flight. Orange ground.*

2852 Willow *Chinoiserie pagodas, Willow tree, bridge, and a fence. Usually a pair of kissing birds in flight. Pale Blue ground.*

2853 Blush Ware - Peony *Peony like flowers*

2854 Willow *Chinoiserie pagodas, Willow tree, bridge, and a fence. Usually a pair of kissing birds in flight. Pale blue ground.*

2857 Pheasant and Rose *Bird on rose tree. Blue ground.*

2858 Kingfisher *Kingfishers, sitting and flying. Blue ground.*

2858 Willow *Chinoiserie pagodas, Willow tree, bridge, and a fence. Usually a pair of kissing birds in flight. Pale blue ground.*

2863 Gallant *Lady and Dandy with gazebo in garden. Pale yellow ground.*

2863 Blush Ware - Rose *Flowers*

2864 Gallant *Lady and Dandy with gazebo in garden. Red, orange ground.*

2866 Bird & Tree Peony *Small bird on Peony*

like blossoms. White ground.

2867 Gallant *Lady and Dandy with gazebo in garden. Matt pale blue ground.*

2868 Gallant *Lady and Dandy with gazebo in garden. Yellow ground.*

2869 Gallant *Lady and Dandy with gazebo in garden. Matt orange ground.*

2872 Gallant *Lady and Dandy with gazebo in garden. Yellow ground.*

2872 Gallant *Lady and Dandy with gazebo in garden. Pink ground.*

2872 Blush Ware - Rose *Flowers*

2872 Blush Ware - Tulips *Flowers*

2880 Temple *Oriental scene of figures in temple with large circular doorway. Ornate trees with black stems. Red ground with black frieze.*

2880 Temple without Temple *Plain pattern with Temple frieze. Red ground with black frieze.*

2881 Mikado *Chinoiserie pagodas, bridges, oriental ladies and usually a pair of kissing birds. Matt black ground with terracotta frieze.*

2882 Persian *Persian design of figures in a temple, usually two white birds by water. Desert scene and palm trees. Persian back stamp. Powder blue ground.*

2883 Persian *Persian design of figures in a temple, usually two white birds by water. Desert scene and palm trees. Persian back stamp. Blue lustre ground.*

2884 Persian *Persian design of figures in a temple, usually two white birds by water. Desert scene and palm trees. Persian back stamp. Blue lustre ground.*

2885 Orchard *Sprays of orchard fruits with blossom. Blue lustre ground.*

2886 Orchard *Sprays of orchard fruits with blossom. Blue lustre ground.*

2887 Dragon *Chinese dragons and symbols. Blue lustre ground.*

2893 Gallant *Lady and Dandy with gazebo in garden. Matt black ground with mother of pearl interior.*

2896 Trailing *Spays of blossom on creamy yellow ground.*

2903 Dragon *Chinese dragons and symbols. Blue ground.*

2905 Dancers *Figures dancing with pan pipes and small birds flying around. White ground and red frieze.*

2907 Magpies *Magpie on tree branch and sometimes also others flying around. Blue ground.*

2907 Magpies *Magpie on tree branch and sometimes also others flying around. Matt red ground.*

2908 Magpies *Magpie on tree branch and sometimes also others flying around. Yellow ground.*

2908 Magpies *Magpie on tree branch and sometimes also others flying around. Orange ground.*

2909 Fruit Bough *Peach like fruit and slender leaves on tree. Blue ground.*

2910 Mikado *Chinoiserie pagodas, bridges, oriental ladies and usually a pair of kissing birds. Matt black ground with green frieze.*

2911 Magpies *Magpie on tree branch and sometimes also others flying around. Orange lustre ground.*

2912 Magpies *Magpie on tree branch and sometimes also others flying around. Orange ground.*

2913 Cretonne *Oriental tree with red crested bird. Matt black ground and yellow band.*

2914 Mikado *Chinoiserie pagodas, bridges, oriental ladies and usually a pair of kissing birds. Black ground with green frieze.*

2917 Plain *Matt black with orange lustre interior to cup. Carlton China.*

2920 Fruit Branch *Fruit and branch on Orange and White ground.*

2922 Sunrise *Matt black and orange lustre exterior with fine enamelled border design.*

2923 Blush Ware - Heather *Flowers.*

2924 no name *Chinoiserie design on brown ground.*

2926 no name *Flowers and foliage on cream ground.*

2927 Mikado *Chinoiserie pagodas, bridges, oriental ladies and usually a pair of kissing birds. Also has a Temple pattern Frieze. Red ground with pinkish frieze.*

2927 Mikado without Mikado *Temple pattern frieze but plain body. Red ground with pinkish frieze.*

2928 Temple *Oriental scene of figures in temple with large circular doorway. Ornate trees some with black stems, sometimes a gold sun. Yellow ground.*

2929 Temple *Oriental scene of figures in temple with large circular doorway. Ornate trees some with black stems, sometimes a gold sun. Gloss bright blue with matt black frieze.*

2930 Chrysanthemum *Realistic Chrysanthemum flowers on a blue ground. Look at newsletter 8 Nov 2005.*

2931 Berries and Bands *Multicoloured berries on multicoloured bands. Orange ground.*

2932 Stork and Bamboo *Two storks (one drinking) in pool. Bamboo shoots with green leaves. Blue lustre ground.*

2933 Stork and Bamboo *Two storks (one drinking) in pool. Bamboo shoots with green leaves. Matt orange ground.*

2934 Stork and Bamboo *Two storks (one drinking) in pool. Bamboo shoots with green leaves. White gloss ground.*

2935 Scalloped Lace *Black granite type border on yellow ground with black frieze.*

2936 Chinese Tea Garden *Oriental scene of figures in pagoda garden. Blue ground.*

2939 Flies *Brightly coloured butterflies on yellow ground.*

2940 no name *Lustre orange and mother of pearl ground.*

2941 Temple *Oriental scene of figures in temple with large circular doorway. Ornate trees some with black stems, sometimes a gold sun. Green ground with black lower frieze.*

2944 Moonlight Cameo *Orange medallion with figures playing with bubbles in the moonlight. Matt black ground.*

2944 Moonlight Cameo *White medallion with figures playing with bubbles in the moonlight. Orange ground.*

2945 Moonlight Cameo *Deep blue medallion with figures playing with bubbles in the moonlight. Dark orange ground.*

2946 Moonlight Cameo *Pale blue medallion with figures playing with bubbles in the moonlight. Orange ground.*

2947 Moonlight Cameo *Pale blue medallion with figures playing with bubbles in the moonlight. Black ground.*

2948 Chinaland *Complex chinoiserie design with underglaze enamels. Pagoda, terraces,*

trees, figures and usually mountains. Coloured W&R backstamp. Orange lustre ground.

2949 Chinaland *Complex chinoiserie design with underglaze enamels. Pagoda, terraces, trees, figures and usually mountains. Mottled green lustre ground.*

2950 Chinaland *Complex chinoiserie design with underglaze enamels. Pagoda, terraces, trees, figures and usually mountains. Dark blue lustre ground.*

2953 Gallant *Lady & Dandy in garden. Blue ground.*

2954 Gallant *Lady & Dandy in garden. Orange ground.*

2956 Gallant *Lady & Dandy in garden. Yellow ground.*

2957 no name *Chinese scene with figures, cloisonne.*

2960 Moonlight Cameo *White medallion with figures playing with bubbles in the moonlight. Orange ground.*

2961 Citrus Fruit *Oranges and other fruit on white ground.*

2962 The Hunt *Hunting Scene on white ground.*

2964 Moonlight Cameo *White medallion with figures playing with bubbles in the moonlight. Blue ground.*

2969 Moonlight Cameo *Pale blue medallion with figures playing with bubbles in the moonlight. Green ground.*

2971 Temple *Oriental scene of figures in temple with large circular doorway. Ornate trees some with black stems, sometimes a gold sun. Emerald green ground with black frieze.*

2972 Chinoiserie *Chinese figures in pagodas. Deep blue ground.*

2975 Magpies *Magpie on tree branch and sometimes also others flying around. Green ground.*

2976 Magpies *Magpie on tree branch and sometimes also others flying around. Cream, yellow ground.*

2978 Mikado *Chinoiserie pagodas, bridges, oriental ladies and usually a pair of kissing birds. Matt black ground with brown frieze.*

2979 Embellished Gilt *Orange lustre or matt black ground, ornate gold border.*

2980 Moonlight Cameo *White medallion with figures playing with bubbles in the moonlight. Brown, orange ground.*

2990 New Mikado *Chinese figures, pagoda, bridge and trees. Sometimes has two cranes and punt like boat. Powder blue lustre ground with border.*

2993 Dragon *Pink dragon on blue glazed ground.*

3003 Temple *Oriental scene of figures in temple with large circular doorway. Ornate trees some with black stems, sometimes a gold sun. Red lustre ground.*

3013 no name *Orange lustre ground with wide white frieze.*

3014 Chinaland *Complex chinoiserie design with underglaze enamels. Pagoda, terraces, trees, figures and usually mountains. Pale blue lustre ground.*

3015 Chinaland *Complex chinoiserie design with underglaze enamels. Pagoda, terraces, trees, figures and usually mountains. Red lustre ground.*

3016 Parrots *Multicoloured parrot and coloured friezes. Green ground.*

3017 Parrots *Multicoloured parrot and coloured*

friezes. Matt black ground.

3018 Parrots *Multicoloured parrot and coloured friezes. Blue lustre ground.*

3019 Galleon *Galleon ship sailing on waves. Blue ground.*

3020 Galleon *Galleon ship sailing on waves. Green ground.*

3023 New Flies *Spiders web and butterfly. Dark blue lustre ground.*

3024 New Flies *Spiders web and butterfly. Mottled orange ground.*

3025 New Flies *Spiders web and butterfly. Light blue lustre ground.*

3026 Temple *Oriental scene of figures in temple with large circular doorway. Ornate trees some with black stems, sometimes a gold sun. White, cream ground with green frieze.*

3026 no name *Birds, trees on vellum ground.*

3027 Temple *Oriental scene of figures in temple with large circular doorway. Ornate trees some with black stems, sometimes a gold sun. Cream ground with black frieze.*

3028 New Flies *Spiders web and butterfly. Rouge ground.*

3033 Almond Blossom *White blossom on blue ground.*

3033 Shagreen *Black band with gold speckles above green ground.*

3037 Parrots *Brightly coloured parrots and coloured friezes. Orange lustre ground.*

3041 Apple and Blossom *Apple and blossom on blue lustre ground.*

3042 Orange Embossed *Oranges and leaves on dark blue lustre ground.*

3043 Violets *Gilt design on dark blue lustre ground.*

3046 Bird & Pine Cone *Coloured birds in pine trees with pine cones. Dark blue lustre ground.*

3047 Temple *Oriental scene of figures in temple with large circular doorway. Ornate trees some with black stems, sometimes a gold sun. Off white ground with terracotta frieze.*

3048 Mikado *Chinoiserie pagodas, bridges, oriental ladies and usually a pair of kissing birds. Pale cream ground with blue frieze.*

3048 Temple *Oriental scene of figures in temple with large circular doorway. Ornate trees some with black stems, sometimes a gold sun. Pale cream ground with pale blue frieze.*

3049 Mayflower *Flower heads and foliage on mottled blue ground with pale yellow border.*

3050 Persian Flowers or Turkish *Persian stylised floral heads and leaves. Enamelled flower design. Blue lustre ground.*

3052 Orange Embossed *Oranges and leaves on white lustre ground.*

3053 Shagreen *Gold band with blue speckles above orange ground.*

3054 Shagreen *Matt black with yellow and gilt honeycomb like band.*

3056 Shagreen *Grey band with dark grey speckles above blue, grey ground.*

3057 Shagreen *Black band with gold speckles above jade green ground or rouge ground.*

3063 Embellished Gilt *Plain yellow with intricate gilt border.*

3064 Orchard *Sprays of oranges, cherries and other fruits with blossom and leaves. Orange ground.*

3065 Plain *Plain Pink.*

3065 Persian *Persian design of figures in a temple, usually two white birds by water.*

Desert scene and palm trees. Terracotta ground with black frieze.

3067 Persian *Persian design of figures in a temple, usually two white birds by water. Desert scene and palm trees. Ivory ground with black frieze.*

3068 Persian *Persian design of figures in a temple, usually two white birds by water. Desert scene and palm trees. Pale cream ground with blue frieze.*

3069 Shagreen *Orange and gilt speckles on red ground.*

3069 Persian *Persian design of figures in a temple, usually two white birds by water. Desert scene and palm trees. Yellow ground..*

3071 Persian Flowers or Turkish *Enamelled flower design. Powder Blue ground.*

3073 Swallow & Cloud *Swallow or swallows in flight with gold ornate cloud. Blue lustre ground.*

3074 Swallow & Cloud *Swallow or swallows in flight with gold ornate cloud. Red lustre ground.*

3075 Moonlight *Figures playing with bubbles in the moonlight. Pale ground.*

3075 Swallow & Cloud *Swallow or swallows in flight with gold ornate cloud. Mottled matt orange ground.*

3076 Moonlight *Figures playing with bubbles in the moonlight. Orange lustre ground.*

3077 Meadow *Orange ground and enamelled floral border.*

3078 Meadow *Yellow ground and enamelled floral border.*

3078 Embellished Gilt *Plain with intricate gilt border.*

3087 Temple *Oriental scene of figures in temple with large circular doorway. Ornate trees some with black stems, sometimes a gold sun. Cream ground with dark frieze.*

3093 Temple Flowers

3095 Parrots *Brightly coloured parrots and coloured friezes. Purple ground.*

3115 Cameo Wren *Wren on branch set in cameo. Orange ground.*

3116 Persian Flowers or Turkish *Gilt and enamelled flower design. Blue ground.*

3118 Moonlight *Figures playing with bubbles in the moonlight. Dark Orange ground.*

3127 Moonlight *Figures playing with bubbles in the moonlight. Green ground.*

3129 Temple *Oriental scene of figures in temple with large circular doorway. Ornate trees some with black stems, sometimes a gold sun. Orange lustre ground with black frieze.*

3130 Temple *Oriental scene of figures in temple with large circular doorway. Ornate trees some with black stems, sometimes a gold sun. Light green ground with black frieze.*

3130 Temple *Oriental scene of figures in temple with large circular doorway. Ornate trees some with black stems, sometimes a gold sun. Powder blue ground.*

3131 Persian *Persian design of figures in a temple, usually two white birds by water. Desert scene and palm trees. Persian back stamp. Red ground.*

3134 Swallow & Cloud *Swallow or swallows in flight with gold ornate cloud. Blue Lustre ground.*

3134 Swallow & Cloud *Swallow or swallows in flight with gold ornate cloud. Green ground.*

3137 New Mikado *Chinese figures, pagoda,*

bridge and trees. Sometimes has two cranes and punt like boat. Green ground.

3141 Landscape Tree *Blossom, birds and umbrella shaped trees with green foliage. Light ground.*

3142 Landscape Tree *Blossom, birds and umbrella shaped trees with orange foliage. Light ground.*

3143 Paradise Bird & Tree with Cloud *Bird of Paradise with long plumed tail flying across clouds and among oriental trees. Red ground.*

3144 Paradise Bird & Tree with Cloud *Bird of Paradise with long plumed tail flying across clouds and among oriental trees. Mottled pale blue ground.*

3145 Dragon in Cartouche *Dragon in black panel on red ground plus decorative frieze.*

3146 Dragon in Cartouche *Dragon in black panel on mottled dark red ground plus decorative frieze.*

3147 Paradise Bird & Tree *Bird of Paradise with long plumed tail flying among oriental trees. Matt black ground.*

3149 Paradise Bird & Tree with Cloud *Bird of Paradise with long plumed tail flying across clouds and among oriental trees. Red ground.*

3150 Paradise Bird & Tree *Bird of Paradise with long plumed tail flying among oriental trees. Red ground with black frieze.*

3151 Paradise Bird & Tree *Bird of Paradise with long plumed tail flying among oriental trees. Gloss yellow ground.*

3154 Paradise Bird & Tree with Cloud *Bird of Paradise with long plumed tail flying across clouds and among oriental trees. Orange ground.*

3155 Paradise Bird & Tree *Bird of Paradise with long plumed tail flying among oriental trees. Gloss blue ground.*

3155 no name *Good Luck motif on coral ground.*

3157 Paradise Bird & Tree *Bird of Paradise with long plumed tail flying among oriental trees. Gloss orange ground.*

3158 Mikado *Chinoiserie pagodas, bridges, oriental ladies and usually a pair of kissing birds. Matt black ground.*

3159 Paradise Bird & Tree *Bird of Paradise with long plumed tail flying among oriental trees. Pale blue ground.*

3161 Mayflower *Flower heads and foliage on blue ground with yellow border.*

3165 Mayflower *Flower heads and foliage on mottled blue ground with yellow border.*

3173 Lace Frieze *Yellow, black with ornate border.*

3174 Swallow & Cloud *Swallow or swallows in flight with gold ornate cloud. Red ground.*

3178 Mikado in Cartouche *Chinoiserie pagodas, bridges, oriental ladies and usually a pair of kissing birds. Orange ground.*

3179 no name *Chines figures and pagodas with frieze on rust ground.*

3185 Temple *Oriental scene of figures in temple with large circular doorway. Ornate trees some with black stems, sometimes a gold sun. Red ground.*

3188 no name *Stylised flowers and trees. Mottled red ground.*

3190 Cubist Butterfly *Bold stylised flowers, berries and butterflies. Matt red ground.*

3191 Bird of Paradise *Bird of Paradise with long plumed tail flying among oriental trees. Blue,* pink lustre ground.

3193 Prunus *Spays of prunus blossom on pale blue ground.*

3194 Cubist Butterfly *Bold stylised flowers, berries and butterflies. Blue ground.*

3195 Cubist Butterfly *Bold stylised flowers, berries and butterflies. Orange ground.*

3196 Chinese Bird *Exotic bird with curly tail, flower and cloud motifs. Blue lustre ground.*

3197 Chinese Bird *Exotic bird with curly tail, flower and cloud motifs. Blue ground.*

3198 Chinese Bird *Exotic bird with curly tail, flower and cloud motifs. Rouge ground.*

3199 Chinese Figures *Oriental scene of figures, tree and sometimes pagodas. Blue ground.*

3201 Mikado *Chinoiserie pagodas, bridges, oriental ladies and usually a pair of kissing birds. Green ground and black frieze.*

3202 Paradise Bird & Tree *Bird of Paradise with long plumed tail flying among oriental trees. Pale green ground plus enamels.*

3222 Chinoiserie *Figures, Pagodas, Bridges. Pale lemon ground and border.*

3223 Cubist Butterfly *Bold stylised flowers, berries and butterflies. Green ground.*

3225 Corolla *White flower heads on dark blue gloss ground.*

3226 Corolla *White flower heads on red, orange ground.*

3227 Corolla *White flower heads on blue ground.*

3228 Corolla *White flower heads on yellow ground.*

3229 Spots *White spots on blue.*

3231 Spots *White spots on green.*

3233 Cubist Butterfly *Bold stylised flowers, berries and butterflies. Green ground.*

3234 Floral Scallops *Overlapping scallop shapes containing five coloured petals of a flower, handcraft. Cream ground.*

3235 Shamrock *Three petalled large blue flowers, handcraft. White ground with blue borders.*

3236 Floribunda *Orange flowers and leaves on blue and white ground.*

3237 Dragon and Cloud *Oriental dragon amongst stylised ornate clouds. Deep blue ground and gilt.*

3238 Forest Tree *Exotic birch like trees. Slender tree rising to a wide pendulous canopy of foliage. Deep blue lustre ground.*

3239 Forest Tree *Exotic birch like tree. Slender tree rising to a wide pendulous canopy of foliage. Glazed yellow ground.*

3240 Forest Tree *Exotic birch like trees. Slender Tree rising to a wide pendulous canopy of foliage. Matt terracotta ground.*

3241 Paradise Bird & Tree *Bird of Paradise with long plumed tail flying among oriental trees. Mottled red ground.*

3242 Flowering Papyrus *Geometric handcraft design in blue, yellow, mauve and black on white ground.*

3243 Swallow & Cloud *Swallow or swallows in flight with gold ornate cloud. Matt blue ground.*

3244 Forest Tree *Exotic birch like trees. Slender tree rising to a wide pendulous canopy of foliage. Matt blue ground with mauve foliage.*

3244 Forest Tree *Exotic birch like trees. Slender tree rising to a wide pendulous canopy of foliage. Green ground with mauve foliage.*

3248 Forest Tree *Exotic birch like trees. Slender tree rising to a wide pendulous canopy of foliage. Grey ground with dark green foliage.*

3249 Flower and Fruit *Large Fruit on a branch together with Petal design.*

3250 Forest Tree *Exotic birch like trees. Slender tree rising to a wide pendulous canopy of foliage. Mottled blue ground with orange foliage.*

3250 Dutch *Handcraft with windmill like pattern, blue, yellow, mauve and black on white ground.*

3251 Dragon *Red dragons with symbols and shapes. Blue ground.*

3252 Paradise Bird & Tree with Cloud *Bird of Paradise with long plumed tail flying across clouds and among oriental trees. Matt cream and mauve ground.*

3253 Forest Tree *Exotic birch like trees. Slender tree rising to a wide pendulous canopy of foliage. Blue ground.*

3254 Forest Tree *Exotic birch like trees. Slender tree rising to a wide pendulous canopy of foliage. Red lustre ground.*

3255 Orchid *Central floral medallion with star containing Orchid. Mauve Blue, Green Yellow and Black stripes, handcraft. Blue gloss ground.*

3259 no name *Similar to Flowering Papyrus.*

3265 Forest Tree *Exotic birch like trees. Slender tree rising to a wide pendulous canopy of foliage. Matt cream and mauve ground.*

3270 Diaper *Matt white ground.*

3271 Marigold *Blue, cream and mauve flowers outlined in blue (Asters?). Handcraft.*

3272 Cherry *Crude stems and leaves behind yellow and red cherries. Flowers and leaves on blue ground.*

3273 Delphinium *Blue delphinium flowers and leaves, handcraft. White or pinky white ground.*

3274 Chinese Bird & Cloud *Exotic bird with curly tail, flower and cloud motifs. Matt blue mosaic ground.*

3275 Chinese Bird & Cloud *Exotic bird with curly tail, flower and cloud motifs. Matt orange ground.*

3275 Chinese Bird & Cloud *Exotic bird with curly tail, flower and cloud motifs. Matt green ground.*

3276 no name *Cream ground similar to 3498 Iris.*

3278 Honesty *Stylised Honesty branches. Royal Blue ground.*

3279 Tree & Swallow *Swallows flying past slender stemmed tree with wide canopy of pendulous foliage. Matt pale blue ground with blue and green foliage.*

3280 Tree & Swallow *Swallows flying past slender stemmed tree with wide canopy of pendulous foliage. Matt blue ground with orange foliage.*

3281 Tree & Swallow *Swallows flying past slender stemmed tree with wide canopy of pendulous foliage. Matt cream and mauve ground.*

3282 Tree & Swallow *Swallows flying past slender stemmed tree with wide canopy of pendulous foliage. Light blue ground with green, blue and orange foliage.*

3283 Forest Tree *Exotic birch like trees. Slender tree rising to a wide pendulous canopy of foliage. Matt blue ground with orange foliage.*

3283 Tree & Swallow *Swallows flying past slender stemmed tree with wide canopy of pendulous foliage. Matt blue ground with lilac foliage.*

3284 no name *Matt blue/orange/yellow, diamonds. Handcraft.*

3285 Tree & Swallow *Swallows flying past slender stemmed tree with wide canopy of pendulous foliage. Matt blue ground.*

3289 Marrakesh *Marrakesh Handcraft design in blue, yellow and black.*

3290 Butterfly *Handcraft pattern depicting a butterfly.*

3291 Stellata or Wild Cherry *Cherry blossom star shaped flowers with leaves and brightly coloured berries. Leaves of blues and greens in star shaped pattern.*

3294 Bluebells *Bluebell flowers and usually with snowdrops, primulas and autumn leaves. Light blue/grey ground.*

3296 Chinese Bird *Exotic bird with curly tail, flower and cloud motifs. Black ground.*

3297 Farrago *Handcraft. Flowers and chevrons, geometric pattern. Pink ground.*

3299 Zig Zag *Lightning like, zig zag patterns. Matt buff ground.*

3304 New Chinese Bird *Exotic bird looking back angrily, on pale grey or pale pink ground.*

3305 Carnival *Brightly coloured geometric design with butterfly. Matt pale ground.*

3313 Sunflower Geometric *Sprays of stylised geometric foliage and sunflower heads on blue ground.*

3314 Swallow & Cloud *Swallow or swallows in flight with gold ornate cloud. Orange ground.*

3320 New Chinese Bird & Cloud *Exotic bird looking back angrily, flying past stylised cloud and flowerheads. Matt blue ground .*

3321 New Chinese Bird & Cloud *Exotic bird looking back angrily, flying past stylised cloud and flowerheads. Matt chocolate brown ground.*

3322 New Chinese Bird & Cloud *Exotic bird looking back angrily, flying past stylised cloud and flowerheads. Blue lustre ground.*

3324 Pomona *Citrus type fruit and leaves on a blue ground.*

3325 Orchid *Central floral medallion with star containing Orchid. Yellow Beige, Green Yellow and Black stripes. Matt yellow ground.*

3326 Stellata or Wild Cherry *Cherry blossom star shaped flowers with leaves and brightly coloured berries. Blue ground.*

3327 Chinese Bird & Cloud *Exotic bird with curly tail, flower and cloud motifs. Blue lustre ground.*

3328 Pomona *Citrus type fruit and coloured leaves on a blue ground.*

3331 Dragon and Cloud *Oriental dragon amongst stylised ornate clouds. Matt green ground.*

3332 Dragon and Cloud *Oriental dragon amongst stylised ornate clouds. Gloss red ground.*

3333 Dragon and Cloud *Oriental dragon amongst stylised ornate clouds. Matt blue ground.*

3333 Sunflower Geometric *Sprays of stylised geometric foliage and sunflower heads on blue lustre ground.*

3334 Sunflower Geometric *Sprays of stylised geometric foliage and sunflower heads on orange ground.*

3337 Bookends - Two Tone *Bookends in two*

colours, brown and black.

3339 Sunflower Geometric *Sprays of stylised geometric foliage and sunflower heads on pale grey/blue ground.*

3341 Daisy & Stripe

3350 Paradise Bird & Tree *Bird of Paradise with long plumed tail flying among oriental trees. Matt mottled blue ground.*

3351 Dragon and Cloud *Oriental dragon amongst stylised ornate clouds. Red ground.*

3352 Jazz *Geometric design with brightly coloured lightning flashes, bands and small bubbles. Red lustre ground.*

3353 Jazz *Geometric design with brightly coloured lightning flashes, bands and small bubbles. Orange lustre ground.*

3354 Feathertailed Bird and Flower *Bird of paradise on stylised blossom bough. Matt pale blue ground.*

3355 Feathertailed Bird and Flower *Bird of paradise on stylised blossom bough. Matt green ground.*

3356 Lightning *Lightning like, zig zag patterns in two tone blue. Blue ground.*

3357 Lightning *Lightning like, zig zag patterns in matt tan, black, orange with silver strip.*

3358 Gentian *Large blue flower heads with black stamens, handcraft. Blue ground.*

3359 Stag *Handcraft with realistic animal leaping in front of the Sun. Brown ground.*

3360 River Fish *Beautiful realistic looking fish swimming amongst gilt seaweed. Powder blue ground.*

3361 Jazz *Geometric design with brightly coloured lightning flashes, bands and small bubbles. Blue lustre ground.*

3362 Farrago *Handcraft. Flowers and chevrons, geometric pattern. Pink ground.*

3384 Tree & Swallow *Swallows flying past slender stemmed tree with wide canopy of pendulous foliage. Grey ground.*

3385 Floral Comets *Stylised flowerheads and triple banded comets tails on matt pale green ground.*

3387 Floral Comets *Stylised flowerheads and triple banded comets tails on matt green ground.*

3388 Fantasia *Exotic bird with swallow like tail amongst exotic flowers and foliage. Matt pale blue ground.*

3389 Fantasia *Exotic bird with swallow like tail amongst exotic flowers and foliage. Matt mauve ground.*

3390 Garden *Spires of Daisy like flowers in many colours. Matt green ground.*

3392 Moonlight Cameo *Blue medallion with figures playing with bubbles in the moonlight. Light Orange ground.*

3394 Birds on Bough *Birds with plumed tail sitting on branch with foliage. Pale blue ground.*

3396 Garden *Spires of Daisy like flowers in many colours. Gloss green ground.*

3397 no name *Small flowers, leaves, petals and triangle shapes on cream ground.*

3400 Fantasia *Exotic bird with swallow like tail amongst exotic flowers and foliage. Blue matt ground.*

3401 Floral Comets *Stylised flowerheads and triple banded comets tails. Pale blue ground.*

3404 Tutankhamen *Egyptian figures and motifs in colours and gilt. Gloss Light & Dark Blue.*

3405 Floral Comets *Stylised flowerheads and triple banded comets tails. Matt blue ground.*

3406 Fantasia *Exotic bird with swallow like tail amongst exotic flowers and foliage. Blue gloss ground.*

3408 Rudolf's Posy *Pattern of large and small flowerheads with leaves.*

3411 Scroll *Swirling patterns of shapes and curves, multi-coloured. Blue ground.*

3412 Aurora *Multi-coloured bold, bulbous cloud like shapes outlined in gilt on blue ground. Handcraft.*

3413 Garden *Spires of Daisy like flowers in many colours. Matt pale blue ground.*

3414 Lazy - Daisy *Simple flower heads large and small. Orange ground.*

3415 Sagitta *Cloud shaped flowers and blue stylised trees. Matt pinky brown.*

3416 Arrowhead *Abstract design of feathery leaves and flowers. Matt pale blue ground.*

3417 Cherry *Crude stems and leaves behind yellow and red cherries. Flowers and leaves on yellow ground.*

3418 Holly *Multi colour (orange and brown etc) abstract design.*

3420 Metropolis *Stylised city skyline with mauve and pink details. Matt pale blue ground.*

3421 Fantasia *Exotic bird with swallow like tail amongst exotic flowers and foliage. Dark blue ground.*

3422 Floral Comets *Stylised flowerheads and triple banded comets tails. Oven blue ground.*

3423 Parkland *Bold simple tree with enamelled dense foliage of autumn colours on matt blue ground.*

3424 Prickly Pansy *Stylised landscape, trees and pansy like flowers in matt finish. Pale brown ground.*

3427 Fantasia *Exotic bird with swallow like tail amongst exotic flowers and foliage. Blue matt ground.*

3428 Floral Comets *Stylised flowerheads and triple banded comets tails. Blue gloss ground.*

3431 Jigsaw *Stylised flower heads with spikey leaves and a patchwork of patterns. Matt green ground.*

3433 Garden *Spires of daisy like flowers in many colours. Blue lustre ground.*

3438 Garden *Spires of daisy like flowers in many colours. Blue lustre ground.*

3439 Jaggered Bouquet *Bouquet of stylised flowers and spikey leaves. Rouge ground.*

3440 Camouflage *Yellow, green & grey squiggles.*

3445 Neapolitan *Circles of rims with variety of colours. Pale pink ground.*

3446 no name *Matt pink ground with large flower heads. Handcraft.*

3447 Explosion *Extravagant starburst design in blue, black, silver, gold. Matt grey ground.*

3448 Peach Melba *Large orange flower heads, with blue foliage. Pale blue ground.*

3449 Prickly Pansy *Stylised landscape, trees and Pansy like flowers on lustre orange ground.*

3450 Awakening *Stylised sunrise design, cloud with jagged centres and ornate sun. Matt light brown ground.*

3451 Victorian Lady *Crinoline lady with parasol in garden.*

3452 Explosion & Butterfly *Star shaped colourful exploding flower heads and butterfly. Powder blue ground.*

3452 Awakening *Stylised sunrise design, cloud with jagged centres and ornate sun. Matt green ground.*

3453 Awakening *Stylised sunrise design, cloud with jagged centres and ornate sun. Matt light blue ground.*

3454 Explosion *Extravagant starburst design in blue, black, silver, gold. Matt grey ground.*

3455 Prickly Pansy *Stylised landscape, trees and Pansy like flowers. Lustre red mottled ground.*

3456 Awakening *Stylised sunrise design, cloud with jagged centres and ornate sun. Mottled red ground.*

3457 Jaggered Bouquet *Bouquet of stylised flowers and spikey leaves. Matt green ground.*

3458 Towering Castle *Fantasy Castle with trees and rocks in the foreground in white, brown, blue, and yellow colours.*

3459 Peach Melba *Large orange flower heads, with blue foliage. Orange ground*

3462 Humming Bird *Elaborately decorated exotic bird and floral decoration with enamels. Pale blue ground.*

3462 Humming Bird without Bird *Elaborately decorated with enamels as in 3462.*

3463 no name *Abstract flower and clouds design.*

3465 Shadow Imprint *Primula like flowers on mauve or lilac ground.*

3469 Cubist Butterfly *Bold stylised flowers, berries and butterflies. Semi-matt blue ground.*

3470 Stork and Bamboo *Two storks (one drinking) in pool. Bamboo shoots with green leaves. Matt orange ground.*

3471 Garden *Spires of Daisy like flowers in many colours. Mottled cork coloured ground.*

3474 Garden *Spires of Daisy like flowers in many colours. Mottled grey coloured ground.*

3475 Garden *Spires of Daisy like flowers in many colours. Orange ground.*

3476 Garden *Spires of Daisy like flowers in many colours. Mottled orange ground.*

3477 Garden *Spires of Daisy like flowers in many colours. Glazed yellow/pink ground.*

3478 Garden *Spires of Daisy like flowers in many colours. Glazed orange ground.*

3479 Garden *Spires of Daisy like flowers in many colours. Glazed orange ground.*

3487 Delphinium *Blue delphinium flowers and leaves, handcraft. Light mottled blue ground.*

3489 Jaggered Bouquet *Bouquet of stylised flowers and spikey leaves.*

3491 Victorian Lady *Crinoline lady with parasol in garden. Blue ground.*

3494 Awakening *Stylised sunrise design, cloud with jagged centres and ornate sun. Orange lustre ground.*

3495 New Mikado *Chinese figures, pagoda, bridge and trees. Sometimes has two cranes and punt like boat. Vivid green ground.*

3496 Awakening *Stylised sunrise design, cloud with jagged centres and ornate sun. Matt green ground.*

3497 Awakening *Stylised sunrise design, cloud with jagged centres and ornate sun.*

3498 Iris *Iris like flower design. Blue and white ground.*

3499 Prickly Pansy *Stylised landscape, trees and pansy like flowers. Orange ground.*

3500 Sylvan Glade *Simple trees in glade design, red border to edge of piece. Cream ground.*

3501 Garden *Spires of Daisy like flowers in*

many colours. Matt brown ground.

3502 Seagulls *Handcraft with realistic seagulls.*

3503 Jazz Poppy *Sprays of flowers and foliage in blue and pink, handcraft. Yellow ground.*

3504 Rose Marie *Large flower head design in enamels. Matt green ground.*

3505 Magical Tree (Rosetta) *Design of stylised trees with spangled trunk and large flowerheads by a lily pond. Orange ground.*

3506 Gypsy *Gypsy like lady dancing. Dark blue ground.*

3507 Iceland Poppy *Design of ornamental grasses, poppies and leaves. Matt green ground.*

3508 Wind & Flower *Large stylised flowers in variety of bright colours, handcraft. Cream and blue ground.*

3509 no name *Leaf green ground with underglaze tree in green and black.*

3510 Ensign *Blue lustre ground with ornate border.*

3517 Autumn Trees & Ferns *Stylised trees and ferns. White, cream ground.*

3519 Freehand Red Sunflower *Pattern with multi-coloured diagonal swirl and large flower heads below. Pale ground.*

3522 Apple Blossom *Black and grey branches with pink Apple blossom like flowers, handcraft. Matt pale blue ground.*

3523 Parkland *Bold simple tree with enamelled dense foliage of autumn colours. Matt pale blue ground.*

3524 Parkland *Bold simple tree with enamelled dense foliage of autumn colours. Matt green ground.*

3525 Clematis *Large multi-coloured Clematis flower heads, handcraft. Mottled light ground.*

3526 New Delphinium *Spires of Delphiniums in blue, pink, green and black. Blue matt ground.*

3527 Chinese Bird *Exotic bird with curly tail, flower and cloud motifs. Mottled pale orange ground.*

3528 Oranges *Oranges on black ground.*

3529 Crested Bird and Water Lily *Exotic oriental crested bird perched on a water lily. Blue lustre ground.*

3530 Crested Bird and Water Lily *Exotic oriental crested bird perched on a water lily. Red lustre ground.*

3532 Bookends - Fan *Bookends in fan shape design coloured purple, yellow and green.*

3533 Bookends - Fan *Bookends in fan shaped design in black, brown, orange and green.*

3535 Bookends - Asymmetric Flower *Bookends with flower heads in brown with green and yellow petal heads.*

3536 Crested Bird and Water Lily *Exotic oriental crested bird perched on a water lily. Mottled red ground.*

3537 Bookends - Saddleback *Bookends in Saddleback design in blue and grey.*

3542 no name *Apple Blossom.*

3544 Chinese Bird *Exotic bird with curly tail, flower and cloud motifs. Orange ground.*

3545 Clematis *Large multi-coloured Clematis flower heads, handcraft. Beige / brown ground.*

3546 Diamond *Diamond shape and design in gilt on pale blue and ivory.*

3547 Diamond *Diamond shape and design in gilt on green and black.*

3549 Diamond *Diamond shape and design in*

green and gilt on cream ground.

3550 Diamond *Diamond shape and design in gilt on black and cream.*

3551 Eclipse *Geometric design on red ground.*

3552 Deco Fan *Brightly coloured fan design with pink rim and bottom border. Terracotta ground.*

3553 Strata *Diagonal wavy stripes in gilt, beige, green and white. Matt black ground.*

3554 Ziggarette *Vertical stripes of green yellow blue gold, descending from top rim. Black ground.*

3555 Entangled Droplets *Brightly coloured enamelled beads on a gloss blue ground. Handcraft.*

3557 Fan *Fan of brightly coloured and ornately decorated panels with clouds of dots. Ascending above exotic circular flowerheads. Blue ground.*

3558 Fan *Fan of brightly coloured and ornately decorated panels with clouds of dots. Ascending above exotic circular flowerheads. Red ground.*

3562 Nightingale *Singing Nightingale bird perched on a stem with a variety of colourful stylised flowers in red, yellow and blue. Dark green ground.*

3563 Tree & Cottage *Cottage with smoking chimney in glade below stylised tree. Matt blue ground.*

3564 Fairy Shadow *Motif of Fairy with delicate wings playing and casting shadows, also bands containing colourful flowerheads. Blue lustre ground.*

3565 Kaleidescopic *Geometric shapes of patterns, stars and circles in profusion of brightly coloured enamels. Rouge ground.*

3566 Geometrica *Modern Art design with geometric right-angle shapes, overlapping squares and patterns with wavy lines. Blue ground.*

3567 Russian *Vibrant pattern of concentric circles in many colours. Stylised sun and*

bands of colour with leaves. Border has geometric pattern like saw teeth.

3568 Nightingale Garden *Large stylised brightly coloured flower heads. Black ground.*

3569 Green Trees *Trees and foliage in shades of green. Green ground.*

3570 Mondrian *Coloured squares and chevrons. Matt turquoise ground.*

3571 Fruit *Fruit (pears, grapes etc) on blue ground.*

3574 Fairy Shadow *Geometric shapes of patterns, stars and circles in profusion of brightly coloured enamels. Mustard ground.*

3576 Fairy Shadow *Motif of Fairy with delicate wings playing and casting shadows, also bands containing colourful flowerheads. Red lustre ground.*

3581 Garden *Spires of Daisy like flowers in many colours. Matt orange/brown ground.*

3587 Medley *Bands of bright colours, blue, green, yellow, orange, red and purple.*

3588 Flower Medley *Bands of bright colours, blue, green, yellow, orange, red and purple plus a simplistic pattern of shapes.*

3589 Hiawatha *Large simplistic flowerheads in bold bright colours with feathers. Black ground.*

3590 Hiawatha *Large simplistic flowerheads in bold bright colours with feathers. Black ground.*

3591 Medley *Bands of colours, yellow, orange and terracotta.*

3592 Gazania *Large simplistic flower heads and leaves.*

3593 Medley *Bands of bright colours, blue, green, yellow, orange, red and purple plus a simplistic pattern of shapes.*

3594 Dragon & Traveller *Dragon & traveller. Oriental Dragon confronting a chinese traveller. Terracotta ground.*

3594 Dragon & Traveller *Dragon & traveller. Oriental Dragon confronting a chinese traveller. Mustardy yellow ground.*

Medley - Pattern 3587
Bowl from the Kosniowski Collection
£30 - £50

221

3595 Dragon & Traveller *Dragon & traveller. Oriental Dragon confronting a chinese traveller. Turquoise ground.*

3596 Flower Medley *Bands of bright colours plus a simplistic pattern of shapes.*

3597 Dragon & Traveller *Dragon & traveller. Oriental Dragon confronting a chinese traveller. Blue lustre ground.*

3598 Nightingale *Singing Nightingale bird perched on a stem with a variety of colourful stylised flowers in red, yellow and blue. Blue lustre ground.*

3599 Medley *Bands of colours, yellow, orange, green, purple, blue and black.*

3600 Medley *Bands of colours, purple, blue, grey and black.*

3601 Melange *Large stylised flowerheads ornately decorated with leaves. Blue ground.*

3601 Melange *Large stylised flowerheads ornately decorated with leaves. Pink ground.*

3603 no name *Daisies, colours on blue ground.*

3606 Dahlia & Butterfly *Bright yellow flower heads and butterflies with mottled green over blue ground.*

3609 Garden *Spires of Daisy like flowers in many colours. Matt red ground.*

3639 Lace Cap Hydrangea *Decorative Lace type design with Hydrangea flower heads and leaves. Light ground.*

3641 Forest Tree *Exotic birch like trees. Slender tree rising to a wide pendulous canopy of foliage. Matt cream ground.*

3643 Victorian Garden *Garden scene - similar to 3451 (Crinoline lady with parasol in garden) but without lady.*

3645 Rosetta *Stylised flowers on trees with black and white bark. Orange ground.*

3645 Fairy Dell *Scene with trees, snow and rabbits.*

3646 Iceland Poppy *Designs of grasses, ornamental poppies and leaves.*

3648 Forest Tree *Exotic birch like trees. Slender tree rising to a wide pendulous canopy of foliage. Mauve, cream ground, with green and yellow foliage.*

3650 Sylvan *Stippled effect painted in green and blue.*

3651 Scimitar *Geometric design of arches, bands and semi-circular shapes containing colourful patterns and flowers on mottled blue, green, pink background. Blue ground.*

3652 Scimitar *Geometric design of arches, bands and semi-circular shapes containing colourful patterns and flowers on mottled blue, green, pink background. Blue ground.*

3653 Mandarins Chatting *Two Chinese figures talking under Mandarin tree with beautiful coloured enamels and flowers. Second tree with detailed foliage and spikey leaves. Red frieze. Gloss black ground.*

3654 Mandarins Chatting *Two Chinese figures talking under Mandarin tree with beautiful coloured enamels and flowers. Second tree with detailed foliage and spikey leaves. Green frieze. Gloss black ground.*

3655 Jazz Stitch *Geometric design of shapes some containing a stitch effect in orange, black and yellow. Light ground.*

3656 Dragon & Traveller *Dragon & traveller. Fierce dragon decorated in many beautiful enamels, confronting chinese traveller also nearby is a pretty weeping tree. Dark blue ground.*

3657 Chevrons *Geometric design in green,*

black and silver.

3658 Carre *Abstract design of black squares with silver borders. Green lustre ground.*

3659 Carre *Abstract design of black squares. Orange lustre ground.*

3660 Dragon & Traveller *Dragon & traveller. Fierce dragon decorated in many beautiful enamels, confronting chinese traveller also nearby is a pretty weeping tree. Yellow ground.*

3661 Norwegian Flowers *Simplistic variety of flowers growing from green base. Matt blue ground.*

3662 Liberty Stripe *Mauve, grey and pale blue separated by gold band.*

3663 Summer Medley *Variety of brightly coloured flowers, some with spikey petals. Handcraft on black reserve.*

3665 Norwegian Lady *Multicoloured simple flower heads. Blue ground.*

3665 Fairy Dell *Scene with trees, snow and rabbits.*

3667 Tiger Lily *Large stylised lily flowers design in blue, orange, yellow, pink and black colours. Frieze with tooth shaped pattern.*

3668 Norwegian Miss *Image of a Norwegian girl surrounded by flowers. Blue ground.*

3669 Candy Flowers *Anemone type flowerheads on mottled pale blue ground.*

3671 Chevrons *Geometric design on orange lustre ground.*

3672 Mandarin Tree *Mandarin tree in beautiful*

coloured enamels and flowers. Second tree with detailed foliage and spikey leaves. Blue ground and blue frieze.

3672 Mandarins Chatting *Two Chinese figures talking under Mandarin tree with beautiful coloured enamels and flowers. Second tree with detailed foliage and spikey leaves. Gloss blue ground.*

3673 Daisy *Daisies on a blue ground.*

3675 Mandarins Chatting *Two Chinese figures talking under Mandarin tree with beautiful coloured enamels and flowers. Second tree with detailed foliage and spikey leaves. White/Cream ground, red frieze.*

3678 Diamond *Diamond shape and design in gilt on black and yellow.*

3680 Mandarins Chatting *Two Chinese figures talking under Mandarin tree with beautiful coloured enamels and flowers. Second tree with detailed foliage and spikey leaves. Green and yellow ground.*

3681 Bathing Belle *Handle formed as arched near naked female figure. White and dark blue.*

3684 Bathing Belle *Handle formed as arched near naked female figure. White, red, gold and black.*

3688 Bathing Belle *Handle formed as arched near naked female figure. Green and black*

3690 Intersection *Red, black, gilt stripe on cream ground.*

3691 Daisy *Daisies on gloss green ground.*

Norwegian Miss - Pattern 3668
Charger from the Dulcie Agnes Joyce Memorial Collection
Image courtesy of www.nicholnack.com.au
£1,250 - £1,500

3692 Lightning *Lightning flashes of zig-zag lines. Orange, black and gilt.*

3693 Daisy *Daisies on matt dark blue, light green ground.*

3694 Anemone *Large stylised flower heads with spikey shaped petals and leaves. Mottled orange ground.*

3695 Egyptian Fan *Elaborate geometric flower heads arranged in fan shapes and spires of brightly coloured flowers. Red lustre ground.*

3696 Egyptian Fan *Elaborate geometric flower heads arranged in fan shapes and spires of brightly coloured flowers. Blue lustre.*

3696 Egyptian Fan *Elaborate geometric flower heads arranged in fan shapes and spires of brightly coloured flowers. Green ground.*

3697 Egyptian Fan *Elaborate geometric flower heads arranged in fan shapes and spires of brightly coloured flowers. Matt light blue ground.*

3698 Egyptian Fan *Elaborate geometric flower heads arranged in fan shapes and spires of brightly coloured flowers. Gloss light blue ground.*

3699 Rainbow Fans *Semi circular open fan shapes containing wavy patterns and exotic flower heads. Bands of colours as a rainbow. Orange ground.*

3700 Rainbow Fans *Semi circular open fan shapes containing wavy patterns and exotic flower heads. Bands of colours as a rainbow. Gloss turquoise ground.*

3701 Mandarin Tree *Mandarin tree in beautiful coloured enamels and flowers. Second tree with detailed foliage and spikey leaves. Red frieze and black ground.*

3702 Mandarin Tree *Mandarin tree in beautiful coloured enamels and flowers. Second tree with detailed foliage and spikey leaves. Green frieze and black ground.*

3703 Mandarin Tree *Mandarin tree in beautiful coloured enamels and flowers. Second tree with detailed foliage and spikey leaves. Red frieze and cream ground.*

3713 Rainbow Fans *Semi circular open fan shapes containing wavy patterns and exotic flower heads. Bands of colours as a rainbow. Gloss blue ground.*

3714 Daisy *Daisies on dark blue / mottled pale blue ground.*

3715 Sylvan *Terracotta marks on dark cream ground.*

3716 Lightning *Lightning flashes.*

3718 Sylvan *Yellow, brown ground, vertical brush strokes with mottled effect.*

3719 Mandarin Tree *Mandarin tree in beautiful coloured enamels and flowers. Second tree with detailed foliage and spikey leaves. Green Frieze and cream, yellow ground.*

3720 Bands *Two tone green bands.*

3721 Rainbow Fans *Semi circular open fan shapes containing wavy patterns and exotic flower heads. Bands of colours as a rainbow. Pale blue ground.*

3729 Christmas Tree *Stylistic design of a Christmas Tree together with an ornate border. Orange ground.*

3742 Primula *Primula flowers in pale mauve & pink.*

3745 Primula *Primula flowers on pink, mauve ground.*

3746 Primula *Primula flowers on pale peach ground.*

3753 Galleon *Large Galleon like sailing ship. Pale blue, grey ground.*

3765 Red Devil *Red devil (Mephistopheles) beneath a spangled tree with pendant foliage and blossoms like eye motifs. Large brightly coloured exotic flowers with spear shaped leaves. Gloss turquoise ground.*

3765 Devils Copse *Mottled exotic tree with pendant foliage and blossoms like eye motifs. Large brightly coloured exotic flowers with spear shaped leaves. Gloss turquoise ground.*

3766 Autumn Leaf *Spray of leaves in Autumn hues of pink, green and orange. Pink mauve ground.*

3767 Red Devil *Red devil (Mephistopheles) beneath a spangled tree with pendant foliage and blossoms like eye motifs. Large brightly coloured exotic flowers with spear shaped leaves. Wedgewood blue ground.*

3767 Devils Copse *Mottled exotic tree with pendant foliage and blossoms like eye motifs. Large brightly coloured exotic flowers with spear shaped leaves. Wedgewood blue ground.*

3768 Gum Tree *Flowers, spikey leaves and seed pods hanging from a tree. Pale blue ground.*

3769 Red Devil *Red devil (Mephistopheles) beneath a spangled tree with pendant foliage and blossoms like eye motifs. Large brightly coloured exotic flowers with spear shaped leaves. Pale yellow ground.*

3769 Devils Copse *Mottled exotic tree with pendant foliage and blossoms like eye motifs. Large brightly coloured exotic flowers with spear shaped leaves. Pale yellow ground.*

3770 Old Stone Ware *Ribbed vase, blue, green.*

3770 Old Stone Ware *Book ends, blue.*

3771 Drip Ware *Running paint pattern. Ribbed*

vase, blue, brown, cream.

3772 Drip Ware *Running paint pattern. Ribbed vase, brown, cream.*

3773 Drip Ware *Running paint pattern. Ribbed running yellow, green.*

3774 Bell *Large stylised flower heads in multicoloured enamels and patterns with harebells curving out. One flowerhead contains a Bluebell. Detailed lace like triangular panels of pretty flowers. Cream gloss ground.*

3775 Old Stone Ware *Ribbed light blue.*

3776 Old Stone Ware *Running blue matt.*

3777 Old Stone Ware *Matt stone.*

3778 Old Stone Ware *Greenish grey.*

3779 Old Stone Ware *Dark Pink.*

3780 Old Stone Ware *Matt mauve.*

3781 Old Stone Ware *Blue Matt.*

3782 Old Stone Ware *Running design light and dark blue matt ground.*

3783 Old Stone Ware *Matt stone*

3784 Old Stone Ware *Running design blue grey matt ground design.*

3785 Bell *Large stylised flower heads in multicoloured enamels and patterns with harebells curving out. One flowerhead contains a Bluebell. Detailed lace like triangular panels of pretty flowers. Matt pale blue ground.*

3786 Bell *Large stylised flower heads in multicoloured enamels and patterns with harebells curving out. One flowerhead contains a Bluebell. Detailed lace like triangular panels of pretty flowers. Matt pale green ground.*

3787 Devils Copse *Mottled exotic tree with pendant foliage and blossoms like eye motifs. Large brightly coloured exotic flowers with spear shaped leaves. Dark blue ground.*

3788 Bell *Large stylised flower heads in multicoloured enamels and patterns with harebells curving out. One flowerhead contains a Bluebell. Detailed lace like triangular panels of pretty flowers. Red Lustre ground.*

3789 Gum Tree *Flowers, spikey leaves and seed pods hanging from a tree. Matt blue ground.*

3790 Gum Tree *Flowers, spikey leaves and seed pods hanging from a tree. Green, yellow ground.*

3791 Mandarin Tree *Mandarin tree in beautiful coloured enamels and flowers. Second tree with detailed foliage and spikey leaves. Grey ground.*

3792 Bell *Large stylised flower heads in multicoloured enamels and patterns with harebells curving out. One flowerhead contains a Bluebell. Detailed lace like triangular panels of pretty flowers. Blue ground.*

3793 Mandarin Tree *Mandarin tree in beautiful coloured enamels and flowers. Second tree with detailed foliage and spikey leaves. Ivory ground.*

3794 Gum Tree *Flowers, spikey leaves and seed pods hanging from a tree. Matt pale green.*

3795 Gilt Scallop *Rouge and black with border of scalloped edging in gilt of enamelled drops.*

3796 Bathing Belle *Handle formed as arched near naked female figure. Blue ground with green handles and borders.*

3801 Herbaceous Border *Spires of hollyhocks, foxgloves and pansy like flowers in a flowerbed. Multi-coloured on black and white ground.*

3802 Autumn Daisy *Daisy flowerheads and leaves with a pattern of brushstrokes. Yellow ground.*

3803 Modern Crocus *Medley of bright coloured bands and black border. Flowerheads of slender crocus shaped petals arranged in a circle with coloured leaves. Mauve brushstoke pattern. Pale green ground.*

3804 Old Stone Ware *Matt pale green.*

3809 Devils Copse *Mottled exotic tree with pendant foliage and blossoms like eye motifs. Large brightly coloured exotic flowers with spear shaped leaves. Turquoise blue ground.*

3810 Embossed - Oak Tree *Oak Tree with leaves and old gnarled trunk on concentric circles. Blue ground.*

3811 Embossed - Oak Tree *Oak Tree with acorns and an old gnarled trunk on concentric circles. Fawn ground.*

3812 Wagon Wheels *Exotic circular flower heads ornately decorated with enamels and leaves on stems. Pale green ground.*

3813 Wagon Wheels *Exotic circular flower heads ornately decorated with enamels and leaves on stems. Mottled pink ground.*

3814 Wagon Wheels *Exotic circular flower heads ornately decorated with enamels and leaves on stems. Red lustre ground.*

3815 Needlepoint *Flower heads enamelled in embroidery like patterns. Bands and crescents of enamelled colours like lace. Dark blue ground.*

3816 Needlepoint *Flower heads enamelled in embroidery like patterns. Bands and crescents of enamelled colours like lace. Maroon ground.*

3817 Devils Copse *Mottled exotic tree with pendant foliage and blossoms like eye motifs. Large brightly coloured exotic flowers with spear shaped leaves. Matt turquoise ground.*

3818 Hollyhocks *Spires of brightly coloured Hollyhocks, Pale green ground.*

3819 Hollyhocks *Spires of brightly coloured Hollyhocks. Pale blue ground.*

3820 Hollyhocks *Spires of brightly coloured Hollyhocks. Black ground.*

3827 Hollyhocks *Spires of brightly coloured Hollyhocks. Pale green ground.*

3829 Old Stone Ware *Ribbed design in pink.*

3830 Old Stone Ware *Ribbed design, semi-glazed in blue.*

3837 Delphinium *Blue delphinium flowers and leaves, handcraft. Beige ground.*

3838 Gum Tree *Flowers, spikey leaves and seed pods hanging from a tree. Matt light brown.*

3839 Autumn Breeze *Stoneware design, flowers heads on pink and beige ground.*

3840 Autumn Breeze *Stoneware design, flower heads on pale bluish pink with green edge.*

3841 Neapolitan *Light green, light brown and light violet.*

3842 Neapolitan *Stoneware, purple, mauve, green, pink.*

3843 Plain *Green with gold band.*

3843 New Mikado *Plain green but with New Mikado pattern. Chinese figures, pagoda, bridge and trees. Sometimes has two cranes*

and punt like boat. Green ground.

3844 Plain *Plain pale blue with gilt.*

3845 Medley *Pink, green, blue and brown bands.*

3846 Plain *Black lustre ground with wide band of gilding to borders.*

3847 Old Stone Ware *Ribbed style in matt brown.*

3848 no name *Pale green ground, flowers yellow orange green purple blue.*

3849 Plain *Black gloss ground with wide band of gilding to borders.*

3852 Sketching Bird *Exotic tree with pendant foliage and decoratively enamelled kingfisher like bird flying by. Pale blue lustre ground.*

3854 Hollyhocks *Spires of Hollyhocks in enamels. Powder blue ground.*

3855 Bell *Large stylised flower heads in multicoloured enamels and patterns with harebells curving out. One flowerhead contains a Bluebell. Detailed lace like triangular panels of pretty flowers. Gloss blue green.*

3857 Leaf *Design of Leaves and small flower heads decorated in enamels. Powder blue ground.*

3858 Tendrillon *Design of swirling patterns with leaves and tendrils in white and gilt. Black gloss ground.*

3859 Devils Copse *Mottled exotic tree with pendant foliage and blossoms like eye motifs. Large brightly coloured exotic flowers with spear shaped leaves. Red ground.*

3860 New Mikado *Chinese figures, pagoda, bridge and trees. Sometimes has two cranes and punt like boat. Blue ground.*

3861 Leaf *Design of Leaves and small flower heads decorated in enamels. Red ground.*

3862 Bluebells *Bluebell flowers with snowdrops, primulas and autumn leaves. Ruby Lustre.*

3863 Garden Gate *Deco tree, bushes and flowers with path leading to garden gate. Pale green ground.*

3865 Spring *Spring flowers depicted on a tree in many bright colours, handcraft. Grey ground.*

3866 Wisteria *Wisteria like flowers trailing from tree with leaves. Pale blue ground.*

3867 New Laburnam *Laburnham like flowers trailing from tree with leaves. Pale turquoise ground, yellow flowers.*

3867 New Laburnam *Laburnham like flowers trailing from tree with leaves. Pale turquoise ground, lilac flowers.*

3868 Vogue *Design of simple primula and hydrangea flowers. Pale matt green ground.*

3872 Bluebells *Bluebell flowers with snowdrops, primulas and autumn leaves. Pink, blue glazed.*

3873 Leaf *Design of Leaves and small flower heads decorated in enamels. Matt pale blue ground.*

3874 Bluebells *Bluebell flowers with snowdrops, primulas and autumn leaves. Mottled grey ground.*

3875 Bluebells *Bluebell flowers with snowdrops, primulas and autumn leaves. Light blue matt ground.*

3876 Embossed - Rock Garden *Simple embossed primula like flowers heads. Spires of flowers with stone shaped patterns. Grey ground.*

3877 Old Stone Ware *Ribbed style on blue*

3878 Old Stone Ware *Ribbed style on matt jade green ground slightly mottled.*

3879 Old Stone Ware *Ribbed style on brown ground.*

3883 Beehives *Mottled grey ground.*

3884 Humming Bird with Tree *Elaborately decorated exotic bird hovering under weeping tree with floral decoration. Rouge ground.*

3884 Beehives *Ivory matt ground.*

3885 Spring *Flowering tree on mottled stone glaze ground.*

3886 Moderne *Moderne set - Matt light & dark blue ground.*

3886 Dancing Deer *Embossed Deer.*

3887 Moderne *Moderne set - Matt blue with dark blue or Matt grey with gold or Matt blue with fawn or Matt grey with pink.*

3888 Moderne *Moderne set - Matt blue with or without gold.*

3889 Sketching Bird *Exotic tree with pendant foliage and decoratively enamelled kingfisher like bird flying by. Rouge ground.*

3890 Sketching Bird *Exotic tree with pendant foliage and decoratively enamelled kingfisher like bird flying by. Matt Cream ground.*

3891 Sketching Bird *Exotic tree with pendant foliage and decoratively enamelled kingfisher like bird flying by. Cream ground.*

3891 Sketching Bird with no Bird *Exotic tree with pendant foliage. No bird. Cream ground.*

3892 Persian Garden *Sprays of exotic enamel flowers and foliage, some in spires with star like heads. Sometimes a magical tree with a variety of flowerheads. Blue ground.*

3893 Persian Garden *Sprays of exotic enamel flowers and foliage, some in spires with star like heads. Sometimes a magical tree with a variety of flowerheads. Black ground.*

3894 Persian Garden *Sprays of exotic enamel flowers and foliage, some in spires with star like heads. Sometimes a magical tree with a variety of flowerheads. Matt green ground.*

3895 Chinaland *Complex chinoiserie design with underglaze enamels. Pagoda, terraces, trees, figures and usually mountains. Green lustre ground.*

3896 Old Stone Ware *Yellow/Cream ribbed*

3897 Spring *Deco tree and small flower heads. Peach ground.*

3900 Incised Square *Incised geometric simplistic flower patterns, some flowerheads are square shaped. Also has some wavy lines. Beige ground.*

3901 Incised Diamond *Incised geometric simplistic flower patterns, some flowerheads are diamond shaped. Also has some wavy lines. Pale blue ground.*

3902 Hammered Pewter *Dimpled, turquoise, green, yellow ground.*

3904 Old Stone Ware *Grey Ribbed.*

3905 Incised Diamond *Incised geometric simplistic flower patterns, some flowerheads are diamond shaped. Also has some wavy lines. Beige ground.*

3907 Sketching Bird *Exotic tree with pendant foliage and decoratively enamelled kingfisher like bird flying by. Pale ice blue lustre ground.*

3908 Crab & Lobster Ware *Aero green.*

3909 Ring Posy Bowls *Powder blue.*

3910 Mikado *Chinoiserie pagodas, bridges,*

oriental ladies and usually a pair of kissing birds. Matt black with green frieze.

3910 Crab & Lobster Ware *Straw.*

3911 Plain *Plain cream with black or gold edging.*

3912 Spots *Turquoise polka dots on cream ground.*

3913 Floral Mist *Floral wispy flower design in blue, yellow and green. Light ground.*

3915 Mirage *Simplistic abstract pattern on cream ground.*

3916 Spots *Yellow polka dots on beige ground.*

3917 Drip Ware *Running paint pattern in green, yellow and blue on cream ground.*

3918 Leaf and Catkin *Leaf and Catkin on white ground.*

3919 Leaf and Catkin *Leaf and Catkin on matt pale green.*

3920 Old Stone Ware *Splashes of blue and brown on grey.*

3922 Wild Duck *Duck with shadow flying over wild grasses and shrubs. Rouge ground.*

3923 Wild Duck *Duck with shadow flying over wild grasses and shrubs. Cream ground.*

3924 Wild Duck *Duck with shadow flying over wild grasses and shrubs. Pale blue ground.*

3925 Summer Flowers *Array of summer flowers and leaves. Matt blue ground.*

3926 Summer Flowers *Array of summer flowers and leaves. Yellow ground with green frieze.*

3927 Summer Flowers *Array of summer flowers and leaves. Cream ground.*

3927 Wild Duck *Duck with shadow flying over wild grasses and shrubs. Pale green ground.*

3929 Will o'wisp *Wavy pattern in mauve with wisps of paint in pale green and brown. Cream ground.*

3933 Plain *Plain rouge deepening to brown with gilt.*

3939 Will o'wisp *Wavy pattern in mauve with wisps of paint in pale green and brown. Yellow green ground.*

3943 Tube Lined Tree *Tube lined tree with hanging foliage in yellow, mauve and green. Cream ground.*

3944 Tube Lined Tree *Tube lined tree with hanging foliage in yellow, mauve and green. Pale matt green ground.*

3945 Tube Lined Flower *Tube lined flower in blue and green with thistle like flower in yellow. Cream ground.*

3946 Hazelnut *Hazelnuts and leaves. Pale mauve, grey ground.*

3947 Wild Duck *Duck with shadow flying over wild grasses and shrubs. Stippled green lustre ground.*

3948 Flower & Falling Leaf *Exotic complex geometric flower heads with leaves swirling and falling over. Matt pale turquoise ground.*

3949 Flower & Falling Leaf *Exotic complex geometric flower heads with leaves swirling and falling over. Rouge ground.*

3950 Flower & Falling Leaf *Exotic complex geometric flower heads with leaves swirling and falling over. Pale cream ground.*

3951 Sketching Bird *Exotic tree with pendant foliage and decoratively enamelled kingfisher bird flying by. Gloss pale green ground.*

3952 Flower & Falling Leaf *Exotic complex geometric flower heads with leaves swirling and falling over. Blue ground.*

3952 Sketching Bird *Exotic tree with pendant foliage and decoratively enamelled kingfisher like bird flying by. Powder blue ground.*

3953 Galleon *Large Galleon sailing ship on waves. Blue, cream ground.*

3955 Rayure *Black circular stripes on Moderne shape. Pale green ground.*

3956 Jacobean Figures *Beautiful design containing Jacobean Figures with shadows. Gloss green ground*

3956 Jacobean Figures *Beautiful design containing Jacobean Figures with shadows. Pale blue ground*

3957 Galleon *Large Galleon sailing ship on waves. Pale blue, mauve ground.*

3957 Jacobean Figures *Beautiful design containing Jacobean Figures with shadows.*

3977 Engine Turned Ware *Ribbed style in gloss pink ground.*

3978 Engine Turned Ware *Ribbed style in gloss green ground.*

3979 Engine Turned Ware *Ribbed style in matt green ground.*

3980 Engine Turned Ware *Ribbed style in matt yellow ground.*

3981 Engine Turned Ware *Ribbed style in matt blue ground.*

3982 Engine Turned Ware *Ribbed style in matt white or cream ground.*

3982 Sunflower *Large Sunflower heads. Black ground.*

3986 no name *Stylised flowers on cream ground.*

3989 Eden (Tiger Tree) *Exotic tree with gnarled trunk and lobes and pendulous hanging foliage with pretty flowers. The foliage also rises from the base in spires. Blue lustre ground.*

3990 no name *Seedheads, flowers on cream ground.*

3993 Embossed - Buttercup *Design in shape of Yellow Buttercup in embossed style. Cream, yellow ground.*

3994 Embossed - Buttercup *Design in shape of Pink Buttercup and embossed style. Pink ground.*

3996 Sunflower *Large Sunflower heads. Black ground.*

3997 Forest Night *Large trees with pendulous hanging leaves. Dark blue ground.*

3998 Old Stone Ware *Dark Green.*

3999 Engine Turned Ware *Ribbed style in matt grey ground.*

4000 Plain *Burnt Orange with Gold*

4001 Plain *Almond with Gold*

4002 Cherry Blossom *Cherry Blossom. Burnt Orange ground*

4003 Cherry Blossom *Cherry Blossom. Almond ground*

4009 Plain *Plain lustre, Rouge Royale.*

4011 Plain *Plain cobalt blue with gilt edging.*

4011 Spots *Spots on cobalt blue ground.*

4012 Tube Lined Marigold *Tubular raised edge flowerheads in red, orange and green with dark leaves. Mottled cream ground.*

4013 Plain *Plain Vert Royale with gilt.*

4014 Harebells *Harebell flowers edged with gilt. Green ground.*

4015 Harebells *Harebell flowers edged with gilt. Pale green ground.*

4016 Harebells *Harebell flowers edged with gilt. Pink ground.*

4017 Secretary Bird *Exotic bird with fan shaped tail feathers and long legs similar to a road runner, under a decorative tree in enamels. Orange ground.*

4018 Secretary Bird *Exotic bird with fan shaped tail feathers and long legs similar to a road runner, under a decorative tree in enamels. Red ground.*

4019 Animal (Squirrel, Deer or Fox) *Decorative landscape with woodland animals either a Squirrel, Deer or Fox. Green ground.*

4021 Plain *Plain blue and mauve lustre ground in mottled effect with gilt.*

4030 Carlton China - Peony *Flower design.*

4037 Plain *Plain jade green with gilt.*

4040 Leaves *Design of pale coloured leaves. Pale blue ground.*

4042 Wild Duck *Duck with shadow flying over wild grasses and shrubs. Pale pink ground.*

Ruby red ground

3958 Summer Flowers *Array of summer flowers and leaves. Cream ground.*

3959 Triple Band *Wash bands in satin, yellow and brown.*

3960 Sketching Bird *Exotic tree with pendant foliage and decoratively enamelled kingfisher bird flying by. Green ground.*

3965 Heron & Magical Tree *Heron flying past large ornamental tree. Cream Lustre ground.*

3965 Plain *Rouge Royale.*

3966 Lace Cap Hydrangea *Lace type design with Hydrangea flower heads and leaves. Green ground.*

3967 Lace Cap Hydrangea *Lace type design with Hydrangea flower heads and leaves. Red ground.*

3968 Blossom & Spray *Blossom spray and small enamelled flower heads with gilt leaves. Powder blue ground.*

3969 Lace Cap Hydrangea *Lace type design with Hydrangea flower heads and leaves. Pink lustre ground.*

3970 Shabunkin *Ornamental brightly enamelled fish with flowing fins amongst exotic seabed plants. Pale blue or grey ground.*

3971 Shabunkin *Ornamental brightly enamelled fish with flowing fins amongst exotic seabed plants. Green and Ivory ground.*

3972 Hollyhocks *Spires of hollyhocks in enamels. Orange ground.*

3973 Hollyhocks *Spires of brightly coloured hollyhocks. Green ground.*

3974 Tube Lined Poppy & Bell *Tube lined poppies and bell flowers. Matt blue ground.*

3975 Persian Rose *Gilt tube lining of flower heads and bell flowers. Mushroom ground.*

3976 Banded and Crosstitch *Moderne design with bands of circles and wavy patterns. Pale cream ground.*

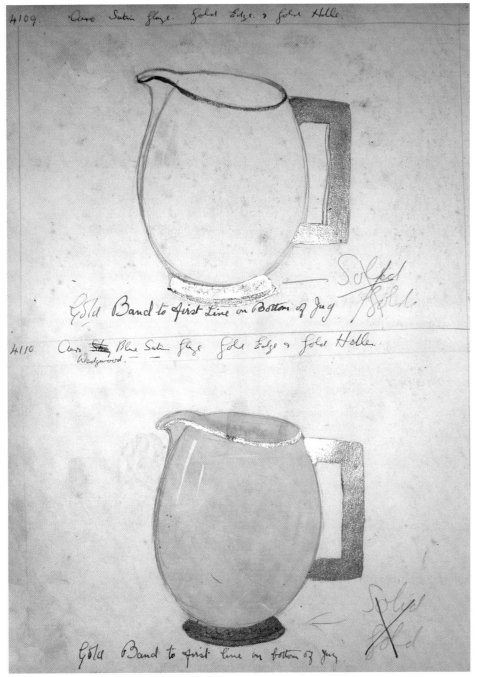

4109. *Cream Satin glaze. Gold Edge & Gold Helle.*

Gold Band to first Line on Bottom of Jug — *Solid Gold*

4110 *Cream Blue Satin glaze Gold Edge & Gold Helle.*
Wedgwood.

Gold Band to first line on bottom of Jug — *Solid Gold*

4045 Blossom & Spray *Blossom spray and small enamelled flower heads with gilt leaves. Red lustre ground.*

4047 Blossom & Spray *Blossom spray and small enamelled flower heads with gilt leaves. Blue mottled ground.*

4060 no name *Black bands and pink glaze.*

4076 Tyrolean Bands *Multi-coloured circular bands in various sizes and wavy lines.*

4077 Vertical Stripes *Large vertical stripes and sometimes smaller horizontal stripes on base in gilt. Cream ground.*

4078 Vertical Stripes *Large vertical stripes and sometimes smaller horizontal stripes on base in gilt. Yellow ground.*

4079 Vertical Stripes *Large vertical stripes and sometimes smaller horizontal stripes on base in gilt. Green ground.*

4080 Vertical Stripes *Large vertical stripes and sometimes smaller horizontal stripes on base in gilt. Gloss pink ground with black and gold.*

4081 Beanstalk *Plant with large leaves like a beanstalk. Pale blue ground.*

4083 Vertical Stripes *Large vertical stripes and sometimes smaller horizontal stripes on base in russet brown stripe. Cream ground.*

4084 Vertical Stripes *Large vertical stripes and sometimes smaller horizontal stripes on base in green. Cream ground.*

4092 Heatwave *Diagonal bands of colours in orange and yellow and many fine wavy lines.*

4100 Plain *Plain pale green with gold.*

4103 Spider's Web *Cobwebs with fruiting berries on branch, also flowers (harebells) and dragonflies. Pale green ground.*

4104 New Mikado *Chinese figures, pagoda, bridge and trees. Sometimes has two cranes and punt like boat. Pale green ground.*

4105 Black Crow *Colourful scene with black crows.*

4106 Secretary Bird *Exotic bird with fan shaped tail feathers and long legs similar to a road runner, under a decorative tree in enamels. Pale blue ground.*

4107 Secretary Bird *Exotic bird with fan shaped tail feathers and long legs similar to a road runner, under a decorative tree in enamels. Green ground.*

4108 Heron & Magical Tree *Heron flying past large ornamental tree. Pale green ground.*

4108 Plain *Plain pale green with gilt.*

4108 Temple *Oriental scene of figures in temple with large circular doorway. Ornate trees some with black stems, sometimes a gold sun. Pale green ground.*

4109 Plain *Plain cream with gold highlight.*

4109 Spider's Web *Cobwebs with fruiting berries on branch, also flowers (harebells) and dragonflies. Matt white ground.*

4109 New Mikado *Chinese figures, pagoda, bridge and trees. Sometimes has two cranes and punt like boat. Cream ground with gilt.*

4110 Plain *Plain pale blue with gilt.*

4117 Bird of Paradise *Bird of Paradise with long plumed tail flying among oriental trees. Red ground.*

4118 Bird of Paradise *Bird of Paradise with long plumed tail flying among oriental trees. Powder Blue ground.*

4119 Primula and Leaf *Primula flowers in bright colours and a butterfly. Rouge ground.*

4120 Primula and Leaf *Primula flowers in bright colours and a butterfly. Pale yellow ground.*

4121 Primula and Leaf *Primula flowers in bright colours and a butterfly. Pale green ground.*

4122 Butterfly *Butterfly and grasses. Cream ground.*

4123 Butterfly *Butterfly and grasses. Vibrant green ground.*

4125 Babylon *Profusion of foliage and leaves cascading down with pretty bell and star flowers. Large star shaped flowerhead ornately decorated in enamels. Yellow, green ground.*

4125 Heron & Magical Tree *Heron flying past large ornamental tree. Blue & green lustre ground.*

4126 Babylon *Profusion of foliage and leaves cascading down with pretty bell and star flowers. Large star shaped flowerhead ornately decorated in enamels. Rouge red ground.*

4128 Banded *Circles and plain green.*

4130 Banded *Yellow highlights on white ground.*

4136 Harebells *Harebell flowers edged with gilt. Pale green ground.*

4137 Babylon *Profusion of foliage and leaves cascading down with pretty bell and star flowers. Large star shaped flowerhead ornately decorated in enamels. Matt Orange ground.*

4138 Tube Lined Fields and Trees *Tube lined landscape scene with curving and bulbous fields, trees and hills. Blue ground.*

4139 Daisies *Large and small blue flower heads. Pale blue, green ground.*

4140 Azalea *Large design of Azalea flowerheads. Pale green ground.*

4141 Plain *Plain pink ground with gilt.*

4142 Plain *Plain pink ground with gilt.*

4146 Plain *Plain pale yellow ground with gilt.*

4149 Plain *Plain cream.*

4150 Heron & Magical Tree *Heron flying past large ornamental tree. Red ground.*

227

4201. as 4119 Cut Over Blue Lustre Spink X Bank in Darby not Black X green

4202. Hero as 3965. Gold Pt on Ruby Lustre Cock Patt.

4153 Heron & Magical Tree *Heron flying past large ornamental tree. Pale yellow ground.*

4154 Harebells *Harebell flowers edged with gilt. Orange ground.*

4155 Primula and Leaf *Primula flowers in bright colours and a butterfly. Pale green ground.*

4156 Crocus and Cloud *Realistic crocuses with clouds on a cream ground.*

4157 Plain *Pale pink with gold handles.*

4157 Plain with Leaves *Pale pink with white leaves.*

4158 Babylon *Profusion of foliage and leaves cascading down with pretty bell and star flowers. Large star shaped flowerhead ornately decorated in enamels. Plain pale yellow ground.*

4158 Plain *Plain pale yellow ground with gilt.*

4159 Heron & Magical Tree *Heron flying past ornamental tree. Rouge ground.*

4160 Heron & Magical Tree *Heron flying past ornamental tree. Blue, green ground.*

4161 Fighting Cocks *Two cockerels displaying in the fighting position amongst a beautiful display of flowers. Orange lustre ground.*

4162 Tube Lined Tulip *Tube lined tulip flowers and leaves. Green ground.*

4163 Spangle Tree or Tiger Tree *Stylised tree with black shadow and hanging green foliage with small flower heads. Yellow ground.*

4166 Plain *Plain green with gilt.*

4168 Babylon *Profusion of foliage and leaves cascading down with pretty bell and star flowers. Large star shaped flowerhead ornately decorated in enamels. Powder blue ground.*

4168 Carlton China - Greek Keys *Simple gilt border design.*

4178 Plain *Gilt on grey ground.*

4179 Plain *Plain mauve with gilt.*

4181 Plain *Plain rouge with gilt.*

4182 Heron & Magical Tree *Heron flying past ornamental tree. Salmon ground.*

4183 Plain *Plain pale green, gilt handles.*

4184 Fighting Glade *Fighting Cocks pattern with no Cocks. Display of flower heads. Bluish, pink ground.*

4185 Pastoral *Slender tree with orange and blue flowerheads also has large leaves. Pale green ground.*

4186 Fighting Cocks *Two cockerels displaying in the fighting position amongst a beautiful display of flowers. Pale blue lustre ground.*

4188 Plain *Plain pale grey ground with gilt.*

4189 Babylon *Profusion of foliage and leaves cascading down with pretty bell and star flowers. Large star shaped flowerhead ornately decorated in enamels. Pink ground.*

4190 no name *Pink flowers, yellow green foliage. Pale green ground.*

4191 Cinquefoil *Yellow and purple flowers, green foliage. Pale green ground.*

4192 Iceland Poppy *Designs of grasses, ornamental poppies and leaves. Pale gloss yellow ground.*

4192 Cinquefoil *Yellow and purple flowers, green foliage. Pale yellow ground.*

4193 Iceland Poppy *Designs of grasses, ornamental poppies and leaves. Pale gloss green ground.*

4194 Iceland Poppy *Designs of grasses, ornamental poppies and leaves. Pale lemon ground.*

4198 Fighting Glade *Fighting Cocks pattern with no Cocks. Display of flowers heads. Pale green ground.*

4199 Fighting Cocks *Two cockerels displaying in the fighting position amongst a beautiful display of flowers. Deep blue lustre ground.*

4201 Primula and Leaf *Primula flowers in bright colours and a butterfly. Blue lustre ground*

4202 Fighting Cocks *Two cockerels displaying in the fighting position amongst a beautiful display of flowers. Ruby lustre ground.*

4204 Temple *Oriental scene of figures in temple with large circular doorway. Ornate trees some with black stems, sometimes a gold sun. Cream gloss ground.*

4205 Temple *Oriental scene of figures in temple with large circular doorway. Ornate trees some with black stems, sometimes a gold sun. Pale green ground.*

4208 Temple *Oriental scene of figures in temple with large circular doorway. Ornate trees some with black stems, sometimes a gold sun. Dark red ground.*

4211 Sketching Bird *Exotic tree with pendant foliage and decoratively enamelled kingfisher bird flying by. Gloss light green ground.*

4212 Fighting Glade *Fighting Cocks pattern with no Cocks. Display of flowers heads. Rouge ground.*

4213 New Anemone *Anemone flowers in bright colours and leaves. Pale yellow ground.*

4214 Temple *Oriental scene of figures in temple with large circular doorway. Ornate trees some with black stems, sometimes a gold sun. Deep pink ground.*

4215 Starflower *Flowers with geometric spires*

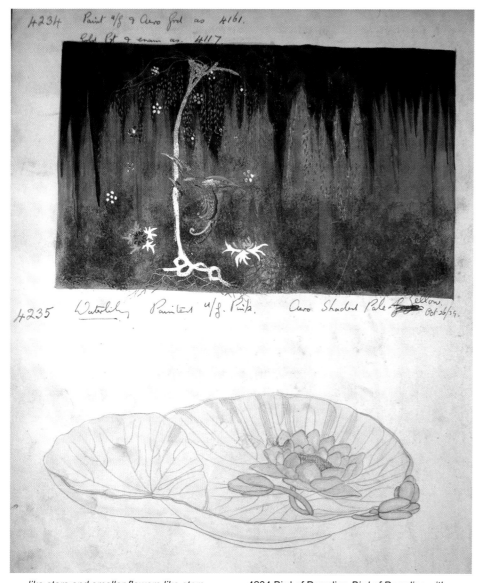

4234   Paint a/g & Aero Grd as 4161.
    Gold Pt & enam as. 4117.

4235   Waterlily   Painted a/g. Pink.   Aero Shaded Pale Yellow. Oct 26/39.

like stars and smaller flowers like stars cascading down. *Rouge ground.*

4216 Starflower *Flowers with geometric spires like stars and smaller flowers like stars cascading down. Light blue ground.*

4217 Tree & Clouds *Stylised tree with gnarled trunk and pendulous foliage trailing down and clouds in the background. Red ground.*

4218 Leaf & Dots *Dots and posies of leaves. Deep pink ground.*

4219 New Anemone *Anemone flowers in bright colours and leaves. Pale green ground.*

4220 Iceland Poppy *Designs of grasses, ornamental poppies and leaves. Pale green ground.*

4221 Iceland Poppy *Designs of grasses, ornamental poppies and leaves. Yellow ground.*

4223 Spots *Pale with orange spots.*

4224 Spots *Royal blue with light blue spots.*

4225 Spots *Rouge Royale with spots.*

4226 Spots *Pale pink with green spots.*

4227 Spots *Pale yellow with spots.*

4228 Iceland Poppy *Designs of grasses, ornamental poppies and leaves. Green ground.*

4231 New Anemone *Anemone flowers in bright colours and leaves. Yellow ground.*

4232 Spots *Pale yellow with orange spots.*

4234 Bird of Paradise *Bird of Paradise with long plumed tail flying among oriental trees. Mottled blue and orange lustre ground.*

4235 Embossed - Water Lily *Embossed Water Lily. Pale yellow and pink.*

4235 Carlton China - no name *Blue Flowers.*

4239 Bird of Paradise *Bird of Paradise with long plumed tail flying among oriental trees. Pale blue ground.*

4241 Eden (Tiger Tree) *Exotic tree with gnarled trunk and lobes and pendulous hanging foliage with pretty flowers. The foliage also rises from the base in spires. Rouge ground.*

4242 Eden (Tiger Tree) *Exotic tree with gnarled trunk and lobes and pendulous hanging foliage with pretty flowers. The foliage also rises from the base in spires. Purple ground.*

4242 Spider's Web *Cobwebs with fruiting berries on branch, flowers (harebells) and dragonflies. Pale blue lustre ground.*

4243 Spider's Web *Cobwebs with fruiting berries on branch, flowers (harebells) and dragonflies. Blue, grey ground.*

4243 Rabbits at Dusk *Rabbits playing amongst grasses shown in silhouette, under tall trees with green foliage. Orange ground.*

4244 Spider's Web *Cobwebs with fruiting berries on branch, flowers (harebells) and dragonflies. Powder blue ground.*

4245 New Anemone *Anemone flowers in bright colours and leaves. Mauve / pink / blue.*

4246 Daydream *Large flower heads in blue with yellow centre also has a frieze of blue scrolls, handcraft. White ground.*

4247 Rabbits at Dusk *Rabbits playing amongst grasses shown in silhouette, under tall trees with green foliage. Mottled orange ground.*

4247 Rabbits at Dusk *Rabbits playing amongst grasses shown in silhouette, under tall trees with green foliage. Mottled pink ground.*

4248 Eden Canopy *Pendulous hanging foliage with pretty flowers from an exotic tree. Rouge ground.*

4249 Rabbits at Dusk *Rabbits playing amongst grasses shown in silhouette, under tall trees with green foliage. Orange ground.*

4249 Eden Canopy *Pendulous hanging foliage with pretty flowers from an exotic tree. Blue ground.*

4252 Spider's Web *Cobwebs with fruiting berries on branch, flowers (harebells) and dragonflies. Rouge ground.*

4254 Spider's Web *Cobwebs with fruiting berries on branch, flowers (harebells) and dragonflies. Rouge Royale ground.*

4257 Rabbits at Dusk *Rabbits playing amongst grasses shown in silhouette, under tall trees with green foliage. Pale green ground.*

4258 Plain *Stiff strong pink and gold.*

4259 Spider's Web *Cobwebs with fruiting berries on branch, flowers (harebells) and dragonflies. Pale pink ground.*

4260 Figurine - Monica *Carlton China Figurine.*

4261 Figurine - Monica *Carlton China Figurine.*

4262 Figurine - Curtsy *Carlton China Figurine.*

4264 Figurine - Nan *Grandmother figurine with shawl, bonnet and basket of flowers.*

4268 Figurine - Nell *Carlton China Figurine.*

4269 Figurine - Nell *Carlton China Figurine.*

4270 Figurine - Peggy *Carlton China Figurine.*

4271 Figurine - Peggy *Carlton China Figurine.*

4273 Figurine - Joan *Carlton China Figurine in pink and green carrying a fan.*

4273 Heron & Magical Tree *Heron flying past large ornamental tree. Pink ground.*

4274 Plain *Plain dark blue lustre.*

4275 Figurine - Grandma *Carlton China Figurine.*

4276 Figurine - Grandma *Carlton China Figurine.*

4277 Marguerite Daisy *Yellow daisy like flowers with green serrated leaves like nettle leaves. Yellow ground.*

4278 Palm Blossom *Flower heads.*

4279 Lilac *Realistic Lilac flowers and leaves. Pale green ground.*

4280 New Storks *Two crane like birds wading in a lake under trees with pendulous hanging foliage. Rouge ground.*

4281 Beech Nut *Leaves & nuts, cream ground.*

4282 Beech Nut *Leaves & nuts, pale brown ground.*

4283 New Storks *Two crane like birds wading in a lake under trees with pendulous hanging foliage. Green, pink, purple lustre ground.*

4284 Plain *Purple Lustre plain.*

4285 Embossed - Foxglove *Embossed Foxglove on Yellow*

4286 Silk Sands *Contour lines as in a silk pattern or left by the sea on the sands. Light green ground with gilt.*

4286 Embossed - Foxglove *Embossed Foxglove on Green*

4.303 Stencilied blown green blue in tipped shaded in black on top. Blown Green Lid inside. Solid Hilts, Gold.

Shaded top & Bottom in black.

4304 Stork Patt. Blown Lid Green Shaded at top & bottom in black Gold Printed.

4287 Silk Sands *Contour lines as in a silk pattern or left by the sea on the sands. Light yellow ground with gilt.*

4289 Silk Sands *Contour lines as in a silk pattern or left by the sea on the sands. Light cream ground with gilt.*

4291 Contours *Pale blue ground with darker dashes and gilt.*

4292 Tree & Clouds *Cream/pink ground, stylised gnarled tree and clouds.*

4293 Heron & Magical Tree *Heron flying past ornamental tree. Pale blue or pale pink ground.*

4294 Carlton China - Arrow Border *Simple arrows around edge design on either Blue or Dark Pink.*

4297 Palm Blossom *Flower heads on mottled red ground.*

4298 Palm Blossom *Flower heads on orange ground.*

4301 Figurine - Joan *Carlton China Figurine.*

4302 Figurine - Grandma *Carlton China Figurine.*

4303 Tree & Clouds *Stylised gnarled tree and clouds on blue ground.*

4304 New Storks *Two crane like birds wading in a lake under trees with pendulous hanging foliage. Green ground.*

4305 Harvest Fruit *Fruit on a white ground with a net type background and a black border. Also found under Carlton China.*

4310 Lilac *Realistic Lilac flowers and leaves. Pale green ground.*

4313 Heron & Magical Tree *Heron flying past ornamental tree. Blue ground.*

4314 Figurine - Jean *Carlton China Figurine in blue dress and pink shawl.*

4320 New Mikado *Chinese figures, pagoda, bridge and trees. Sometimes has two cranes and punt like boat. Pale yellow ground.*

4321 Heron & Magical Tree *Heron flying past large ornamental tree. Yellow ground.*

4322 Spots *White spots on Noire Royale.*

4323 Spots *White spots on pink.*

4324 Spots *White spots on French green ground.*

4325 Heron & Magical Tree *Heron flying past ornamental tree. Blue Royale ground.*

4326 Heron & Magical Tree *Heron flying past ornamental tree. Rouge Royal ground.*

4327 Spider's Web *Cobwebs with fruiting berries on branch, flowers (harebells) and dragonflies. Pale yellow ground.*

4328 New Mikado *Chinese figures, pagoda, bridge and trees. Sometimes has two cranes and punt like boat. Pale green ground.*

4329 New Mikado *Chinese figures, pagoda, bridge and trees. Sometimes has two cranes and punt like boat. Pale Ice blue ground.*

4330 Spider's Web *Cobwebs with fruiting berries on branch, flowers (harebells) and dragonflies. Pale pink ground.*

4331 Spider's Web *Cobwebs with fruiting berries on branch, flowers (harebells) and dragonflies. Pale green ground.*

4332 Heron & Magical Tree *Heron flying past ornamental tree. Pink ground.*

4339 New Storks *Two crane like birds wading in a lake under trees with pendulous hanging foliage. Powder blue ground.*

4340 New Storks *Two crane like birds wading in a lake under trees with pendulous hanging foliage. Rouge Royale ground.*

4341 Plain *Plain Cobalt blue with gilt.*

4342 New Storks *Two crane like birds wading in a lake under trees with pendulous hanging foliage. Pale yellow ground.*

4343 New Storks *Two crane like birds wading in a lake under trees with pendulous hanging foliage. Pale green ground.*

4344 New Storks *Two crane like birds wading in a lake under trees with pendulous hanging foliage. Pale pink ground.*

4346 New Mikado *Chinese figures, pagoda, bridge and trees. Sometimes has two cranes and punt like boat. Noir Royale ground.*

4347 Spider's Web *Cobwebs with fruiting berries on branch, flowers (harebells) and dragonflies. Noire Royale ground.*

4348 New Storks *Two crane like birds wading in a lake under trees with pendulous hanging foliage. Noire Royale ground.*

4350 Plain *Plain green with gilt.*

4352 Plain *Blue grey.*

4353 Plain *Matt fawn.*

4354 Sketching Bird *Exotic tree with pendant foliage and decoratively enamelled kingfisher like bird flying by. Ruby Lustre ground.*

4355 Humming Bird with Tree *Elaborately decorated exotic bird and floral decoration. Powder blue ground.*

4355 Sketching Bird *Exotic tree with pendant foliage and decoratively enamelled kingfisher like bird flying by. Powder Blue ground.*

4356 Plain *Plain Vert Royale with gilt.*

4357 Plain *Plain ribbed Bleu Royale.*

4358 no name *Powder blue with border (raised enamel).*

4359 no name *Rouge Royale with border.*

4360 Carlton China - Canterbury Border or New Bluebells *Bluebells and other flowers design on edge.*

4362 New Mikado *Chinese figures, pagoda, bridge and trees. Sometimes has two cranes*

4363 Spider's Web *Cobwebs with fruiting berries on branch, also flowers (harebells) and dragonflies. Mottled green ground.*

4366 Spider's Web *Cobwebs with fruiting berries on branch, flowers (harebells) and dragonflies. Mottled pale blue lustre ground.*

4367 New Storks *Two crane like birds wading in a lake under trees with pendulous hanging foliage. Bleu Royale.*

4368 Embossed - Primula *Embossed primula on yellow ground.*

4369 Embossed - Primula *Embossed primula on green ground.*

4372 Spots *Powder blue with spots.*

4373 Mikado *Chinoiserie pagodas, bridges, oriental ladies and usually a pair of kissing birds. Vert Royale ground.*

4374 New Violets *Violets on pale violet ground.*

4375 Snowdrops *Snowdrops flowers on pale blue ground.*

4376 New Violets *Violets on pale violet ground.*

4376 Sketching Bird *Exotic tree with pendant foliage and decoratively enamelled kingfisher like bird flying by. Bleu Royale ground.*

4377 Fighting Glade *Fighting Cocks pattern with no Cocks. Display of flowers heads. Rouge Royale.*

4379 Spots *Lilac ground with white spots.*

4380 Fighting Cocks *Two cockerels displaying in the fighting position amongst a beautiful display of flowers. Powder blue ground.*

4385 Vine *Vine with leaves and grapes on rouge ground.*

4387 Vine *Vine with leaves and grapes on pale yellow.*

4388 Embossed - Poppy & Daisy *Embossed poppies and daisies. Pale green ground.*

4389 Embossed - Poppy & Daisy *Embossed poppies and daisies. Pale blue ground.*

4391 Kingfisher & Water Lily *Kingfisher perched on the stem of a climbing plant over water lilies. Rouge Royale.*

4393 Sketching Bird *Exotic tree with pendant foliage and decoratively enamelled kingfisher like bird flying by. Vert Royale ground.*

4395 Vine *Vine with leaves and grapes on pale green.*

4397 Plain *Bleu Royale plain with gilt.*

4398 New Mikado *Chinese figures, pagoda, bridge and trees. Sometimes has two cranes and punt like boat. Bleu Royale.*

4399 Spider's Web *Cobwebs with fruiting berries on branch, flowers (harebells) and dragonflies. Bleu Royale ground.*

4400 New Storks *Two crane like birds wading in a lake under trees with pendulous hanging foliage. Bleu Royale.*

4401 Fighting Cocks *Two cockerels displaying in the fighting position amongst a beautiful display of flowers. Bleu Royale.*

4402 Vine *Vine with leaves and grapes on Blue Royale.*

4402 Carlton China - Trellis Border *Simple Frieze pattern on Blue.*

4403 no name *Bleu Royale with border.*

4404 Spots *Pale yellow/green ground with mauve spots.*

4405 Vine *Vine with leaves and grapes on powder blue.*

4406 Spots *Bleu Royale with spots.*

4408 Spots *Green with red spots.*

4411 Vine *Vine with leaves and grapes on pale pink.*

4414 no name *Rouge Royale with bird & tree border (tea & coffee ware only).*

4415 no name *Chinese on Rouge Royale - no enamels.*

4416 New Mikado *Chinese figures, pagoda, bridge and trees. Sometimes has two cranes and punt like boat. Powder blue ground.*

4417 Plain *Vert Royale plain.*

4417 Fighting Cocks *Two cockerels displaying in the fighting position amongst a beautiful display of flowers. Rouge Royale.*

4418 Spots *Vert Royale with white spots.*

4418 Bird of Paradise *Bird of Paradise with long plumed tail flying among oriental trees. Powder Blue ground.*

4419 New Mikado *Chinese figures, pagoda, bridge and trees. Sometimes has two cranes and punt like boat. Vert Royale.*

4419 Carlton China - Reproduction Swansea *Colourful posies of flowers in gilt cartouches with decorative gilt leaves and bands.*

4420 Spider's Web *Cobwebs with fruiting berries on branch, flowers (harebells) and dragonflies. Vert Royale ground.*

4421 New Storks *Two crane like birds wading in a lake under trees with pendulous hanging foliage. Vert Royale ground.*

4421 Carlton China - Bird Cartouche *Birds in a Cartouche pattern.*

4422 Mikado *Chinoiserie pagodas, bridges, oriental ladies and usually a pair of kissing birds. Rouge ground.*

4422 Fighting Cocks *Two cockerels displaying in the fighting position amongst a beautiful display of flowers. Vert Royale.*

4423 Vine *Vine with leaves and grapes on Vert Royale.*

4426 Forest Tree *Exotic birch like trees. Slender tree rising to a wide pendulous canopy of foliage. Mottled blue ground, with mauve, orange and white foliage.*

4427 Embossed - Wild Rose *Embossed Wild Rose on Yellow*

4428 Embossed - Wild Rose *Embossed Wild Rose on Green*

4433 Mikado *Chinoiserie pagodas, bridges, oriental ladies and usually a pair of kissing birds. Rouge ground.*

4434 Mikado *Chinoiserie pagodas, bridges, oriental ladies and usually a pair of kissing birds. Blue ground.*

4435 Water Lily *Water Lily with bullrushes and a dragonfly. Rouge Royale.*

4435 Sketching Bird *Exotic tree with pendant foliage and decoratively enamelled kingfisher like bird flying by. Vert Royale ground.*

4436 Water Lily *Water Lily with bullrushes and a dragonfly. Vert Royale.*

4437 Plain *Cobalt blue.*

4438 no name *Chinese on cobalt blue.*

4439 Spider's Web *Cobwebs with fruiting berries on branch, flowers (harebells) and dragonflies. Cobalt blue ground.*

4440 New Storks *Two crane like birds wading in a lake under trees with pendulous hanging foliage. Cobalt blue ground.*

4441 Vine *Vine with leaves and grapes on cobalt blue.*

4442 Spots *Powder blue with white spots.*

4443 New Storks *Two crane like birds wading in a lake under trees with pendulous hanging*

foliage. Powder blue ground.

4444 Vine *Vine with leaves and grapes, no enamels. Vert Royale ground.*

4445 no name *Rouge Royale with chinese border on edge only - no enamels.*

4446 no name *Chinese on powder blue - no enamels.*

4448 Embossed - Hydrangea *Embossed pink Hydrangea flowers on green.*

4449 Embossed - Hydrangea *Embossed dark blue, mauve and pink Hydrangea flowers on blue.*

4450 no name *Chinese on Vert Royale - no enamels.*

4451 Carlton China - Gothic Border or Gilt Crosses *Simple border pattern on Green.*

4452 no name *Cobalt blue with border (raised enamel red).*

4454 no name *Cobalt blue with border (no raised enamel).*

4455 Duck *Realistic Mallard type ducks flying above Irises and wild grasses. Rouge ground.*

4457 Lily of the Valley *Lily of the valley on Rouge Royale.*

4458 Lily of the Valley *Lily of the valley on Vert Royale.*

4459 Duck *Realistic Mallard type ducks flying above Irises and wild grasses. Vert Royale ground.*

4460 Plain *Vert Royale with gold border.*

4461 Canadian Views *Variety of Canadian views printed in brown and finished in green.*

4461 Carlton China - no name *Simple gilt border pattern on White.*

4462 Canadian Views *Variety of Canadian views printed in black.*

4463 Embossed - Grape *Embossed Grapes, bright green on beige.*

4464 Embossed - Grape *Embossed Grapes, sandy brown on beige.*

4472 no name *Vert Royale with chinese border - no enamel.*

4475 Stars *Gold stars on Bleu Royale.*

4479 no name *Powder blue with chinese border.*

4480 Vine *Vine with leaves and grapes on Rouge Royale.*

4481 Vine *Vine with leaves and grapes on cobalt blue.*

4482 Carlton China - Tidal Border *Simple gilt border pattern on Blue.*

4484 Plain *Noire Royale.*

4487 no name *Bleu Royale with chinese border - no enamels.*

4488 Lily of the Valley *Lily of the valley on Noire Royale.*

4489 Nosegay *Pretty gilded and enamelled border design Rouge Royale.*

4490 Duck *Realistic Mallard type ducks flying above Irises and wild grasses. Black ground.*

4491 Kingfisher & Water Lily *Kingfisher perched on the stem of a climbing plant over water lilies. Noire Royale.*

4492 Water Lily *Water Lily with bullrushes and a dragonfly on Noire Royale.*

4499 Duck *Realistic Mallard type ducks flying above Irises and wild grasses. Cobalt blue ground.*

4500 Duck *Realistic Mallard type ducks flying above Irises and wild grasses. Pale pink ground.*

4501 Duck *Realistic Mallard type ducks flying above Irises and wild grasses. Pale yellow ground.*

4509. BLACKBERRY ON JADE GREEN. (Enamel as 4020)

4502 Duck *Realistic Mallard type ducks flying above Irises and wild grasses. Pale green ground.*

4503 Duck *Realistic Mallard type ducks flying above Irises and wild grasses. Powder blue ground.*

4503 Carlton China - Orange Tree or Coppice Tree *with orange coloured fruit.*

4504 Embossed - Hazel Nut *Embossed Hazel Nut on Matt Cream*

4505 Embossed - Hazel Nut *Embossed Hazel Nut on Green*

4506 Plain *Plain Jade green.*

4507 New Storks *Two crane like birds wading in a lake under trees with pendulous hanging foliage. Jade green ground.*

4508 New Mikado (Part) *Chinese figures, pagoda, bridge and trees. Sometimes has two cranes and punt like boat. Jade Green.*

4509 Spider's Web *Cobwebs with fruiting berries on branch, flowers (harebells) and dragonflies. Jade green ground.*

4510 Carlton China - no name *Simple border pattern on Blue.*

4511 Spots *Jade green with spots.*

4512 Vine *Vine with leaves and grapes on Noire Royale.*

4513 no name *Turquoise & pink, gold edge & foot only - shell ware only.*

4514 Nosegay *Pretty gilded and enamelled border design on Vert Royale.*

4514 Carlton China - Gothic Border or Gilt Crosses *Simple but pretty border pattern on blue.*

4515 Nosegay *Pretty gilded and enamelled border design on Noire Royale.*

4515 Crepes *Speckled blue with gold frieze design.*

4515 Carlton China - Vine Border *Bunches of grapes in border on Blue.*

4516 Carlton China - Nosegay *Pretty gilded and enamelled border design on Blue.*

4517 Nosegay *Pretty gilded and enamelled border design on Pale pink.*

4517 Carlton China - Gothic Border or Gilt Crosses *Simple but pretty border pattern on blue.*

4518 Nosegay *Pretty gilded and enamelled border design on pale yellow.*

4519 Nosegay *Pretty gilded and enamelled border design on pale green.*

4520 Twin Tone *Twin-tone jade green, salmon pink interior.*

4520 no name *Gold edge & foot only, shellware only.*

4521 Twin Tone *Twin-tone jade green, salmon pink interior.*

4521 no name *Full Gold, shellware only.*

4522 Twin Tone *Twin-tone jade green, yellow interior.*

4522 no name *Gold edge & foot only, shellware only.*

4523 Twin Tone *Twin-tone jade green, yellow interior.*

4523 no name *Full gold, shellware only.*

4525 Twin Tone *Pink and grey edged in gilt.*

4526 Carlton China - Crocus or Spring Border *Crocuses on white ground.*

4527 Nosegay *Pretty gilded and enamelled border design on jade green.*

4527 Carlton China - Summer Border or Cottage Flowers *Summer or Cottage flowers on edge.*

4528 Nosegay *Pretty gilded and enamelled border design on powder blue.*

4532 Twin Tone *Black and yellow.*

4534 Carlton China - Dragons *Blue Dragons on White.*

4536 Carlton China - Canterbury Border or New Bluebells *Bluebells and other flowers design on edge.*

4539 Fish & Seaweed *Fish swimming by coral on greyish ground.*

4544 Carlton China - no name *Fruit design.*

4550 Carlton China - New Mikado *Chinese figures, pagoda, bridge and trees. Sometimes has two cranes and punt like boat.*

4551 Twin Tone *Twin-tone Green*

4552 Twin Tone *Twin-tone Grey*

4553 Twin Tone *Brown and Cream*

4556 no name *Gold leaf on jade green.*

4557 no name *Gold leaf on Noire Royale.*

4558 no name *Gold leaf on Rouge Royale.*

4559 Twin Tone *Twin-tone jade green, yellow interior.*

4560 Kingfisher & Water Lily *Kingfisher perched on the stem of a climbing plant over water lilies. Pale yellow ground.*

4561 Kingfisher & Water Lily *Kingfisher perched on the stem of a climbing plant over water lilies. Pale green ground.*

4562 Kingfisher & Water Lily *Kingfisher perched on the stem of a climbing plant over water lilies. Jade green ground.*

4563 Water Lily *Water Lily with bullrushes and a dragonfly. Pale yellow ground.*

4564 Water Lily *Water Lily with bullrushes and a dragonfly. Pale green ground.*

4565 Water Lily *Water Lily with bullrushes and a dragonfly. Jade green ground.*

4566 Water Lily *Water Lily with bullrushes and a dragonfly. Powder blue ground.*

4574 Carlton China - Pendant Bubbles *Enamelled pendant design.*

4576 Carlton China - Gothic Band *Simple band design between blue and cream.*

4577 Carlton China - Blue & Gold *Blue and gold bands.*

4578 Carlton China - Springtime *Garden flowers and bluebirds on pale ground.*

4580 Kingfisher & Water Lily *Kingfisher perched on the stem of a climbing plant over water lilies. Powder blue ground.*

4581 Windswept *Leaves on matt cream and brown.*

4581 Carlton China - no name *Simple double gold band design on blue.*

4582 Windswept *Leaves on matt cream and sage green.*

4583 Windswept *Leaves on glossy pale blue and bottle green.*

4592 no name *Mutli-coloured flower heads, green leaves.*

4599 Plain *Turquoise*

4601 Twin Tone *Twin-tone Chartreuse*

4603 Kingfisher & Water Lily *Kingfisher perched on the stem of a climbing plant over water lilies. Vert Royale ground.*

4603 Carlton China - no name *Swirled gold pattern on blue and white.*

4604 Water Lily *Water Lily with bullrushes and a dragonfly. Bleu Royale ground.*

4605 Duck *Realistic Mallard type ducks flying above Irises and wild grasses. Bleu Royale ground.*

4605 Carlton China - Enchanted Garden *Trees and birds design.*

4606 Kingfisher & Water Lily *Kingfisher perched on the stem of a climbing plant over water lilies. Bleu Royale ground.*

4607 Kingfisher & Water Lily *Kingfisher perched on the stem of a climbing plant over water lilies. Pale pink.*

4608 Duck *Realistic Mallard type ducks flying above Irises and wild grasses. Pastel blue ground.*

4608 Carlton China - Playing Cards or Bridge Set *Images of playing cards and symbols.*

4609 Pin Stripe *Pin Stripe on Lime Green*

4609 Carlton China - Orchard Walk *Crinoline lady surrounded by flowers.*

4610 Pin Stripe *Pin Stripe on brown*

4611 Pin Stripe *Pin Stripe on sand colour*

4611 Carlton China - Gallant *Lady and Gent.*

4614 Carlton China - English Rose *Design with roses.*

4614 Twin Tone *Black and orange*

4614 Carlton China - Spider Flower or Cornflower *Design with thistle like flowers.*

4615 Twin Tone *Grey and pink.*

4616 Twin Tone *Green and stripe*

4617 Twin Tone *Orange and yellow with spots*

4618 Twin Tone *Brown and cream.*

4618 Carlton China - English Rose *Design with roses.*

4620 Embossed - Hazel Nut *Embossed Hazel Nut on Blue*

4621 Embossed - Foxglove *Embossed Foxglove on Peach/Chartreuse*

4622 Windswept *Leaves on dusky pink and pale blue.*

4623 Plain *Leaf Green*

4624 Plain *Blue*

4625 Plain *Leaf Brown*

4626 Plain *Black*

4627 Plain *Chartreuse*

4628 Plain *Lavender*

4629 no name *Pagoda on Noire Royale.*

4632 Carlton China - no name *Flowers in the border design.*

4633 Langouste *Lobster design on Cream ground.*

4634 Langouste *Lobster design on Chartreuse (green) ground.*

4636 Allium *White design on brownish red ground.*

4636 Carlton China - Trailing Lobelia *Red flowers with gold swirls.*

4637 Carlton China - Trailing Lobelia *Blue flowers with gold swirls.*

4639 Carlton China - New Wisteria *Wisteria design.*

4641 Eastern Splendour *Figure in turban with castle and or slave under tree with hanging foliage. Rouge Royale ground.*

4642 Eastern Splendour *Figure in turban with castle and or slave under tree with hanging foliage. Noire Royale ground.*

4643 Eastern Splendour *Figure in turban with castle and or slave under tree with hanging foliage. Vert Royale ground.*

4644 Eastern Splendour *Figure in turban with castle and or slave under tree with hanging foliage. Powder blue ground.*

4644 Carlton China - Spider Flower or Cornflower *Design with thistle like flowers.*

4645 Eastern Splendour *Figure in turban with castle and or slave under tree with hanging foliage. Bleu Royale ground.*

4645 Carlton China - Spider Flower or Cornflower *Design with thistle like flowers.*

4646 Eastern Splendour *Figure in turban with castle and or slave under tree with hanging foliage. Pale yellow ground.*

4647 Eastern Splendour *Figure in turban with castle and or slave under tree with hanging foliage. Pale green ground.*

4648 Carlton China - Honeysuckle *Orange Honeysuckle flowers.*

4649 Carlton China - Cherries *Design with bunches of Cherries.*

4650 Carlton China - no name *Colourful Harebell like flowers.*

4651 Carlton China - no name *Simple colourful design.*

4653 Carlton China - Hibiscus *Enamelled red flowers.*

4654 Carlton China - no name *Blue flower swag design.*

4655 Carlton China - Target *Design that looks like three arrows shot into a target.*

4657 Carlton China - no name *Blue and orange petals.*

4658 Carlton China - Imari *Aztec like symmetric design in blue and red on white.*

4660 Carlton China - Floral Band *Colourful flowers and a blue band.*

4664 Carlton China - Field Scabious *Flowers.*

4665 Carlton China - no name *Blue and white with gilt edges.*

4668 Carlton China - Love-in-a-Mist *Blue and pink flowers.*

4671 Carlton China - Bordered Baubles *Design with baubles in border.*

4672 Plain *Matt While*

4675 Carlton China - Orchard *Enamelled trees and flowers.*

4676 Bamboo *Bamboo and hanging foliage on white ground.*

4676 Carlton China - Strawberry Tree *Tree resembling a strawberry on a white ground.*

4678 Mikado *Chinoiserie pagodas, bridges, oriental ladies and usually a pair of kissing birds. Vert Royale ground.*

4683 Carlton China - Butterfly *Pretty abstract Butterfly design.*

4693 Carlton China - Sunshine *White gloss ground with groups of small flowers.*

4710 Plain *Matt Black*

4710 Carlton China - no name *Pale green band and gold swirls.*

4717 Dragon *Golden dragons on a white ground.*

4722 Carlton China - Chintz Tulip *Flowers in gilt design.*

4723 Carlton China - Lace *Lace pattern on white ground.*

4727 Carlton China - Gilt Festoon *Gilt design on white and yellow.*

4733 Pearl Insignia *Symmetric design of circles (beads), curved triangles and flower heads. White ground.*

4734 Pearl Insignia *Symmetric design of circles (beads), curved triangles and flower heads. Brownish ground.*

4734 Carlton China - Gothic Border or Gilt Crosses *Simple but pretty border pattern on yellow.*

4735 Carlton China - Gothic Border or Gilt Crosses *Simple but pretty border pattern on pale green.*

4741 Carlton China - Blue & Gold *Blue and gold.*

4744 Carlton China - Bright Sunshine *Flower design.*

4753 Carlton China - New Delphinium *Delphinium flowers.*

4754 Carlton China - Springtime *Garden flowers and bluebirds on pale ground.*

4758 Carlton China - Swags of Flowers *Gilt design.*

4761 Carlton China - Spring Medley *Garden flowers, similar to Sunshine.*

4762 Carlton China - Diamond Band *Diamonds in border design.*

4763 Carlton China - Strawberry Tree *Tree resembling a strawberry on a white ground.*

4764 Carlton China - Weeping Willow *Stylized design with flowers, tree and bird.*

4769 Bamboo *Bamboo and hanging foliage on blue ground.*

4769 Carlton China - Strawberry Tree *Tree resembling a strawberry on a blue ground.*

4775 Carlton China - Springtime *Garden flowers and bluebirds on pale ground.*

4777 Carlton China - Pimpernel or Lilac Posy *Pretty flower design on pale mauve ground.*

4783 Plain with Floral *Floral patterns on white insets on blue with gold highlights. Powder blue ground.*

4785 no name *Printed floral design on pale green ground.*

4794 New Bird of Paradise *Buds, blossom, birds of paradise and butterflies. Rouge ground.*

4794 Carlton China - no name *Garden scene with flowers, bush and tree.*

4795 New Bird of Paradise *Buds, blossom, birds of paradise and butterflies. Mottled blue ground.*

4799 Carlton China - Carlton China - Chinese Figures *Oriental scene of figures, tree and sometimes pagodas.*

4801 Malvern *Medallion with bird and fruit on a yellow ground.*

4801 Carlton China - River Fish *Beautiful realistic looking fish swimming amongst gilt seaweed. Blue ground.*

4805 Pheasant *like bird and flowers with gilt and enamels. Black ground.*

4805 Carlton China - Canterbury Border or New Bluebells *Bluebells and other flowers design on edge.*

4805 Mikado *Chinoiserie pagodas, bridges, oriental ladies and usually a pair of kissing birds. Black ground*

4805 New Bird of Paradise *Buds, blossom, birds of paradise and butterflies. Black ground.*

4808 Thistle Heads *Thistle heads on red ground.*

4809 Thistle Heads *Thistle heads on powder blue ground.*

4812 Carlton China - Floral Spray *Sprigs of flowers.*

4813 Carlton China - Butterflies & Seaweed *Butterflies and foliage.*

4818 Carlton China - Floral Trumpet *Flowers in trumpet shape.*

4821 Carlton China - Enamelled Berries or Berry Cluster *Berries with floral design on a cobalt blue ground.*

4823 Carlton China - Tulip Garden *Tulips.*

4824 Carlton China - Posies *Posies of flowers.*

4838 Carlton China - Festive Border *Garland of flowers that resemble festive lights.*

4841 Plain *Mottled grey with gilt.*

4861 Carlton China - Meadow Tree *Stylized tree in blue grass meadow.*

4864 Carlton China - Fantail Birds on Branch *Birds on foliage on white ground.*

4865 Carlton China - Enamelled Berries or Berry Cluster *Berries with floral design on a yellow border.*

4870 Carlton China - Enamelled Berries or Berry Cluster *Berries with floral design on a green border.*

4876 Carlton China - Meadow Tree *Stylized tree in grey grass meadow.*

4878 Carlton China - Afternoon Stroll *Lady and hanging leaf design.*

4879 Carlton China - Bouquet *Stylised flowers.*

4880 Carlton China - New Garden *Spires of Daisy like flowers in many colours. Powder blue ground.*

4881 Carlton China - New Garden *Spires of Daisy like flowers in many colours.*

4885 Carlton China - New Garden *Spires of Daisy like flowers in many colours.*

4886 Carlton China - Enamelled Berries or Berry Cluster *Berries with floral decorations on blue and cream.*

4888 Carlton China - Spider Flower or Cornflower *Design with thistle like flowers.*

4889 Carlton China - Zig-Zag Tree *Stylized trees with angled trunks.*

4894 Carlton China - Vine Border *Bunches of grapes in border.*

4897 Carlton China - Bouquet *Bouquet of flowers.*

4900 Carlton China - Fantail Birds on Branch *Birds on foliage on white ground.*

4901 Malvern *Medallion with bird and fruit on a blue ground.*

4903 Carlton China - Sylvan Trees *Topiary trees.*

4904 Carlton China - Cottage Garden or Hollyhocks *Flower beds of cottage flowers.*

4905 Carlton China - no name *Deco angular shapes.*

4906 Carlton China - Chinese Lanterns *Bold angular shapes with tiny flower heads.*

4907 Enchantment Medallion *Medallions of romantic scenes. Rouge Royale ground.*

4907 Carlton China - Starburst Tree & Birds *Stylized star shaped trees with fantailed birds on a white ground.*

4908 Enchantment Medallion *Lady and Dandy in Garden with Gazebo. Powder blue ground.*

4908 Carlton China - Spring Flower *Floral design with a display that looks like a Christmas Tree.*

4909 Malvern *Medallion with bird and fruit. White medallions on black ground.*

4909 Carlton China - Celebration or Technicolour Posies *Colourful posies.*

4910 Carlton China - Canterbury Border or New Bluebells *Bluebells and other flowers design on edge.*

4911 Carlton China - Summer Border or Cottage Flowers *Summer or Cottage flowers on edge.*

4912 Carlton China - Zig-Zag Tree *Stylized trees with angled trunks.*

4913 Carlton China - Starburst Tree & Birds *Stylized star shaped trees with fantailed birds on a blue ground.*

4914 Dragon *Green Dragon on white ground.*

4916 Carlton China - no name *Gilt decoration on blue ground over white.*

4923 Aquilegia *Flowers, including Aquilegia type flowers on a white ground.*

4923 Carlton China - Summer Posy *Flowers.*

4925 Carlton China - New Delphinium *Delphinium flowers.*

4927 Carlton China - Wild Garden *Flowers and trees.*

4928 Carlton China - Hanging Baubles *Baubles hanging design.*

4929 Carlton China - Charleston *Deco emblems.*

4934 Pheasant *Pheasant like bird and flowers with gilt and enamels. Red ground.*

4935 Pheasant *Pheasant like bird and flowers on blue ground with a matt sheen plus enamelled and gilded decoration.*

4940 Carlton China - Rainbow *Deco rainbow like pattern on a cream ground.*

4942 Carlton China - Bud Eye *Floral display with buds.*

4943 Carlton China - Rainbow *Deco rainbow like pattern on a white ground.*

4947 Garden of Tranquillity *Two figures, one lying down, some flower heads on rouge ground.*

4948 Carlton China - Black Eye *Stylistic flower with black eyed centre.*

4958 Carlton China - Papaver or Poppy *Realistic poppies on yellow.*

4961 Carlton China - New Harebells *Realistic Harebells.*

4961 Carlton China - Digitalis *Realistic Foxgloves.*

4963 Carlton China - Dahlia *Dahlia on cream or white.*

4966 Carlton China - New Garden *Spires of Daisy like flowers in many colours.*

4977 Carlton China - Papaver or Poppy *Realistic Poppies on white ground.*

4979 Carlton China - Orange Tree *Tree with Orange coloured fruit.*

4983 Carlton China - Aster *Trio of brightly coloured Asters.*

4985 Carlton China - Summer Posy *Blossom flowers.*

4986 Carlton China - Autumn Trees *Pendulous trees on a white ground.*

4987 Carlton China - Love-in-a-Mist *Red and yellow flowers.*

4988 Carlton China - Susan *Red flowers with five petals named after the flower Black Eyed Susan.*

4989 Carlton China - Flower and Cloud *Flower flying on small cloud.*

4990 Carlton China - Bright Daisy or Powder Puff *Colourful daisies on white ground.*

4991 Carlton China - Crooked Tree *Tree with berries.*

4992 Carlton China - Sweet Pea *Orange Sweet Peas on white ground.*

4993 Carlton China - Sweet Pea *Blue Sweet Peas on white ground.*

4994 Carlton China - Sweet Pea *Orange Sweet Peas on white ground.*

4995 Carlton China - Enamelled Berries or Berry Cluster *Berries with floral design on white.*

4998 Carlton China - Birds and Trees or Autumn Trees *Birds and Trees on a white ground.*

5000 Carlton China - Clematis *Bold Clematis flowers.*

5001 Carlton China - Moon House *House with a Moon on a mottled sky.*

5002 Carlton China - Gloaming *Silhouette version of Bird & Trees (4998).*

5019 Carlton China - Deco Wave *Deco curves and waves. Orange, Black and Gold.*

5023 Carlton China - Deco Wave *Deco curves and waves. Turquoise, Black and Gold.*

The following patterns have unknown pattern numbers.

???? Bird of Paradise *Bird of Paradise with long plumed tail flying among oriental trees. Pale green ground.*

???? Chinese Lanterns *Floral decoration with Chinese Lanterns and a Dragon Fly. Rouge ground.*

???? Cock & Peony *Two cockerels standing amongst foliage. Also has a variety of beautifully enamelled flowers including peonies. Armand Lustre backstamp. Mottled orange ground. Armand.*

???? Denim *Blue denim jeans and shirt.*

???? Fairy Carnival *Beautiful design of Fairies. Extremely rare!*

???? Fairy Dell *Scene with trees, snow and rabbits.*

???? Forest Tree *Exotic birch like trees. Slender tree rising to a wide pendulous canopy of foliage. Matt blue ground with orange and green foliage.*

???? Gallant *Lady and Dandy, matt black ground.*

???? Glacielle Ware *Glacielle Ware comes in about 4 or 5 different animals / bird designs.*

???? Glade *Pan like figure with shadow in forest glade with spires of flowers. Matt blue ground.*

???? Hatching *Hatched pattern above brown.*

???? Heinz *Orange running down green ground.*

???? Honesty *Stylised Honesty branches. Orange ground.*

???? Humming Bird *Elaborately decorated exotic bird and floral decoration. Blue lustre ground.*

???? New Rainbow *Multicolored Rainbow pattern.*

???? Owls *Realistic Owls with a moon.*

???? Paradise Bird & Tree with Cloud *Bird of Paradise with long plumed tail flying across clouds and among oriental trees. Mustardy Yellow ground.*

???? Peach Blossom *Pink blossom sprays on pale blue ground.*

???? Primula and Leaf *Primula flowers in bright colours and a butterfly. Pale blue ground.*

???? Rain Forest *Storks in Forest.*

???? Rainbow Portal *Bird sitting on a bough and a cameo with multicoloured stripes. White or pale yellow ground.*

???? River Fish *Beautiful realistic looking fish swimming amongst gilt seaweed. Rouge ground.*

???? Carlton China - River Fish *Beautiful realistic looking fish swimming amongst seaweed. Blue ground.*

???? Silk Sands *Contour like lines on pink ground with gilt.*

???? Sketching Bird *Exotic tree with pendant foliage and exotic bird flying by. Bleu Royale.*

???? Sketching Bird *Exotic tree with pendant foliage and exotic bird flying by. Matt pale green ground.*

???? Tree & Swallow *Swallows flying past slender stemmed tree with wide canopy of pendulous foliage. Matt cream ground.*

???? Tutankhamen *Gloss Light Blue & Yellow. Egyptian Motifs in colours and gilt.*

List of Pattern Numbers by Pattern Name

Allium: 4636
Almond Blossom: 1905, 2445, 3033
Anemone: 3694
Animal (Squirrel, Deer or Fox): 4019
Apple Blossom: 3522
Apple and Blossom: 3041
Aquilegia: 4923
Arrowhead: 3416
Aurora: 3412
Autumn Breeze: 3839, 3840
Autumn Daisy: 3802
Autumn Leaf: 3766
Autumn Trees & Ferns: 3517
Awakening: 3450, 3452, 3453, 3456, 3494, 3496, 3497
Azealea: 4140
Babylon: 4125, 4126, 4137, 4158, 4168, 4189
Bamboo: 4676, 4769
Banded: 4128, 4130
Banded and Crosstitch: 3976
Bands: 3720
Barge: 2519
Basket of Flowers: 2124, 2151, 2184, 2185, 2189
Basket of Fruit: 2539, 2556
Bathing Belle: 3681, 3684, 3688, 3796
Beanstalk: 4081
Beech Nut: 4281, 4282
Beehives: 3883, 3884
Bell: 3774, 3785, 3786, 3788, 3792, 3855
Berries and Bands: 2446, 2454, 2460, 2461, 2931
Bird: 421
Bird & Chequered Border: 2218, 2221
Bird & Pine Cone: 3046
Bird & Tree Peony: 595, 2466, 2866
Bird of Paradise: 3191, 4117, 4118, 4234, 4239, 4418
Birds and Blossom: 2089
Birds on Bough: 2794, 3394
Black Crow: 4105
Blossom & Spray: 3968, 4045, 4047
Bluebells: 3294, 3862, 3872, 3874, 3875
Blush Ware: 110, 253, 524, 585, 649, 670, 708, 732, 975, 1075, 1219, 1230, 1246, 1340, 1358, 1414, 1509, 1518, 1572, 1621, 1624, 1653, 1664, 1681, 1739, 1747, 1749, 1752, 1786, 1799, 1848, 1863, 1902, 1928, 1935, 1942, 2040, 2339, 2366, 2659
Blush Ware - Arvista: 428, 476, 561, 1031, 1057, 1630, 1652, 1879, 1946, 1990, 2561, 2562
Blush Ware - Azalea: 347
Blush Ware - Camellia: 184, 425, 843, 848, 849, 860, 1153, 2300, 2700
Blush Ware - Carnation: 483, 1038, 1041, 1582, 1693, 1732, 1733, 2486
Blush Ware - Carnation Spray: 621, 1242
Blush Ware - Catalpa: 661
Blush Ware - Cherry Blossom: 2406
Blush Ware - Chrysanthemum: 401, 405, 406, 407, 409, 504, 1089, 1091, 1372, 2407, 2410
Blush Ware - Cistus: 52, 74, 1474, 1769, 1804, 2494, 2798
Blush Ware - Clematis: 821, 826
Blush Ware - Convolvulous: 376, 2662, 2669
Blush Ware - Cornflower: 709

Blush Ware - Cornucopia: 637, 653, 739, 832, 1162, 2083, 2086, 2474
Blush Ware - Daffodil: 641
Blush Ware - Dahlia: 682, 683, 735, 878, 1653, 1741, 1878, 1982, 2458
Blush Ware - Daisies: 2224, 2227
Blush Ware - Daisy: 686
Blush Ware - Diadem: 1650
Blush Ware - Dianthus: 438, 458
Blush Ware - Dog Rose: 1400, 1524
Blush Ware - Floral: 2377
Blush Ware - Gladioli: 1750
Blush Ware - Heather: 418, 1166, 1713, 1742, 2455, 2713, 2718, 2757, 2923
Blush Ware - Hibiscus: 634, 638, 639, 839, 1635, 2021, 2166, 2510, 2687
Blush Ware - Honeysuckle: 1601
Blush Ware - Honfleur: 666, 921, 1002
Blush Ware - Impatiens: 2560
Blush Ware - Iris: 2833
Blush Ware - Marguerite: 1655, 2301
Blush Ware - Mixed Cottage: 1795
Blush Ware - Nasturtium: 2154, 2749
Blush Ware - Nouveau Poppies: 838, 886, 888
Blush Ware - Pansy: 914
Blush Ware - Peony: 186, 194, 538, 945, 949, 1034, 1658, 1661, 1682, 1683, 1685, 1832, 1839, 1853, 1865, 1869, 1996, 2691, 2853
Blush Ware - Petunia: 491, 694, 695, 698, 1451, 1453, 1467, 1810, 1966, 1987, 2007, 2179
Blush Ware - Picotees: 624
Blush Ware - Poppy: 206, 303, 305, 306, 307, 1015, 1770
Blush Ware - Poppy Spray: 1042
Blush Ware - Primula: 2309
Blush Ware - Queen Victoria: 856
Blush Ware - Rose: 2863, 2872

Blush Ware - Rose Bud: 403
Blush Ware - Rose Garland: 348, 438, 1186
Blush Ware - Roses: 439, 913, 1221
Blush Ware - Royal May: 508, 509, 602, 1229
Blush Ware - Sweet Violet: 142
Blush Ware - Tulips: 578, 2872
Blush Ware - Violet: 237, 1283, 1315, 1332
Blush Ware - Wild Rose: 659, 1123, 1125, 1609, 1918, 1919, 1939, 1947, 1974, 1986, 2215
Bookends - Asymmetric Flower: 3535
Bookends - Fan: 3532, 3533
Bookends - Saddleback: 3537
Bookends - Two Tone: 3337
Brodsworth: 2586
Butterfly: 3290, 4122, 4123
Cameo Wren: 3115
Camouflage: 3440
Canadian Views: 4461, 4462
Candy Flowers: 3669
Carlton China - Afternoon Stroll: 4878
Carlton China - Arrow Border: 4294
Carlton China - Aster: 4983
Carlton China - Autumn Trees: 4986
Carlton China - Bird Cartouche: 4421
Carlton China - Birds and Trees or Autumn Trees: 4998
Carlton China - Black Eye: 4948
Carlton China - Blue & Gold: 4577, 4741
Carlton China - Bordered Baubles: 4671
Carlton China - Bouquet: 4879, 4897
Carlton China - Bright Daisy or Powder Puff: 4990
Carlton China - Bright Sunshine: 4744
Carlton China - Bud Eye: 4942
Carlton China - Butterflies & Seaweed: 4813
Carlton China - Butterfly: 4683
Carlton China - Canterbury Border or New

Awakening - Pattern 3450

Jug from the Kosniowski Collection

£750 - £1,000

Bluebells: 4360, 4536, 4805, 4910
Carlton China - Carlton China - Chinese Figures: 4799
Carlton China - Celebration or Technicolour Posies: 4909
Carlton China - Charleston: 4929
Carlton China - Cherries: 4649
Carlton China - Chinese Lanterns: 4906
Carlton China - Chintz Tulip: 4722
Carlton China - Clematis: 5000
Carlton China - Cottage Garden or Hollyhocks: 4904
Carlton China - Crocus or Spring Border: 4526
Carlton China - Crooked Tree: 4991
Carlton China - Dahlia: 4963
Carlton China - Deco Wave: 5019, 5023
Carlton China - Diamond Band: 4762
Carlton China - Digitalis: 4961
Carlton China - Dragons: 4534
Carlton China - Enamelled Berries or Berry Cluster: 4821, 4865, 4870, 4886, 4995
Carlton China - Enchanted Garden: 4605
Carlton China - English Rose: 4614, 4618
Carlton China - Fantail Birds on Branch: 4864, 4900
Carlton China - Festive Border: 4838
Carlton China - Field Scabious: 4664
Carlton China - Floral Band: 4660
Carlton China - Floral Spray: 4812
Carlton China - Floral Trumpet: 4818
Carlton China - Flower and Cloud: 4989
Carlton China - Gallant: 4611
Carlton China - Gilt Festoon: 4727
Carlton China - Gloaming: 5002
Carlton China - Gothic Band: 4576
Carlton China - Gothic Border or Gilt Crosses: 4451, 4514, 4517, 4734, 4735
Carlton China - Greek Keys: 4168
Carlton China - Hanging Baubles: 4928
Carlton China - Hibiscus: 4653
Carlton China - Honeysuckle: 4648
Carlton China - Imari: 4658
Carlton China - Lace: 4723
Carlton China - Love-in-a-Mist: 4668, 4987
Carlton China - Meadow Tree: 4861, 4876
Carlton China - Moon House: 5001
Carlton China - New Delphinium: 4753, 4925
Carlton China - New Garden: 4880, 4881, 4885, 4966
Carlton China - New Harebells: 4961
Carlton China - New Mikado: 4550
Carlton China - New Wisteria: 4639
Carlton China - Nosegay: 4516
Carlton China - Orange Tree: 4979
Carlton China - Orange Tree or Coppice: 4503
Carlton China - Orchard: 4675
Carlton China - Orchard Walk: 4609
Carlton China - Papaver or Poppy: 4958, 4977
Carlton China - Pendant Bubbles: 4574
Carlton China - Peony: 4030
Carlton China - Pimpernel or Lilac Posy: 4777
Carlton China - Playing Cards or Bridge Set: 4608
Carlton China - Posies: 4824
Carlton China - Rainbow: 4940, 4943
Carlton China - Reproduction Swansea: 4419
Carlton China - River Fish: 4801
Carlton China - Spider Flower or Cornflower: 4614, 4644, 4645, 4888
Carlton China - Spring Flower: 4908
Carlton China - Spring Medley: 4761
Carlton China - Springtime: 4578, 4754, 4775
Carlton China - Starburst Tree & Birds: 4907, 4913

Carlton China - Strawberry Tree: 4676, 4763, 4769
Carlton China - Summer Border or Cottage Flowers: 4527, 4911
Carlton China - Summer Posy: 4923, 4985
Carlton China - Sunshine: 4693
Carlton China - Susan: 4988
Carlton China - Swags of Flowers: 4758
Carlton China - Sweet Pea: 4992, 4993, 4994
Carlton China - Sylvan Trees: 4903
Carlton China - Target: 4655
Carlton China - Tidal Border: 4482
Carlton China - Trailing Lobelia: 4636, 4637
Carlton China - Trellis Border: 4402
Carlton China - Tulip Garden: 4823
Carlton China - Vine Border: 4515, 4894
Carlton China - Weeping Willow: 4764
Carlton China - Wild Garden: 4927
Carlton China - Zig-Zag Tree: 4889, 4912
Carlton China - no name: 4235, 4461, 4510, 4544, 4581, 4603, 4632, 4650, 4651, 4654, 4657, 4665, 4710, 4794, 4905, 4916
Carnation: 1981
Carnival: 3305
Carre: 3658, 3659
Cartouche of Flowers: 2033, 2216
Chequered Border: 128
Cherry: 3272, 3417
Cherry Blossom: 4002, 4003
Chevrons: 3657, 3671
Chinaland: 2948, 2949, 2950, 3014, 3015, 3895
Chinese Bird: 3196, 3197, 3198, 3296, 3527, 3544
Chinese Bird & Cloud: 3274, 3275, 3275, 3327
Chinese Figures: 3199
Chinese Quail: 522
Chinese Tea Garden: 2936
Chinoiserie: 2752, 2755, 2810, 2972, 3222
Chinoiserie design: 2359
Chintz: 2046, 2047, 2069

Chorisia: 1846
Christmas Tree: 3729
Chrysanthemum: 1775, 2930
Cinquefoil: 4191, 4192
Citrus Fruit: 2961
Clematis: 3525, 3545
Cock & Peony: 2250, 2280, 2281, 2282, 2285, 2287, 2288, 2308, 2398, 2816
Cock & Peony Spray: 2405
Contours: 4291
Cornflower: 2385, 2392
Corolla: 3225, 3226, 3227, 3228
Crab & Lobster Ware: 3908, 3910
Crepes: 4515
Crested Bird and Water Lily: 3529, 3530, 3536
Cretonne: 2913
Crocus and Cloud: 4156
Cubist Butterfly: 3190, 3194, 3195, 3223, 3233, 3469
Dahlia & Butterfly: 3606
Daisies: 4139
Daisy: 3673, 3691, 3693, 3714
Daisy & Stripe: 3341
Dancers: 2905
Dancing Deer: 3886
Dancing Figures: 614, 2178, 2284
Daydream: 4246
Deco Fan: 3552
Delphinium: 3273, 3487, 3837
Devils Copse: 3765, 3767, 3769, 3787, 3809, 3817, 3859
Diamond: 3546, 3547, 3549, 3550, 3678
Diaper: 3270
Dragon: 2006, 2053, 2062, 2064, 2066, 2067, 2102, 2103, 2818, 2887, 2903, 2993, 3251, 4717, 4914
Dragon & Traveller: 3594, 3594, 3595, 3597, 3656, 3660
Dragon and Cloud: 3237, 3331, 3332, 3333, 3351

Diamond - Pattern 3678
Large Flared Bowl from the Kosniowski Collection
£600 - £800

Dragon in Cartouche: 3145, 3146
Drip Ware: 3771, 3772, 3773, 3917
Duck: 4455, 4459, 4490, 4499, 4500, 4501, 4502, 4503, 4605, 4608
Dutch: 3250
Eastern Splendour: 4641, 4642, 4643, 4644, 4645, 4646, 4647
Eclipse: 3551
Eden (Tiger Tree): 3989, 4241, 4242
Eden Canopy: 4248, 4249
Egyptian Fan: 3695, 3696, 3696, 3697, 3698
Eighteenth Tee: 2630, 2633, 2636
Embellished Gilt: 2979, 3063, 3078
Embossed - Buttercup: 3993, 3994
Embossed - Foxglove: 4285, 4286, 4621
Embossed - Grape: 4463, 4464
Embossed - Hazel Nut: 4504, 4505, 4620
Embossed - Hydrangea: 4448, 4449
Embossed - Oak Tree: 3810, 3811
Embossed - Poppy & Daisy: 4388, 4389
Embossed - Primula: 4368, 4369
Embossed - Rock Garden: 3876
Embossed - Water Lily: 4235
Embossed - Wild Rose: 4427, 4428
Enchantment Medallion: 4907, 4908
Engine Turned Ware: 3977, 3978, 3979, 3980, 3981, 3982, 3999
Ensign: 3510
Entangled Droplets: 3555
Explosion: 3447, 3454
Explosion & Butterfly: 3452
Fairy Dell: 3645, 3665
Fairy Shadow: 3564, 3574, 3576
Fairy and Sunflower: 2369
Fan: 3557, 3558
Fantasia: 3388, 3389, 3400, 3406, 3421, 3427
Farrago: 3297, 3362
Feathertailed Bird and Flower: 3354, 3355
Fighting Cocks: 4161, 4186, 4199, 4202, 4380, 4401, 4417, 4422
Fighting Glade: 4184, 4198, 4212, 4377
Figurine - Curtsy: 4262
Figurine - Grandma: 4275, 4276, 4302
Figurine - Jean: 4314
Figurine - Joan: 4273, 4301
Figurine - Monica: 4260, 4261
Figurine - Nan: 4264
Figurine - Nell: 4268, 4269
Figurine - Peggy: 4270, 4271
First Blush of Day: 1220
Fish & Seaweed: 4539
Flies: 2093, 2095, 2099, 2105, 2109, 2112, 2131, 2133, 2134, 2174, 2420, 2456, 2469, 2473, 2939
Flies Border: 2642
Floral Comets: 3385, 3387, 3401, 3405, 3422, 3428
Floral Mist: 3913
Floral Scallops: 3234
Floribunda: 3236
Flow Blue: 230, 566, 616, 1225, 1274, 1406, 1619, 1631, 1950, 2319
Flow Blue - Arvista: 561
Flow Blue - Catalpa: 547, 1911
Flow Blue - Chrysanthemum: 1635
Flow Blue - Daffodil: 1646
Flow Blue - Diadem: 777
Flow Blue - Dragons & Unicorn: 2787
Flow Blue - Florida: 220
Flow Blue - Flower Garland: 586
Flow Blue - Honfleur: 1639
Flow Blue - Iris: 1422
Flow Blue - May: 876
Flow Blue - Multi- Flowers: 1941

Flow Blue - Petunia: 534
Flow Blue - Poppy: 751, 752, 1006, 1031, 1041, 1960
Flower & Falling Leaf: 3948, 3949, 3950, 3952
Flower Medley: 3588, 3596
Flower and Fruit: 3249
Flowering Papyrus: 3242
Forest Night: 3997
Forest Tree: 3238, 3239, 3240, 3244, 3244, 3248, 3250, 3253, 3254, 3265, 3283, 3641, 3648, 4426
Freehand Red Sunflower: 3519
Fruit: 2560, 2564, 2565, 2567, 3571
Fruit Bough: 2909
Fruit Branch: 2920
Gallant: 2804, 2839, 2863, 2864, 2867, 2868, 2869, 2872, 2872, 2893, 2953, 2954, 2956
Galleon: 3019, 3020, 3753, 3953, 3957
Garden: 3390, 3396, 3413, 3433, 3438, 3471, 3474, 3475, 3476, 3477, 3478, 3479, 3501, 3581, 3609
Garden Gate: 3863
Garden of Tranquillity: 4947
Gazania: 3592
Gentian: 3358
Geometric Clouds: 2212
Geometrica: 3566
Gilt Scallop: 3795
Grecian Figures: 601, 602, 604
Grecian Figures with no Figures: 602
Green Trees: 3569
Gum Tree: 3768, 3789, 3790, 3794, 3838
Gypsy: 3506
Hammered Pewter: 3902
Harebells: 4014, 4015, 4016, 4136, 4154
Harvest Fruit: 4305
Hazelnut: 3946
Heatwave: 4092
Herbaceous Border: 3801
Heron & Magical Tree: 3965, 4108, 4125, 4150, 4153, 4159, 4160, 4182, 4273, 4293, 4313,

4321, 4325, 4326, 4332
Hiawatha: 3589, 3590
Holly: 3418
Hollyhocks: 3818, 3819, 3820, 3827, 3854, 3972, 3973
Honesty: 3278
Humming Bird: 3462
Humming Bird with Tree: 3884, 4355
Humming Bird without Bird: 3462
Iceland Poppy: 3507, 3646, 4192, 4193, 4194, 4220, 4221, 4228
Incised Diamond: 3901, 3905
Incised Square: 3900
Insects: 850
Intersection: 3690
Iris: 3498
Italian Scenes: 2591
Jacobean Figures: 3956, 3956, 3957
Jaggered Bouquet: 3439, 3457, 3489
Jazz: 3352, 3353, 3361
Jazz Poppy: 3503
Jazz Stitch: 3655
Jigsaw: 3431
Kaleidescopic: 3565
Kang Hsi: 596, 599
Kang Hsi Chinoiserie: 2021
Kang Hsi Fish: 597
Kien Lung: 2031, 2053
Kingfisher: 2517, 2530, 2537, 2621, 2858
Kingfisher & Water Lily: 4391, 4491, 4560, 4561, 4562, 4580, 4603, 4606, 4607
Lace Cap Hydrangea: 3639, 3966, 3967, 3969
Lace Frieze: 3173
Landscape Tree: 3141, 3142
Langouste: 4633, 4634
Lazy - Daisy: 3414
Leaf: 3857, 3861, 3873
Leaf & Dots: 4218
Leaf and Catkin: 3918, 3919
Leaves: 4040
Liberty Stripe: 3662

Lace Frieze - Pattern 3173
Cup & Saucer from the Dulcie Agnes Joyce Memorial Collection
Image courtesy of www.nicholnack.com.au
£80 - £120

Lightning: 3356, 3357, 3692, 3716
Lilac: 4279, 4310
Lily of the Valley: 4457, 4458, 4488
Long Tailed Bird and Tree Peony: 2634, 2832, 2834
Lovebirds: 2121, 2326, 2328, 2333, 2782
Magical Tree (Rosetta): 3505
Magpies: 2907, 2907, 2908, 2908, 2911, 2912, 2975, 2976
Malvern: 4801, 4901, 4909
Mandarin Tree: 3672, 3701, 3702, 3703, 3719, 3791, 3793
Mandarins Chatting: 3653, 3654, 3672, 3675, 3680
Marguerite Daisy: 4277
Marigold: 3271
Marrakesh: 3289
Mayflower: 3049, 3161, 3165
Meadow: 3077, 3078
Medley: 3587, 3591, 3593, 3599, 3600, 3845
Melange: 3601, 3601
Metropolis: 3420
Mikado: 1883, 1886, 2199, 2240, 2264, 2270, 2314, 2340, 2355, 2356, 2357, 2361, 2363, 2364, 2370, 2399, 2410, 2422, 2442, 2470, 2881, 2910, 2914, 2927, 2978, 3048, 3158, 3201, 3910, 4373, 4422, 4433, 4434, 4678, 4805
Mikado in Cartouche: 2367, 2368, 3178
Mikado without Mikado: 2927
Mirage: 3915
Modern Crocus: 3803
Moderne: 3886, 3887, 3888
Moderne Lady: 2654
Mondrian: 3570
Moonlight: 3075, 3076, 3118, 3127
Moonlight Cameo: 2944, 2944, 2945, 2946, 2947, 2960, 2964, 2969, 2980, 3392
Neapolitan: 3445, 3841, 3842
Needlepoint: 3815, 3816
New Anemone: 4213, 4219, 4231, 4245
New Bird of Paradise: 4794, 4795, 4805
New Chinese Bird: 3304
New Chinese Bird & Cloud: 3320, 3321, 3322
New Delphinium: 3526
New Flies: 2837, 3023, 3024, 3025, 3028
New Laburnum: 3867, 3867
New Mikado: 2091, 2428, 2727, 2728, 2729, 2740, 2788, 2814, 2815, 2825, 2830, 2990, 3137, 3495, 3843, 3860, 4104, 4109, 4320, 4328, 4329, 4346, 4362, 4398, 4416, 4419
New Mikado (Part): 4508
New Mikado with Lady: 2814
New Mikado without Mikado: 2428, 2814
New Prunus Spray: 2463
New Storks: 4280, 4283, 4304, 4339, 4340, 4342, 4343, 4344, 4348, 4367, 4400, 4421, 4440, 4443, 4507
New Violets: 4374, 4376
Nightingale: 3562, 3598
Nightingale Garden: 3568
Norwegian Flowers: 3661
Norwegian Lady: 3665
Norwegian Miss: 3668
Nosegay: 4489, 4514, 4515, 4517, 4518, 4519, 4527, 4528
Old Stone Ware: 3770, 3770, 3775, 3776, 3777, 3778, 3779, 3780, 3781, 3782, 3783, 3784, 3804, 3829, 3830, 3847, 3877, 3878, 3879, 3896, 3904, 3920, 3998
Old Wisteria: 2191, 2238
Orange Blossom: 2721, 2722, 2723, 2724, 2725
Orange Embossed: 3042, 3052
Oranges: 3528

Moonlight Cameo - Pattern 2944
Large Bowl from the Kosniowski Collection
£300 - £450

Orchard: 2885, 2886, 3064
Orchid: 3255, 3325
Oriental Water Garden: 2477
Palm Blossom: 4278, 4297, 4298
Paradise Bird & Tree: 3147, 3150, 3151, 3155,

3157, 3159, 3202, 3241, 3350
Paradise Bird & Tree with Cloud: 3143, 3144, 3149, 3154, 3252
Parkland: 3423, 3523, 3524
Parrots: 3016, 3017, 3018, 3037, 3095

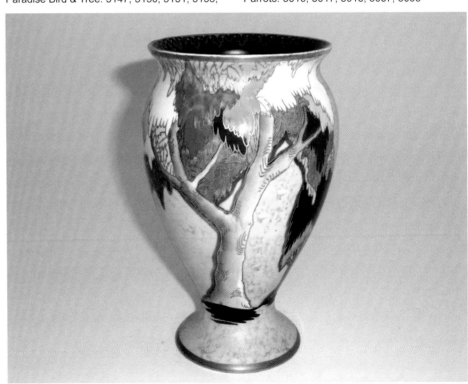

Parkland - Pattern 3523
Small vase from the Kosniowski Collection
£600 - £750

Stork and Bamboo - Pattern 2932
Large Dish from the Kosniowski Collection
£150 - £250

Shapes

Carlton Ware produced thousands of different shapes in their portfolio. Each shape was normally given a number and the design would have been recorded. Records of the shape numbers from 1001 onwards, which were placed in large books, still exist and provide a valuable source of information about Carlton Ware. A list of shapes is given in this chapter. The original records show an illustration of the piece but it's not possible for us to show all of these drawings as that would fill several books. One of our previous books, *Carlton Ware Catalogue & Price Guide*, provided many pictures and details of many of the shapes. That book mainly concentrated on the "embossed" ware about which we have also written elsewhere in this book.

We are aware that some shapes listed have not surfaced, to our knowledge, and therefore may never have been produced by Carlton Ware. Or, possibly, just one piece was made and is now lost.

Records of shape numbers up to 1000 have not been found; possibly they did not exist in a book form and if they did this might have been destroyed when Carlton Ware finally went to the receivers. We have managed to fill in some of the details by physically finding an item with a particular shape number. In addition we have copies of photographs of some of the Vase shapes produced by Carlton Ware. These have been reproduced in the next few pages. Most of these shape numbers are below 1000 and were used by Carlton Ware throughout its lifetime. For example, the Ginger Jar with shape number 125.

We would like to thank Frank Salmon (Francis Joseph) for access to some of the old Carlton Ware records held at The Potteries Museum & Art Gallery, Stoke-on-Trent. Many of the Black & White Photographs are photographs of pages from the records that we took at the Museum.

We have included a Price Guide for the embossed range. For pieces that might have been produced with a variety of different patterns, such as the Ginger Jar, it's not possible to give a price guide as it does depend on the pattern! Some pieces have not been seen and we have therefore not been able to provide a price guide.

129 L/S   129 S/S   153   125 S/S   125 /12"

167   123   128   165   174   226

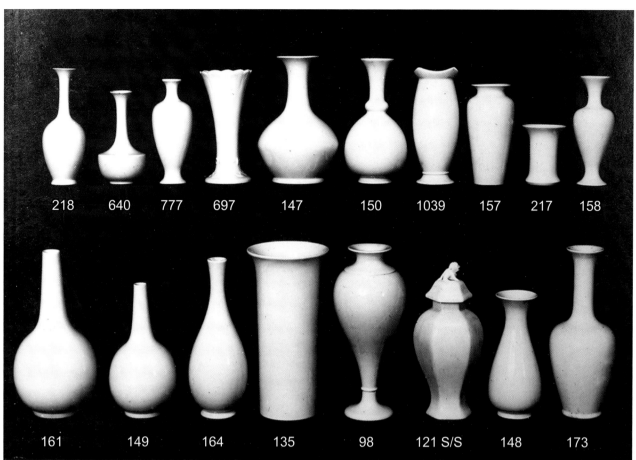

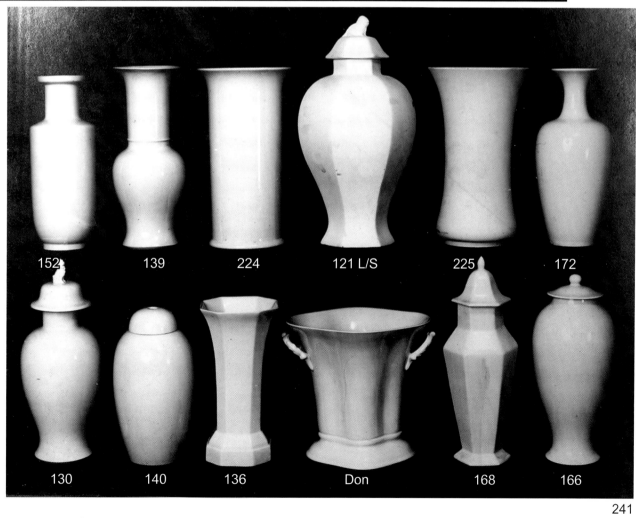

Bowl 198/9"   Tall Cigarette Box Carlton   283   284   Revo Rose Bowl
                          Match Holder

Gondola Salad   Bowl 198/5"   Revo Fruit

326   Cigarette Box   314   Grape Fruit Holder   1039

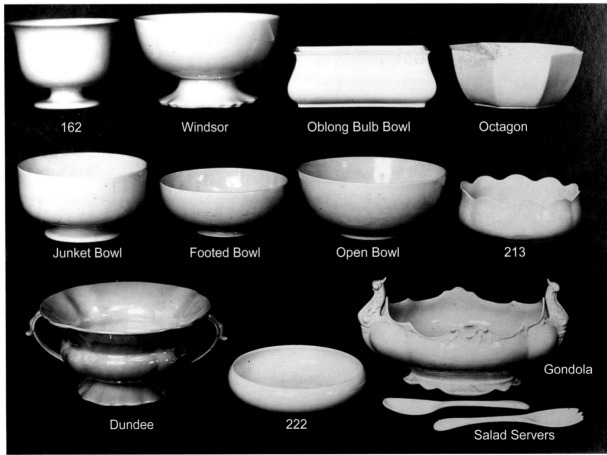

162   Windsor   Oblong Bulb Bowl   Octagon

Junket Bowl   Footed Bowl   Open Bowl   213

Dundee   222   Gondola

                                              Salad Servers

242

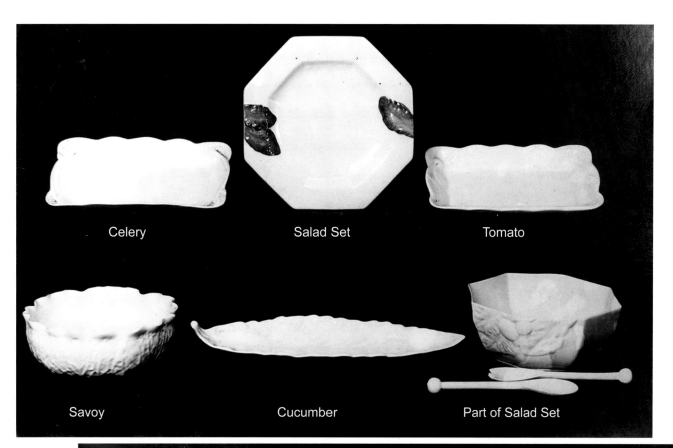

Celery

Salad Set

Tomato

Savoy

Cucumber

Part of Salad Set

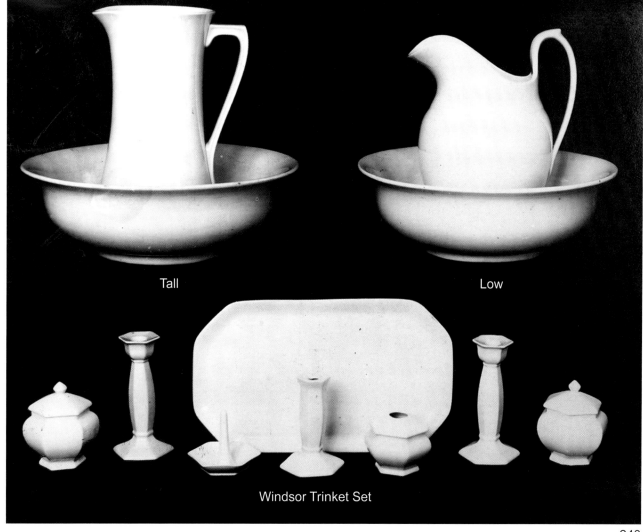

Tall

Low

Windsor Trinket Set

243

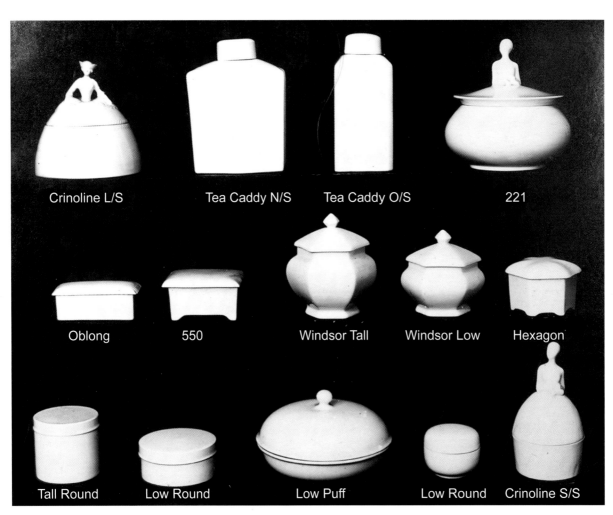

Crinoline L/S   Tea Caddy N/S   Tea Caddy O/S   221

Oblong   550   Windsor Tall   Windsor Low   Hexagon

Tall Round   Low Round   Low Puff   Low Round   Crinoline S/S

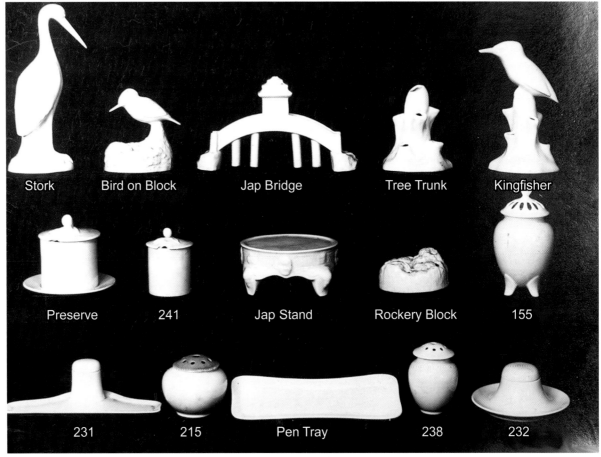

Stork   Bird on Block   Jap Bridge   Tree Trunk   Kingfisher

Preserve   241   Jap Stand   Rockery Block   155

231   215   Pen Tray   238   232

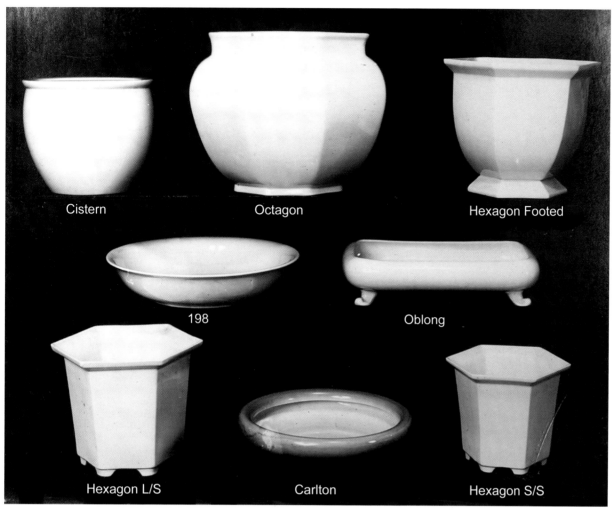

Cistern

Octagon

Hexagon Footed

198

Oblong

Hexagon L/S

Carlton

Hexagon S/S

Some Carlton Ware Ash Trays

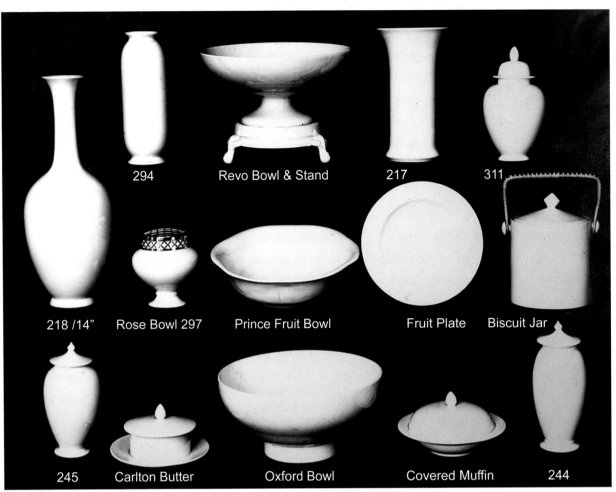

294

Revo Bowl & Stand

217

311

218 /14"

Rose Bowl 297

Prince Fruit Bowl

Fruit Plate

Biscuit Jar

245

Carlton Butter

Oxford Bowl

Covered Muffin

244

Lamp Shade and Stand with New Mikado pattern

List of Shape Numbers with some Prices

98 Vase
111 Conical Vase
121 Bulbous Temple Jar with lid
123 Flower Vase
125 Ginger Jar, 5 sizes
128 Square Vase with narrow stem
129 Bulbous Temple Jar with lid
130 Temple Jar with Lion
135 Vase
136 Octagonal Vase
139 Bulbous Vase
140 Elongated Ginger Jar
144 Conical Ginger Jar
147 Vase
148 Vase
149 Vase
150 Vase
152 Cylindrical Vase with narrower collar
153 Temple Jar with Lion
155 Pot Pourri
157 Vase
158 Vase
161 Vase
162 Urn
164 Vase
165 Trumpet vase
166 Temple Jar with lid
167 Vase
168 Hexagonal Vase with lid
172 Bulbous vase with narrow collar
173 Vase
174 Pregnant Vase
198 Bowl
213 Bowl
215 Pot Pourri
217 Cylindrical Vase
218 Vase
221 Powder Bowl with Lady
222 Bowl
224 Cylindrical vase
225 Curved Cylindrical Vase
226 Vase
231 Pen Holder
232 Ink Holder
238 Pot Pourri
241 Preserve with lid
244 Vase with lid
245 Fruit Basket Small Preserve Pot £45 - £65
245 Vase with lid
283 Vase
284 Vase
294 Vase
297 Rose Bowl
298 Bowl, 4 sizes
304 Lighter
311 Ginger Jar
314 Vase
325 Vase
326 Vase
331 Fruit Jaffa Preserve and Stand £30 - £50
349 Gondola
406 Vase
437 Vase
442 Vase
443 Vase
456 Vase
457 Vase

463 Vase
464 Vase
465 Vase
466 Vase
467 Vase
487 Vase
496 Jug
550 Cigarette Box
620 Old Salad Preserve and Stand £50 - £75
640 Vase
697 Vase
711 Fruit Basket Preserve Pot £55 - £75
743 Vase with Handles
760 Fruit Basket Bowl £30 - £45
761 Fruit Basket Cruet £120 - £170
777 Vase
786 Vase
787 Milk Jug
830 Fruit Basket Jug and Stand £70 - £90
876 Fruit Basket Comport £50 - £80
899 Square Ashtray £20 - £40
925 Anemone Preserve Cover *see 1174*
928 Anemone Tray £75 - £110
932 Anemone Plate £75 - £110
933 Anemone Leaf Tray, one hole for handle £80 - £150
935 Anemone Plate £75 - £110
945 Anemone Biscuit Barrel £250 - £350
946 Anemone Square Salad Bowl & Servers £350 - £450
949 Gum Nut Round Plate £20 - £35
950 Gum Nut Long Tray £25 - £40
952 Gum Nut Preserve Pot £40 - £60
970 Anemone Small Bowl £45 - £70
975 Anemone Flower Jug, Pitcher, 3 sizes £200 - £400
976 Anemone Bowl £75 - £110
978 Anemone Jug £100 - £130
979 Anemone Preserve Base *see 1174*
983 Anemone Cress Dish and Tray £150 - £190
995 Fruit Basket Pitcher £75 - £95
997 Anemone Preserve £120 - £175
1001 Toy Teapot, no 3
1002 Deer Serviette Holder £30 - £50
1003 Dick Whittington
1004 Clergyman Bell £30 - £50
1005 Maid Bell £30 - £50
1006 Page Bell £30 - £50

1007 Dandy Bell £30 - £50

1008 Clergyman Cigarette Box or Preserve £30 - £50
1009 Gum Nut Triangular Tray 9ins £25 - £40
1010 Gum Nut Triangular Tray 7ins £25 - £40
1011 Gum Nut Triangular Tray 6ins £25 - £40
1012 Crinoline Lady Bell £110 - £160
1013 Jug
1014 Anemone Round Plate 4ins £75 - £110
1015 Anemone Round Plate 8ins £75 - £110
1016 Santa Claus & Mickey Mouse
1017 Fairy with Mushroom
1018 Fairy on Leaf
1019 Fairy Kneeling
1020 Fish Band Drummer
1021 Fish Band Fife
1022 Fish Band Trumpet
1023 Fish Band Fiddle
1024 Fish Band Drummer
1025 Fish Band Banjo
1026 Anemone Tea Pot £300 - £420
1027 Anemone Sugar £60 - £85
1028 Anemone Cream £60 - £85
1029 Anemone Cup £150 - £200 with 1030
1030 Anemone Saucer *see 1029*
1031 Anemone Puff (Bowl with feet plus lid) £160 - £190
1032 Anemone Mayonnaise (Puff with spoon) £185 - £265
1033 Anemone Sugar Sifter £90 - £125
1034 Bowl with Bulb Feet
1035 Gum Nut Grapefruit £30 - £60
1036 Gum Nut Toast Rack, 3 bar £30 - £50
1037 Gum Nut Sauceboat £30 - £50 with 1038
1038 Gum Nut Sauceboat Stand *see 1037*
1039 Pear Salt & Pepper £30 - £50
1039 Vase
1040 Gum Nut Sauce Container £30 - £50
1041 Anemone Trinket Tray £75 - £100
1042 Anemone Bee Box £100 - £120
1043 Gum Nut Sugar Bowl £15 - £30
1044 Gum Nut Milk or Creamer £15 - £30
1045 Gum Nut Cruet Set £35 - £60
1046 Old Woman in Shoe
1047 Red Riding Hood
1048 Acorn Salt & Pepper £15 - £30
1049 Mickey Mouse with Sled
1050 Mickey Mouse
1051 Mickey Mouse on Plane
1052 Mickey Mouse
1053 No details
1054 No details
1055 No details
1056 Pip Squeak & Wilfred Band
1057 No details
1058 No details
1059 No details
1060 No details
1061 Pip Squeak & Wilfred Band
1062 Bowl - Velox, similar to Cone Ashtray
1063 Gum Nut Salad Spoon *see 1066*
1064 Gum Nut Salad Fork *see 1066*
1065 Jaffa Sugar £30 - £50
1066 Gum Nut Salad Bowl £50 - £70 with 1063 & 1064
1067 Anemone Vase £100 - £120
1068 Anemone Covered Mug £190 - £250
1069 Anemone Flower Pot £70 - £100
1070 Stone Ware Vase - Rings £15 - £30
1071 Stone Ware Ribbed Vase £15 - £30
1072 Stone Ware Vase £15 - £30
1073 Stone Ware Round Ash Tray, 3 rests £5 - £10
1074 Stone Ware Jug £15 - £30
1075 Stone Ware Vase, 2 handles each side

offset *£15 - £30*
1076 Stone Ware Bowl with 2 handles *£15 - £30*
1077 Stone Ware Vase *£15 - £30*
1078 Stone Ware Beaker *£10 - £20*

1079 Stone Ware Puff Box *£15 - £30*
1080 Stone Ware Candle Stick *£10 - £20*
1081 Stone Ware Bowl on Foot *£15 - £30*
1082 Gum Nut Toast Rack, 5 bar *£40 - £60*
1083 Hand Mirror with Face
1084 Gum Nut Triangular Tray 8ins *£25 - £40*
1085 Thermometer Frame
1086 Gum Nut Rectangular Tray *£25 - £40*
1087 Crinoline Mustard, Salt & Pepper *£75 - £100*
1088 Jaffa Lemon Squeezer, Large Size *£30 - £50*
1089 Gum Nut Leaf Butter *£25 - £45*
1090 Squirrel Tooth Brush Holder
1091 Guardsman Tooth Brush Holder
1092 Sailor Tooth Brush Holder
1093 Soldier Tooth Brush Holder
1094 Oven Ware Preserve or Jam Jar Container
1095 Cancelled

Bluebell Jug - Shape 1099
Jug from Fieldings Auctioneers
£50 - £80

1096 Anemone Butter, small *£45 - £70*
1097 Anemone Morning Tray *£100 - £125 with 1029*
1098 Oak Tree Jug or Pitcher *£120 - £160*
1099 Bluebell Jug *£200 - £300*
1100 Gum Nut Sauceboat, Large Size *£30 - £50 with 1101*
1101 Gum Nut Sauceboat Stand, Large Size *see 1100*
1102 21st Key, Large Size

1103 Stone Ware Dog *£150 - £200*
1104 Stone Ware Vase *£15 - £30*
1105 Stone Ware Vase *£15 - £30*
1106 Stone Ware Ribbed Vase *£15 - £30*
1107 Stone Ware Bowl *£15 - £30*
1108 Stone Ware Vase *£15 - £30*
1109 Stone Ware Vase *£15 - £30*
1110 Stone Ware Bowl *£15 - £30*
1111 Stone Ware Mug *£10 - £20*
1112 Stone Ware Jug *£10 - £20*
1113 Stone Ware Bowl on Foot *£10 - £20*
1114 Stone Ware Owl Cruet *£20 - £35*
1115 Stone Ware Pot *£10 - £20*
1116 Stone Ware Dessert Plate *£10 - £20*
1117 Stone Ware Bulb Bowl *£10 - £20*
1118 Stone Ware Bulb Bowl *£10 - £20*
1119 Stone Ware Tobacco Jar *£20 - £40*
1120 Stone Ware Vase No 5 *£15 - £30*
1121 Stone Ware Vase No 4 *£15 - £30*
1122 Stone Ware Vase /4 *£15 - £30*
1123 Stone Ware Jug, 1 handle *£15 - £30*
1124 Stone Ware Jug, 2 handles *£15 - £30*
1125 Jug, Flat Sided
1126 Gum Nut Mayonnaise Bowl , Unhandled *£35 - £55*
1127 Dimple Jug, Large Size *£10 - £20*
1128 Dimple Ash Tray *£10 - £20*
1129 Tall Round Ash Tray, 2 rests *£20 - £40*
1130 Yale Key
1131 Square Ash Bowl, 4 rests
1132 Cat Toy Tea Ware
1133 Dimple Jug, Small Size
1134 Dimple Jug
1135 Round Ash Bowl
1136 Round Ash Tray, Solid
1137 Rabbit Toy Tea Ware
1138 Crinoline Lady Napkin Holder *£60 - £90*
1139 Posie Bowl, 4 sizes
1140 Stone Ware Jug, No 1 & 2 *£15 - £30*
1141 Oblong Ash Bowl
1142 Triangular Ash Bowl
1143 Oak Tree Ashtray *£40 - £60*
1144 Oak Tree Charger *£100 - £150*

1145 Oak Tree Candlestick, single *£50 - £60*
1146 Oak Tree Jug, 8ins *£100 - £130*
1147 Oak Tree Cigarette Box *£40 - £70*
1148 Oak Tree Bowl, handled *£60 - £90*
1149 Oak Tree Toast Rack, 3 bar *£40 - £50*
1150 Octagonal Shaving Brush Handle
1151 Vase on Foot
1152 Vase, Size 5, 6
1153 Vase, Size 5, 6
1154 Vase, Size 5, 6
1155 Oak Tree Match Holder *£45 - £60*
1156 Vase, Square Top
1157 Vase, Footed Cone
1158 Cat Mug
1159 Cat Fruit Plate
1160 Cat Muffin
1161 Stone Ware Lamp, as vase 1071 *£20 - £30*
1162 Oak Tree Vase *£50 - £70*
1163 Oak Tree Vase, two handled *£80 - £110*
1164 Oak Tree Book Ends *£140 - £170*
1165 Oak Tree Oval Bowl *£30 - £45*
1166 Oak Tree Toast Rack, 5 bar *£50 - £60*
1167 Oak Tree Cheese Dish and Cover *£80 - £100*
1168 Oak Tree Butter, covered, square *£60 - £80*
1169 Oak Tree Leaf Butter *£25 - £35*
1170 Lemon Segmented Dish *£40 - £60*
1171 Stone Ware Vase, as 1071 *£15 - £30*
1172 Stone Ware Vase, as 1072 *£15 - £30*
1173 Oval shaped Bowl, two handled
1174 Anemone Preserve Pot *£120 - £175 with 925 & 979*
1175 Oak Tree Preserve with Base *£60 - £80*
1176 Vase 16ins (/00) 14ins (/0)
1177 Stone Ware Square Box *£20 - £35*
1178 Stone Ware Crinoline Lady *£40 - £70*
1179 Stone Ware Rat *£150 - £200*
1180 Stone Ware Goose *£250 - £300*
1181 Stone Ware Penguin *£150 - £200*

1182 Stone Ware Rabbit *£150 - £200*
1183 Oak Tree Cruet Set *£130 - £160*
1184 Anemone Tea Cup as 1029 *see 1029*
1185 Oak Tree Cream *£35 - £50*
1186 Oak Tree Sugar *£35 - £50*
1187 Oak Tree Leaf Tray (s, m, l) *£25 - £60*
1188 Oak Tree Biscuit *£70 - £100*
1189 Oak Tree Sauceboat and Stand *£40 - £60*
1190 Oak Tree Sugar Sifter *£70 - £90*
1191 Oak Tree Jug, 6ins, 1 pint *£120 - £150*
1192 Oak Tree Double Candlestick *£60 - £70*
1193 Oak Tree Cigarette Holder and Ashtray *£45 - £70*

1194 Oak Tree Triple Tray £50 - £70
1195 Jug, as 1125 but shrunk
1196 Jug
1197 Pelican Cruet £30 - £60
1198 Pot Pourri (Base 1157 with new cover)
1199 Powder Puff (897 with Wicker Knob)
1200 Small Grecian Jug
1201 Jug, Barrel Shape
1202 Scot Toothbrush Holder
1203 Irish Toothbrush Holder
1204 Welsh Toothbrush Holder
1205 Stone Ware Triangular Ash Tray £5 - £10
1206 Cat Ash Tray £10 - £15
1207 Triangular Jug
1208 Oak Tree Bon-bon dish £30 - £50
1209 Lamp, converted from 1105/4

Cigarette or Card Holders

Shape 1210 from the Ian & Jerome Collection

1938 Empire Exhibition in Glasgow £50 - £70

1939/40 New Zealand Centennial £50 - £70

Apple Blossom £150 - £200

1210 Modern Cigarette or Card Holder
1211 Stone Ware Book End £20 - £40
1212 Stone Ware Book End £20 - £40
1213 Mugs & Jugs, Musical Humpty Dumpty
    £100 - £200
1214 Oak Tree Bowl, 3ins £40 - £70
1215 Round Ash Tray
1216 Vase converted to Jug (1181)
1217 Gazelle Candle Stick
1218 Large Round Ash Tray as 1215
1219 Medium Ash Tray
1220 Drip Ash Tray, large size
1221 Drip Ash Tray, small size

1222 Posy Bowl, small size, Ring
1223 Gazelle Pot
1224 Posy Bowl, (1217 covered Vase)
1225 Footed Vase
1226 Fruit Grapefruit slices £10 - £20
1227 Offside Handled Vase
1228 Bowl
1229 Cigarette Holder, Ring
1230 Ashtray, single cigarette rest on each side
    £15 - £20
1231 Vase
1232 Vase, two offset handles each side, 2 sizes
1233 Two Handled Vase, 2 sizes
1234 Two Handled Vase, handles offset, 2 sizes
1235 Three Handled Vase
1236 Oval Dish
1237 Rock Garden Tray, Elliptical £30 - £50
1238 Rock Garden Flower Jug, Tall £110 - £150
1239 Rock Garden Vase, two offset handles
    each side £40 - £60
1240 Rock Garden Posy Bowl £45 - £55
1241 Rock Garden Leaf Butter, small handle,
    large size £20 - £35
1242 Ring 2 handled Vase
1243 Rock Garden Cigarette Vase, unholed
    handles - £40
1244 Rock Garden Vase, offset handle each
    side £50 - £80
1245 Moderne Tea Set £300 - £400
1246 Moderne Coffee Set £300 - £400
1247 Rock Garden Soup Bowl, unholed handles
    £35 - £50
1248 Rock Garden Ashtray £20 - £40
1249 Rock Garden Flower Trough £30 - £45
1250 Rock Garden Jug or Pitcher, two handles
    on one side £40 - £55
1251 Rock Garden Candlestick £35 - £50
1252 Rock Garden Ashtray and Match or
    Cigarette Holder £45 - £60
1253 Rock Garden Vase, Bulbous, handles on
    one side £40 - £60
1254 Rock Garden Vase, offset handles each
    side £40 - £60
1255 Guinness Round Ash Tray £20 - £40
1256 Vase converted to Lamp (1104/4 as Lamp)
1257 Abbotts Choice Jug £15 - £20
1258 Abbotts Choice Ash Tray £15 - £20
1259 Vase with handle from 1140

1260 Mugs & Jugs, Musical Hunting Scene Jug
    £40 - £80
1261 Santa
1262 Rock Garden Cruet Set £80 - £100
1263 Dovecote Range Oblong Jug £20 - £30
1264 Rock Garden Leaf Butter, small handle,
    small size £20 - £35
1265 Rock Garden Preserve with Lid £70 - £90
1266 Blackberry/Raspberry Preserve £80 - £120
1267 Lobster Oval Salad £100 - £160 with 1273
1268 No details
1269 Lobster Round Salad £100 - £160 with
    1273
1270 Crab Butter £20 - £40
1271 Haig Cigar Ash Bowl £10 - £20
1272 Lobster Oblong Dish £30 - £50
1273 Lobster Servers see 1267, 1269
1274 Dolls Head Open Top, 4ins
1275 Ash Tray
1276 Dolls Head Paramount 400
1277 Lobster Preserve £40 - £70
1278 Lobster Round Plate, 4 sizes £20 - £50
1279 Dolls Head Open Top, 6.5ins
1280 Crab & Lobster Triangular Dish £20 - £40
1281 Craven A Square Ash Tray £5 - £10
1282 Guinness Ash Tray with several rests £20
    - £40
1283 Ash Tray
1284 Mugs & Jugs, Musical Hangsman £150
    - £250
1285 Mugs & Jugs, Musical Hangsman £80
    - £150
1286 Diamond Dish, 2 sizes
1287 Rock Garden Sauceboat and Stand £55
    - £85
1288 Dolls Head Paramount 350
1289 Mugs & Jugs, Musical Hunting Scene Mug
    £40 - £80
1290 Incised Ash Tray
1291 Incised Jug as 496
1292 Incised Vase with incised Diamond
1293 Incised Plaque, 12ins
1294 Incised Oval Dish as 1237
1295 Incised Jug as 786
1296 Incised Vase as 443/6ins
1297 Incised Vase as 1176/4ins
1298 Incised Biscuit Jar as 998
1299 Incised Cigarette Box as 923

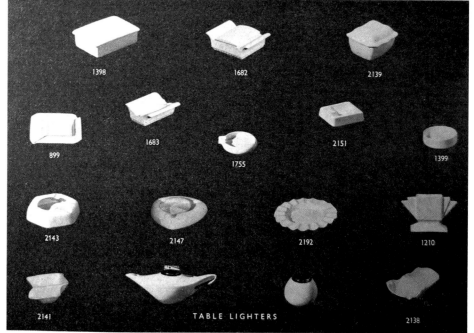

TABLE LIGHTERS

1300 Incised Vase as 466
1301 Incised Bowl as 1062
1302 Incised Preserve & Stand as 800
1303 Incised Ash Tray as 1136
1304 Incised Vase as 442
1305 Incised Triangle Book Ends
1306 Incised Vase as 443/10ins
1307 Incised Ash Tray as 794
1308 Incised Vase as 741
1309 Incised Jug as 788
1310 Incised Posy Bowl
1311 Flower Ring Plain Candlestick
1312 Dolls Head Paramount 300
1313 Punch Egg Timer
1314 Pope Egg Timer
1315 Policeman Egg Timer
1316 Golliwog Egg Timer
1317 Store Jar, as 905, 6ins x 4 ins
1318 Jug, as 814 shrunk handle
1319 Hexagonal Shaving Brush Handle
1320 Incised Posy Bowl, small size
1321 Incised Cigarette Holder, as 1210
1322 Incised Vase, as 1232 large size
1323 Incised Posy Bowl, medium size
1324 Incised Diamond Shape Tray as 1286
1325 Incised Vase as 1227
1326 Incised Double Posy Bowl
1327 Flower Ring, 4 sizes
1328 Royalty King Henry VIII Bowl *£750 - £1,000*
1329 Milk Jug (White & Mackey) *£15 - £30*
1330 Mugs & Jugs, Musical Huntsman Mug Plain *£40 - £80*
1331 Dolls Head Paramount 500
1332 Royalty Confederation Jug *£500 - £750*
1333 Barrel Jug
1334 Crab & Lobster Sauce Boat *£20 - £40*
1335 Crab & Lobster Sauce Stand, small size *£10 - £20*
1336 Rock Garden Lamp *£200 - £250*
1337 Rock Garden Charger or Plaque *£150 - £200*
1338 Crab & Lobster Sauce Container *£15 - £30*
1339 Crab & Lobster 5 bar Toast Rack *£50 - £80*
1340 Modern Triangular Tray, 9ins
1341 Modern Oblong Dish, 3 sizes
1342 Modern Butter, with handle
1343 Modern Round Salad
1344 Dolls Head Paramount 600, size 7
1345 Brush Book
1346 Modern Preserve, 2 sizes
1347 Modern Jug, 3 sizes
1348 Crab & Lobster Low Round Salad *£30 - £60*
1349 Dolls Head Paramount, size 8
1350 Crab & Lobster Shallow Oblong Dish *£30 - £60*
1351 Artists Palette, numbered sample 1
1352 Artists Palette, numbered sample 13
1353 Rock Garden Lamp, unhandled *£200 - £250*
1354 Crab & Lobster Cheese *£30 - £60*
1355 Legs of Man
1356 Rings Jug, as 1112
1357 Rings Vase, 8ins, as 1121
1358 Rings Vase, 8ins, as 1122
1359 Rings Vase , 8ins, as 1109
1360 Rings Vase 2 handles, as 1075
1361 Rings Vase Handled, as 1105
1362 Posy Hoop
1363 VAT 69 Jug
1364 Crab & Lobster 3 Bar Toast Rack *£40 - £70*
1365 Oblong Shallow Tray

1366 Modern Cruet
1367 Curled Lettuce Diamond Dish *£10 - £20*
1368 Dolls Head Paramount Open Top
1369 Posy Bar
1370 Fish Candle Holder
1371 Modern Beaker & Cover
1372 Curled Lettuce Sauce Boat and Tray *£30 - £40*
1373 Flower Bowl, Plate with stem holder
1374 Curled Lettuce Butter *£10 - £20*
1375 Curled Lettuce Oblong Tray *£10 - £20*
1376 Toy Tea Set
1377 Round Ash Tray
1378 Oblong Ash Tray with rests
1379 Oblong Ash Tray
1380 Curled Lettuce Knife *£10 - £20*
1381 Oval Ash Tray, 2 rests
1382 Curled Lettuce Crescent Dish *£10 - £20*
1383 Curled Lettuce Salad Bowl *£30 - £40*
1384 No details
1385 Curled Lettuce Square Plate, 4 sizes *£10 - £20*
1386 Curled Lettuce Triple Tray *£15 - £25*
1387 Circular Butter, 2 ears *£10 - £20*
1388 Vase, 2 sizes
1389 Curled Lettuce Sauce Boat and Tray *£30 - £40*
1390 Curled Lettuce Diamond Tray, less elongated than 1367 *£10 - £20*
1391 Curled Lettuce Salad Servers *£15 - £30*
1392 Curled Lettuce Mayonnaise Bowl & Stand *£30 - £40*
1393 Ash Tray with 3 rests
1394 Modern Cheese
1395 Buttercup Butter *£40 - £70 with 1402*
1396 Strawberry Jam
1397 Bon Bon, as Puff Base 897 to verge
1398 Oblong Cigarette Box, no feet
1399 Card Table Ash Tray
1400 Modern Knife
1401 Modern Spoon
1402 Buttercup Butter Knife *see 1402*
1403 Tulip Spoon, also for Strawberry *£15 - £25*
1404 Tulip Jam or Butter, 2 sizes *£25 - £40*
1405 Shaving Brush Handle, small size
1406 Haig Jug, modernised *£20 - £45*
1407 Wall Pocket Vase
1408 Ash Bowl
1409 Coronation Mug
1410 Footed Bowl
1411 Jug, introduced October 1936
1412 Curled Lettuce Cress Drainer & Tray *£30 - £50*
1413 Candle Stick
1414 Royalty King Edward VIII *£500 - £750*
1415 Cake Plate & Knife
1416 Tulip Jug, 6 sizes *£40 - £90*
1417 Tulip Oval Dish *£30 - £40*
1418 Tulip Preserve *£45 - £75*
1419 Tulip Plate, 3 sizes *£25 - £55*
1420 Tulip Square Jug, 2 sizes *£50 - £70*
1421 Tulip Handled Crescent Plate, 3 sizes *£40 - £80*
1422 Tulip Sugar Sifter *£60 - £95*
1423 Lion Cubs sitting *£400 - £450*
1424 Sea Lion *£300 - £400*
1425 Polar Bear *£300 - £400*
1426 Lioness *£450 - £500*
1427 Lion Cubs lying down *£400 - £450*
1428 Lemonade Jug
1429 Lemonade Beaker
1430 Lion *£450 - £500*
1431 Large Spill
1432 Royalty Sphere *see 1434*

1433 Vase, 9ins
1434 Royalty King George VI *£400 - £600 with 1432*
1435 Royalty Queen Elizabeth *£400 - £600*
1436 Vase, 2 offset handles
1437 Lizard Vase with Neck *£300 - £400*
1438 Lizard Vase without neck *£300 - £400*
1439 Tulip Morning Tea Set (Tea for Two) *£200 - £300*
1440 Scotch Terrier Standing *£100 - £150*
1441 Scotch Terrier Sitting *£100 - £150*
1442 Fox Terrier *£100 - £150*
1443 Round Ash Tray, 6 rests
1444 Round Ash Tray, 7 rests
1445 Spaniel Dog *£100 - £150*
1446 Lamb *£100 - £150*
1447 Stag *£100 - £150*
1448 Fox *£100 - £150*
1449 Mouse on Log *£100 - £150*
1450 Mouse on Nest *£100 - £150*
1451 Sea Gulls *£300 - £400*
1452 Trinket Tray
1453 Tulip Salad *£45 - £75*
1454 Trinket Box
1455 Puff Box, as 1454
1456 Sphere Lamp
1457 Tulip Servers *£30 - £50*
1458 Round Flat Bowl, 14ins
1459 Tulip Cruet *£60 - £95*
1460 Lamp, Jug 1411 converted
1461 Tulip Biscuit *£60 - £95*
1462 Bovril Cup *£20 - £45*
1463 Bovril Cup *£20 - £45*
1464 Guinness Ash Tray, as 1282 *£20 - £40*
1465 Shaving Brush Handle
1466 Lizard on Rock *£300 - £400*
1467 Blue Tits *£300 - £400*
1468 Fish on Stand *£100 - £150*
1469 Alsatian Dogs *£450 - £500*
1470 Group of Sheep *£300 - £400*
1471 Heron in Flight *£300 - £400*
1472 Daisy Jam or Butter *£20 - £40*
1473 Blackberry/Raspberry Jam or Butter *£30 - £45*
1474 Pear Butter *£15 - £25*
1475 Greyhounds *£450 - £500*
1476 Daisy Knife *£15 - £25*
1477 Blackberry/Raspberry Spoon *£20 - £40*
1478 Buttercup Salad Bowl *£90 - £150 with 1479*
1479 Buttercup Salad Bowl Servers *see 1478*
1480 Crab *£100 - £150*
1481 Snake Charmer *£100 - £150*
1482 Buttercup Plate, 6ins, 7ins, 8ins, 9ins *£30 - £75*
1483 Buttercup Bowl, Oval, 3 sizes *£30 - £75*
1484 Shaving Brush Handle
1485 Guinness Oblong Ash Tray *£20 - £40*
1486 Buttercup Preserve & Stand *£90 - £155*
1487 Engine Turned Plate, 4 sizes *£30 - £50*
1488 Engine Turned Vase *£40 - £80*
1489 Engine Turned Vase, 4 sizes *£40 - £80*
1490 Engine Turned Vase *£40 - £80*
1491 Engine Turned Bowl, 7ins *£30 - £50*
1492 Engine Turned Vase, 4 sizes *£40 - £80*
1493 Engine Turned Biscuit Barrel *£50 - £75*
1494 Engine Turned Puff Bowl with lid, as 1495 with no hole in lid *£30 - £50*
1495 Engine Turned Sugar *£30 - £40*
1496 Engine Turned Trinket Box with lid, 2 sizes *£30 - £50*
1497 Engine Turned Vase, 3 sizes *£40 - £80*
1498 Engine Turned Vase, 3 sizes *£40 - £80*
1499 Engine Turned Beaker *£30 - £40*

1500 Engine Turned Cruet £80 - £80
1501 Buttercup Cruet (on a Tomato Cruet Frame) £120 - £180
1502 Engine Turned Cylinder Vase £40 - £80
1503 Pewter Teapot
1504 Pewter Cream
1505 Pewter Sugar
1506 Giraffe £200 - £300
1507 Kangaroo £200 - £300
1508 Borzois Dog £200 - £300
1509 Leopard £200 - £300
1510 Buttercup Triple Tray £100 - £150
1511 Buttercup Bon-Bon Dish £35 - £70
1512 Buttercup Cress Dish and Tray £70 - £110
1513 Buttercup Sauce Boat and Tray £50 - £70
1514 Buttercup Comport £50 - £80
1515 Blackberry/Raspberry Crescent Tray £40 - £60
1516 Blackberry/Raspberry Plate £30 - £45
1517 Vase
1518 Mandarin
1519 Plain Finger Bowl
1520 Water Carrier
1521 Coolie
1522 Buttercup Morning Tea Set (Tea for two) £400 - £600
1523 Buttercup Footed Bowl £50 - £80
1524 Buttercup Jug, 2 sizes £70 - £110
1525 Buttercup Reamer £100 - £150
1526 Buttercup Toast Rack, Combination £120 - £170
1527 Bee Butter Bee Box
1528 Buttercup Sauce Container £50 - £80
1529 Buttercup Crescent Plate, 2 sizes £40 - £70
1530 Buttercup Covered Butter or Cheese £200 - £400
1531 Buttercup Cheese Tray £60 - £100
1532 Buttercup Toast Rack, 5 Bar £80 - £120
1533 Buttercup Toast Rack, 3 Bar £70 - £100
1534 Buttercup Round Butter £30 - £50
1535 Mans Head
1536 Indian Group
1537 Leaf Nut Leaf Knife £10 - £20
1538 Leaf Ivy Leaf Butter £20 - £30
1539 Leaf Vine Leaf Jam or Butter £20 - £30
1540 Old Water Lily Butter £35 - £65 with 1541
1541 Old Water Lily Knife see 1540
1542 Curled Lettuce Cheese Plate £20 - £40
1543 Mugs & Jugs, Musical Flower Mug £80 - £150
1544 Flower Cruet
1545 Blackberry/Raspberry Sandwich Tray £40 - £60
1546 Blackberry/Raspberry Diamond Tray £40 - £60
1547 Blackberry/Raspberry Oblong Tray £40 - £60
1548 Blackberry/Raspberry Covered Cheese £180 - £225
1549 Mugs & Jugs, Musical Ghoules £100 - £200
1550 Fruit Apple Jam £10 - £20
1551 Wild Rose Butter £20 - £40 with 1554 or 1555
1552 Crocus Butter £30 - £70
1553 Crocus Knife £10 - £20
1554 Wild Rose Knife see 1551
1555 Wild Rose Spoon see 1551
1556 Fruit Apple Spoon £10 - £20
1557 Plain Knife Handle
1558 Buttercup Cheese Knife £20 - £30
1559 Blackberry/Raspberry Oval Tray £30 - £50
1560 Blackberry/Raspberry Round Salad £30

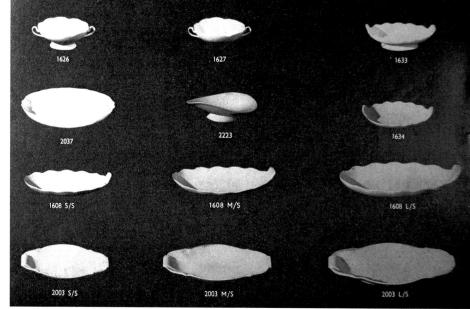

- £50
1561 Engine Turned Lamp, 12ins, no handle £50 - £75
1562 Engine Turned Lamp, 11ins, handled £50 - £75
1563 Modern Tea Set
1564 Blackberry/Raspberry Salad Servers £40 - £60
1565 Blackberry/Raspberry Biscuit Barrel £175 - £225
1566 Coffee Set
1567 Stone Ware Lamp, 1108/2 converted £15 - £30
1568 Lamp, 226/10 converted
1569 Lamp, 456/8 converted
1570 Blackberry/Raspberry Morning Tea Set (Tea for two) £330 - £450
1571 Triangular Tray
1572 Oval Bowl
1573 Engine Turned Lamp, 1502 converted £50 - £75
1574 Buttercup Juicer and Jug £60 - £90
1575 Toy Tea Set
1576 Thistle Butter or Jam £30 - £50

1577 Thistle Butter Knife £15 - £25
1578 Thistle Jam Spoon £15 - £25
1579 Thistle Ashtray £25 - £50
1580 Blackberry/Raspberry Bon-bon dish £30 - £50
1581 Blackberry/Raspberry Fruit £20 - £45
1582 Rita Coffee Set
1583 Buttercup Sugar Shaker £100 - £150
1584 Blackberry/Raspberry Sauceboat and Stand £70 - £90
1585 Buttercup Covered Mug £150 - £200
1586 Blackberry/Raspberry Jug £60 - £90
1587 Buttercup Open Jam, also called Grapefruit £90 - £120
1588 Water Lily Open Jam, also called Grapefruit £100 - £120
1589 Shaving Brush Handle
1590 Engine Turned Ash Tray, 1 rest £30 - £40
1591 Lamp, 443/10 converted
1592 Scotch Cruet
1593 Blackberry/Raspberry Sauce Container £25 - £45
1594 Modern Jug, handle at side
1595 Buttercup Egg Cruet £190 - £260

RITA COFFEE WARE

1596 Modern Salad Servers
1597 Buttercup Butter Pat *£30 - £50*
1598 Blackberry/Raspberry Cruet *£100 - £150*
1599 Blackberry/Raspberry Butter Pat *£20 - £35*
1600 Triangular Salad, as 1571 with foot
1601 Triangular Dessert Plate
1602 Blackberry/Raspberry Jug with Lemon Squeezer *£60 - £85*
1603 Red Currant Butter or Jam *£20 - £30*
1604 Modern Butter Pat
1605 Red Currant Butter Knife *£10 - £20*
1606 Red Currant Jam Spoon *£10 - £20*
1607 Red Currant Preserve *£50 - £80*
1608 Oval Scalloped Dish
1609 Oval Scalloped Comport
1610 Bon Bon Dish, as 1397 with rim at outside edges
1611 Bowl, as 1062 Velox with rim
1612 Ash Tray, as 797 with rim
1613 Buttercup Bulb Bowl, 10ins *£50 - £80*
1614 Apple Blossom Leaf Tray *£30 - £50*
1615 Parisienne Tea Set
1616 Rope Vase *£30 - £50*
1617 Apple Blossom Triangular Tray 4ins, 6ins, 9ins *£30 - £50*
1618 Apple Blossom Preserve *£65 - £95*
1619 Modern Shallow Dish
1620 Glasgow Exhibition Ash Tray
1621 Apple Blossom Butter *£30 - £50*
1622 Octagonal Bon Bon with Foot
1623 Octagonal Bon Bon without Foot
1624 Bird on Horseshoe
1625 Bird on Ring
1626 Footed Bon Bon Dish
1627 Bon Bon Dish without Foot
1628 Footed Bon Bon Dish
1629 Bon Bon Dish without Foot
1630 Rita Tea Set
1631 Oblong Bon Bon Dish Footed
1632 Oblong Bon Bon Dish without Foot
1633 Bon Bon Dish Footed
1634 Bon Bon Dish Footed without Foot
1635 Diamond Bon Bon Dish Footed
1636 Diamond Bon Bon Dish without Foot
1637 Red Currant Leaf Tray *£30 - £50*
1638 Apple Blossom Vase, 3 sizes *£70 - £100*
1639 Cone Sugar Sifter
1640 Rope Vase, rope top & bottom, 3 sizes *£30 - £50*
1641 Rope Vase, rope top & bottom, 3 sizes *£30 - £50*
1642 Rope Vase, rope top & bottom, 3 sizes *£30 - £50*
1643 Rope Vase, rope top & bottom, 3 sizes *£30 - £50*
1644 Rope Vase, rope top & bottom, 2 sizes *£30 - £50*
1645 Rope Vase, rope bottom only, as 1641, 2 sizes *£30 - £50*
1646 Rope Vase, rope bottom only, as 1642, 2 sizes *£30 - £50*
1647 Rope Vase, rope bottom only, as 1643, small size *£30 - £50*
1648 Apple Blossom Vase, Bulbous, 3 sizes *£70 - £100*
1649 Apple Blossom Vase, 3 sizes *£70 - £100*
1650 Apple Blossom Cheese Plate *£35 - £55*
1651 Apple Blossom Cheese Knife *£20 - £30*
1652 Apple Blossom Sauceboat and Stand *£55 - £80*
1653 Apple Blossom Cruet Set *£80 - £100*
1654 Apple Blossom Spoon *£20 - £30*
1655 Apple Blossom Butter Knife *£20 - £30*
1656 Red Currant Leaf Jam *£20 - £30*

1657 Red Currant Preserve, with leaves on side *£40 - £60*
1658 Red Currant Cheese Tray *£30 - £60 with 1659*
1659 Red Currant Cheese Tray Knife *see 1658*
1660 Red Currant Sauceboat and Stand *£30 - £50*
1661 Buttercup Butter Pat Knife *£20 - £30*
1662 Blackberry/Raspberry Butter Pat Knife *£20 - £40*
1663 Apple Blossom Salad Servers *£50 - £70*
1664 Apple Blossom Bon-bon dish *£35 - £50*
1665 Apple Blossom Oval Bowl, 3 sizes *£40 - £70*
1666 Triple Candlestick
1667 Double Candlestick
1668 Apple Blossom Cress Dish *£55 - £80*
1669 Apple Blossom Footed Bowl *£45 - £70*
1670 Apple Blossom Morning Tea Set (Tea for two) *£250 - £400*
1671 Apple Blossom Salad *£75 - £100*
1672 Ash Tray & Cigarette Holder
1673 Cracker Toast Rack
1674 Conical Vase
1675 Conical Vase
1676 Modern Oval Jug
1677 Modern Round Jug
1678 Ash Bowl
1679 Red Currant Double Butter *£30 - £50*
1680 Apple Blossom Double Butter *£40 - £60*
1681 Guinness Menu Stand *£20 - £40*
1682 Cigarette Box
1683 Ash Tray
1684 Pen Tray
1685 Mugs & Jugs, Musical Grandfather Clock *£150 - £250*
1686 Apple Blossom Jug, 2 sizes *£70 - £100*
1687 Apple Blossom Beaker and Cover *£95 - £135*
1688 Apple Blossom Triple Tray *£35 - £60*
1689 Apple Blossom Mayonnaise Bowl, Stand and Ladle *£85 - £120*
1690 Vase
1691 Vase with Wavy Sides
1692 Vase with small handles, two each side, 4 sizes
1693 Vase with small handles, three each side, 4 sizes
1694 Vase with small handles, two each side, 4 sizes
1695 Vase with small handles, two each side, 4 sizes
1696 Apple Blossom Toast Rack *£80 - £110*
1697 Apple Blossom Jug, Tall *£250 - £320*
1698 Judge Serviette Holder *£45 - £80*
1699 Scotchman Serviette Holder *£45 - £80*
1700 Apple Blossom Jug, double handle, 3 sizes *£175 - £250*
1701 Apple Blossom Egg Frame and 4 Egg Cups *£110 - £140*
1702 Judge Bottle Stopper *£40 - £70*
1703 Scotchman Bottle Stopper *£40 - £70*
1704 Apple Blossom Covered Cheese *£175 - £225*
1705 Crinoline Lady Cruet Set *£120 - £180*
1706 Ribbed Toy Tea Set
1707 Apple Blossom Serviette Holder *£40 - £70*
1708 Red Currant Napkin Ring *£40 - £80*
1709 Buttercup Napkin Ring *£100 - £160*
1710 Apple Blossom Vase *£70 - £90*
1711 Double Horse Shoe & Doves
1712 Bowl, Conical, 12ins
1713 Candlestick
1714 Apple Blossom Toy Teaware *£250 - £500*

1715 Bell Posy Holder *£30 - £40*
1716 Humpty Dumpty Lamp
1717 Wedding Cake Fence Cake Decoration
1718 Water Lily Posy Holder *£40 - £60*
1719 Ash Tray, as 1683 without rests
1720 Apple Blossom Morning Set on Tray *£250 - £500*
1721 Vase, as 1675 handled
1722 Vase, two double handles
1723 Apple Blossom Sugar - Toy Set size *£30 - £50*
1724 Wild Rose Wall Pocket *£70 - £100*
1725 Cottage Small House
1726 Gnome, 1.125ins
1727 Fluted Wall Pocket
1728 Apple Blossom Mayonnaise Bowl, unhandled *£40 - £60*
1729 Apple Blossom Pickle Dish *£20 - £30*
1730 Red Currant Jam Pot Holder *£40 - £60*
1731 Gnome
1732 Daffodil Posy Holder *£50 - £70*
1733 Hexagonal Bowl
1734 Double Candle Stick, modelled May 1939
1735 Ribbed Round Bowl
1736 Tulip Posy Holder *£35 - £55*
1737 Storage Jar, 9ins
1738 Water Lily Cruet Set *£100 - £160*
1739 Fruit Lemon Preserve *£20 - £35*
1740 Arum Lily Posy Holder *£40 - £65*
1741 Water Lily Twin Lobed Plate *£50 - £70*
1742 Wedding Cake Fence, large, as 1717 altered for Robin
1743 Wedding Cake Fence, small, from Hunting series
1744 Gladioli Bracket *£200 - £300*
1745 Cottage Windmill
1746 Poppy Bracket *£140 - £170*
1747 Crocus Serving Dish, 2 sizes *£30 - £70*
1748 Tomato Oval Tray *£30 - £50*
1749 Mug, 2 sizes
1750 Water Lily Serving Bowl, Oval Bowl *£50 - £70*
1751 Pyrethrum Jam *£45 - £80 with 1757*
1752 Wallflower Butter or Jam *£45 - £60 with 1763 or 1758*
1753 Anemone Butter *£25 - £35*
1754 Clover/Shamrock Clover Tray *£20 - £40*
1755 Modern Ashtray, 2 rests on one side *£15 - £20*
1756 Apple Blossom Cream, Tall *£35 - £55*
1757 Pyrethrum Spoon *see 1751*
1758 Wallflower Butter Knife *see 1752*
1759 Crocus Comport *£45 - £70*
1760 Crocus Bon Bon Dish *£50 - £80*
1761 Anemone Spoon *£25 - £35*
1762 Anemone Knife *£25 - £35*
1763 Wallflower Jam Spoon *see 1752*
1764 Basket Fruit Basket *£40 - £60*
1765 Crocus Flower Jug, Pitcher, 2 sizes *£200 - £250*
1766 Crocus Bulb Bowl *£60 - £100*
1767 Narcissus Jug *£70 - £120*
1768 Begonia Butter & Knife, Jam & Spoon *£45 - £60 each set*
1769 Forget-me-not Butter & Knife, Jam & Spoon *£45 - £60 each set*
1770 Lady Serviette Holder *£60 - £90*
1771 Campion Butter & Knife, Jam & Spoon *£45 - £60 each set*
1772 Leaf Candle Stick *£10 - £20*
1773 Water Lily Cheese Tray & Knife *£60 - £90*
1774 Water Lily Cress Dish and Tray *£70 - £100*
1775 Basket Handled Flower Basket *£80 - £120*
1776 Water Lily Sauce Boat and Tray *£50 - £80*

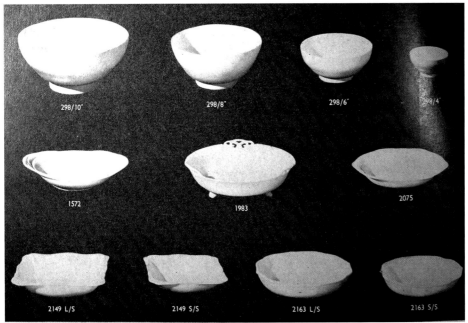

1777 Water Lily Handled Basket £90 - £120
1778 Water Lily Salad Bowl £80 - £120 with 1782
1779 Water Lily Candlestick £30 - £50
1780 Daffodil Candle Holder £45 - £60
1781 Water Lily 3 Lobed Tray £60 - £90
1782 Water Lily Salad Bowl Servers see 1778
1783 Water Lily Plate, 9ins, 6ins £30 - £50
1784 Water Lily Butter or Jam, Knife, Spoon £35 - £65
1785 Wedding Cake Slipper
1786 Water Lily Morning Tea Set (Tea for two) £350 - £500
1787 Water Lily Covered Beaker £90 - £150
1788 Water Lily Jug, 3 sizes £60 - £80
1789 Water Lily Bon Bon £40 - £70
1790 Wedding Cake Pillar, 4.5ins
1791 Wedding Cake Slipper, evening style
1792 Ribbed Toy Tea Set
1793 Wedding Cake Boot
1794 Wedding Cake Double Slipper
1795 Wedding Cake Basket
1796 Wedding Cake Slipper & Dove
1797 Wedding Cake Bell
1798 Water Lily 3 Way Tray £80 - £100
1799 Apple Blossom Toyware £250 - £500
1800 Wedding Cake Corinthian Pillar. 4ins
1801 Water Lily Toast Rack, 5 bar £60 - £100
1802 Polar Bear & Santa Claus
1803 Basket Handled Vase/ Basket, 2 sizes £50 - £80
1804 Water Lily Preserve Pot £50 - £90
1805 Water Lily Biscuit Barrel £150 - £220
1806 Water Lily Jug, Juicer & Tray £50 - £80
1807 Butter, .25lbs, with curved lid
1808 Crocus Mug with Cover £140 - £190
1809 Crocus Preserve Jar with Lid £80 - £120
1810 Basket Handled Vase, 2 sizes £50 - £80
1811 Tulip Candle Holder £25 - £40
1812 War Ship
1813 Nurse
1814 Militia Man
1815 Sailor with Kit Bag
1816 Balloon Barge
1817 Bridal Pair
1818 Doll
1819 Polar Bear
1820 Water Lily Covered Cheese £150 - £200
1821 Tiny Robin

1822 Military Bridal Pair
1823 Santa on Sleigh
1824 Medium Robin
1825 Airman
1826 Anti Aircraft Gun
1827 Snow Baby Falling
1828 Snow Baby Sitting
1829 Snow Baby Lying & Standing
1830 Cupid Sitting
1831 Sailor, movable arms
1832 Crocus Posy Holder, movable arms £60 - £80
1833 Policeman, movable arms
1834 Nurse, movable arms
1835 Soldier, movable arms
1836 Bridegroom, movable arms
1837 Old Bill
1838 Dancing Figure
1839 Figure
1840 Figure with Cape
1841 Airman, movable arms
1842 Skater
1843 Santa
1844 Slipper, as 1796 without Dove
1845 Hitler, movable head
1846 Footballer, movable head
1847 Golfer, movable head
1848 Cottage Church for Windmill series
1849 Girl with bag
1850 Dutch Boy & Girl
1851 Babies on Bear
1852 Eskimo & Hut
1853 Incised Cigarette Box, incised wood grain
1854 Bride, movable arms
1855 Arum Lily Candle Holder £35 - £55
1856 Incised Tray, as 1608 incised
1857 Old Bill, movable head
1858 W A A T, movable head
1859 Fence from Hunting series 757
1860 Large Horse Shoe
1861 Small Horse Shoe
1862 Large Dove
1863 Small Dove
1864 21 on key, medium
1865 Mushroom Bowl
1866 Dogshead Ashtray with Foxhound £5 - £10
1867 Margarite Flower Vase £40 - £60
1868 Lily Flower Vase £25 - £40
1869 Clover/Shamrock Butter £20 - £40

1870 Foxglove Leaf Tray £25 - £35
1871 Incised Bowl, Wood incised
1872 Poppy Flower Vase £25 - £40
1873 Campion Flower Vase £40 - £60
1874 Clover/Shamrock Shamrock Cress Dish & Stand £30 - £50
1875 Foxglove Butter Dish £25 - £35
1876 Basket Salad Bowl £80 - £120 with 1944
1877 Flower Vase
1878 Barley Bowl
1879 Foxglove Salad Bowl & Servers £90 - £150
1880 Coffee Cup
1881 Foxglove Preserve Pot and Cover £60 - £80
1882 Foxglove Flower Jug, Pitcher £130 - £180
1883 Foxglove Morning Tea Set (Tea for two) £300 - £400
1884 Foxglove Handled Basket £75 - £120
1885 Foxglove Jug, 3 sizes £45 - £95
1886 Foxglove Beaker and Cover £90 - 120
1887 Foxglove Cheese Plate and Knife £45 - £75
1888 Foxglove Bon-bon dish £40 - £60
1889 Incised Tray, as 236
1890 Incised Vase, as 1693
1891 Incised Mug, as 1749
1892 Incised Candle Stick, as 1667
1893 Incised Jug, as 1676
1894 Incised Bon Bon, cancelled
1895 Foxglove Toast Rack £70 - £90
1896 Foxglove Cruet Set £70 - £100
1897 Foxglove Sauceboat and Stand £50 - £80
1898 Foxglove Butter & Knife, Jam & Spoon £40 - £60 each set
1899 Ornament Stand No 1, reserved for Hovells
1900 Ornament Stand No 2, reserved for Hovells
1901 Ornament Stand No 3, reserved for Hovells

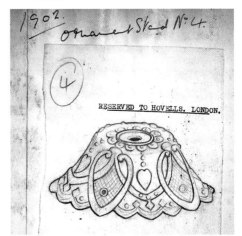

1902 Ornament Stand No 4, reserved for Hovells
1903 Foxglove Oval Bowl, 3 sizes £20 - £50
1904 Foxglove Plate £20 - £40
1905 Wedding Cake Base
1906 Wedding Cake Base
1907 Basket Covered Beaker £100 - £170
1908 Basket Single Handled Sandwich Tray £40 - £60
1909 Basket Bon Bon £30 - £50
1910 Basket Lemon Squeezer £80 - £100
1911 Basket Handled Basket £100 - £150
1912 Basket Preserve Pot and Cover £90 - £120
1913 Basket Cress Dish & Stand £50 - £100
1914 Dogshead Ashtray with Alsatian £5 - £10

1915 Dogshead Ashtray with Spaniel *£5 - £10*
1916 Dogshead Ashtray with Terrier *£5 - £10*
1917 Dogshead Ashtray with Setter *£5 - £10*
1918 Dogshead Ashtray with Bull Dog *£5 - £10*
1919 Covered Butter
1920 Covered Butter for South America
1921 Cup & Saucer
1922 Basket Serving Open Bowl *£40 - £70*
1923 Incised Vase,, 1694/4 incised
1924 Incised Bon Bon with two handles, as 1623
1925 Incised Vase with three handles each side, as 1695E
1926 Incised Oval Tray, as 1572
1927 Incised Vase, as 1694E
1928 Incised Vase, as 1694C
1929 Incised Comport, as 1609
1930 Incised Bon Bon, as 1633
1931 Incised Bon Bon, as 1629
1932 Incised Vase, as 1692D
1933 Incised Butter, as 1387
1934 Incised Candle Stick, as 1713
1935 Incised Preserve and Stand with Modern Sugar
1936 Incised Ash Tray, as 1683
1937 Incised Square Ash Tray, as 899
1938 Incised Vase, as 1695C
1939 Incised Bon Bon, as 1626
1940 Incised Vase, as 1692H
1941 Incised Vase, as 1693G
1942 Incised Vase, as 1695J
1943 Cancelled
1944 Basket Salad Bowl Servers *see 1876*
1945 Shaving Brush Handle
1946 Chestnut Leaf Tray
1947 Daisy Dish, 9ins *£40 - £70*
1948 Wedding Cake Base, as 1906 with holes
1949 Wedding Cake Base, as 1948 with holes lower position
1950 Ash Tray
1951 Daisy Bowl, 6ins *£40 - £70*
1952 Water Lily Ash Tray *£20 - £40*
1953 Clematis Leaf Plate *£30 - £50*
1954 Chestnut Supper Tray
1955 Chestnut Preserve
1956 Chestnut Salad & Servers
1957 Clematis Beaker & Cover *£90 - £120*
1958 Clematis Oval Bowl, 3 sizes *£35 - £65*
1959 Clematis Sauceboat and Stand *£65 - £90*
1960 Clematis Tall Cream *£30 - £50*
1961 Clematis Supper Tray *£30 - £50*
1962 Clematis Cress Dish and Stand *£70 - £95*
1963 Clematis Plate, 2 sizes *£30 - £50*
1964 Clematis Butter *£25 - £40*
1965 Unhandled Beaker, War Office
1966 Worcester Cup & Saucer
1967 Jug, 2 sizes
1968 Opal Cup
1969 Teapot
1970 Unhandled Cup
1971 Opal Cup altered
1972 Mugs & Jugs, Musical Hangsman, Plain Handle *£40 - £80*
1973 Shell Bowl *£30 - £50*
1974 Swirl Coffee Set
1975 Primula Leaf Tray *£20 - £40*
1976 Shell Bon Bon *£20 - £40*
1977 Dish, two handled with a Swirl
1978 Shell Flower Vase, No 1, 6ins *£30 - £50*
1979 Shell Vase, No 2, 6ins *£30 - £50*
1980 Shell Oval Vase *£30 - £50*
1981 Shell Oval Dish *£30 - £50*
1982 Primula Butter or Jam *£30 - £50 with 2052 each set*
1983 Bowl on 3 feet

1984 Vase
1985 Round Ash Tray, 2 protruding rests in centre
1986 Square Ash Tray, 2 protruding rests in centre
1987 Round Flattened Dish, 6 handles
1988 Diamond Dish, 2 handles
1989 Tobacco Jar
1990 Round Box (Powder)
1991 Cherry Preserve *£30 - £50*
1992 Shell Oval Bowl *£40 - £60*
1993 Embossed Flower Vase, cancelled
1994 Shell Butter *£30 - £50*
1995 Wallflower Vase
1996 Shell Jug, 10ins *£40 - £70*
1997 Shell Double Vase *£40 - £70*
1998 Shell Sugar *£30 - £50*
1999 Shell Cream Jug *£30 - £50*
2000 Delphinium Vase
2001 Bon Bon, as 1626
2002 Bon Bon, as 1627
2003 Oval Tray, 3 sizes
2004 Narrow Vase with Folds
2005 Primula Salad Bowl, Fork and Spoon *£100 - £150*
2006 Jug
2007 Bowl
2008 Apple Blossom Lamp *£180 - £250*
2009 Jug
2010 Poppy and Daisy Round Bowl *£60 - £90*
2011 Oval Bon Bon
2012 Primula Cruet *£100 - £150*
2013 Delphinium Shallow Bowl
2014 Delphinium Deeper Bowl
2015 Delphinium Conical Bowl
2016 Delphinium Dish
2017 Delphinium Vase
2018 Delphinium Vase
2019 Delphinium Flower Vase, 3 sizes
2020 Wallflower Sugar
2021 Wallflower Cream
2022 Wallflower Preserve
2023 Wallflower Cruet
2024 Embossed Flower Cup & Saucer
2025 Wallflower Butter
2026 Wallflower Large Oblong Tray
2027 Wallflower Small Oblong Tray
2028 Wallflower Salad Set
2029 Wallflower Triple Tray
2030 Late Buttercup or Buttercup Garland Powder Bowl, Covered Bowl *£40 - £60*
2031 Embossed Birds Tray, 2 handles
2032 Wallflower Egg Cup
2033 Poppy and Daisy Oval Tray *£50 - £80*
2034 Poppy and Daisy Vase, 3 sizes *£80 - £180*
2035 Embossed Flowers Vase, 3 feet
2036 Primula Butter, Triangular *£20 - £35*
2037 Round Bowl
2038 Primula Morning Tea Set (Tea for two) *£250 - £400*
2039 Primula Dish, 4 sizes *£20 - £40*
2040 Primula Long Dish *£25 - £50*
2041 Primula Preserve and Lid *£50 - £80*
2042 Poppy and Daisy Bowl, 3 dips, 3 sizes *£50 - £140*
2043 New Daisy Vase, 2 sizes *£60 - £90*
2044 New Daisy Oval Tray *£60 - £90*
2045 New Daisy Sugar and Cream *£50 - £70 each*
2046 Late Buttercup or Buttercup Garland Oval Tray *£30 - £40*
2047 Late Buttercup or Buttercup Garland Morning Tea Set (Tea Pot, Sugar, etc) *£175 - £250*

2048 Primula Bon-bon dish *£30 - £50*
2049 Primula Sauceboat and Stand *£40 - £60*
2050 Cocktail Cup, metal foot
2051 Poppy and Daisy Bowl/Plate, 2 sizes *£50 - £80*
2052 Primula Jam Spoon & Butter Knife *£20 - £40, also see 1982*
2053 Poppy and Daisy Bon-bon dish *£40 - £70*
2054 Poppy and Daisy Large Footed Bowl, Fluted *£70 - £100*
2055 Late Buttercup or Buttercup Garland Tray *£30 - £50*
2056 New Daisy Preserve *£60 - £90*
2057 Poppy and Daisy Round Vase, 3 sizes *£60 - £160*
2058 Rope Lamp Base *£70 - £100*
2059 Comport, as 2011 Bon Bon
2060 Guinness Round Ash Tray, 3 rests *£20 - £40*
2061 Late Buttercup or Buttercup Garland Jug, 2 sizes *£40 - £60*
2062 Late Buttercup or Buttercup Garland Bon-bon dish *£20 - £30*
2063 Late Buttercup or Buttercup Garland Comport *£40 - £60*
2064 Late Buttercup or Buttercup Garland Salad Bowl *£40 - £60*
2065 Late Buttercup or Buttercup Garland Bread & Butter Plate *£20 - £30*
2066 Late Buttercup or Buttercup Garland Sauceboat and Stand *£40 - £60*
2067 Cocktail Cup with foot
2068 Late Buttercup or Buttercup Garland Bowl *£40 - £60*
2069 Late Buttercup or Buttercup Garland Butter and Knife *£30 - £45*
2070 Round Ash Tray, 3 rests
2071 Square Ash Tray, 4 rests
2072 Bowl, 3 feet
2073 Vase, 2 handles
2074 Late Buttercup or Buttercup Garland Cruet Set *£60 - £90*
2075 Bowl
2076 Bowl, as 2072 with no feet
2077 Salt & Pepper, Modern style modified
2078 Tray, 3 sizes
2079 Poppy and Daisy Lamp Base *£90 - £120*
2080 Fluted Lamp
2081 Plain Lamp
2082 Small Dogs Head from 12ins Vase 130, 1.625ins tall
2083 Large Dogs Head from vase, 2.25ins tall
2084 Musical Bottle
2085 Comport from Tray 2037 with tall and low foot
2086 Hydrangea Vase *£70 - £90*
2087 Shell Tray *£30 - £50*
2088 Oval Bowl
2089 Vase with Ringed feet, 4 sizes
2090 Bon Bon
2091 Dessert Plate from 2085 Comport
2092 Salad Ware Butter *£10 - £20*
2093 Salad Ware Triangular Plate, 3 sizes *£20 - £40*
2094 Salad Ware Salad Bowl & Servers *£50 - £70*
2095 Salad Ware Tray, 3 sizes *£10 - £30*
2096 Salad Ware Sauceboat and Stand *£20 - £40*
2097 Rope Pattern Round Vase
2098 Mug, 4 sizes
2099 Salad Ware Cucumber Tray *£30 - £40*
2100 Rope Pattern Tray
2101 Rope Pattern Butter

2102 Rope Pattern Triangular Ash Tray, 3 rests
2103 Rope Pattern Triangular Vase
2104 Rope Pattern Bon Bon
2105 Rope Pattern Cigarette Box Lid
2106 Rope Pattern Oval Bowl, 3 sizes
2107 Rope Pattern Tall Oval Bowl
2108 Wild Rose Oval Dish 4ins, 6ins, 8ins, 9ins *£30 - £60*
2109 Cherry Oval Plate, 3 sizes *£20 - £40*
2110 Rope Pattern Comport
2111 Rope Pattern Round Vase
2112 Rope Pattern Post Bowl
2113 Ash Bowl, 3 rests
2114 Wild Rose Butter & Knife, Jam & Spoon *£20 - £40 each set*
2115 Wild Rose Morning Tea Set (Tea Pot, Sugar, etc) *£250 - £450*
2116 Wild Rose Oval Bowl, 3 sizes *£40 - £60*
2117 Wild Rose Cruet Set *£70 - £100*
2118 Wild Rose Toast Rack *£60 - £90*
2119 Wild Rose Supper Tray (Long Tray) *£20 - £50*
2120 Wild Rose Preserve with cover *£50 - £80*
2121 Wild Rose Sauceboat and Stand *£50 - £80*
2122 Wild Rose Bon Bon *£45 - £70*
2123 Wild Rose Salad Bowl and Servers *£70 - £90*
2124 Wild Rose Jug, 2 sizes *£60 - £100*
2125 Lobster Plate *£20 - £30*
2126 Cherry Oval Bowl, 3 sizes *£30 - £50*
2127 Cherry Preserve Jar, Lid & Ladle *£50 - £80*
2128 Cherry Tall Cream *£30 - £60*
2129 Cherry Sugar *£30 - £60*
2130 Cherry Cream *£30 - £60*
2131 Salad Ware Cruet *£40 - £60*
2132 Wild Rose Mayonnaise Bowl & Ladle *£70 - £100*
2133 Cherry Plate, 3 sizes *£20 - £40*
2134 Cherry Butter & Knife, Jam & Spoon *£40 - £70 each*
2135 Cherry Cruet Set *£70 - £100*
2136 Cherry Salad Bowl & Servers *£80 - £120*
2137 Cherry Bon Bon *£30 - £50*
2138 Combined Ash Tray & Cigarette Holder
2139 Combined Ash Tray & Cigarette Box, Lid without rests
2140 Rectangular Ash Tray, 2 rests
2141 Cigarette Box and double Ash Tray
2142 Triangular Ash Tray, 3 rests
2143 Hexagonal Ash Tray, 3 rests
2144 Cigarette Box, Tray with Lid
2145 Shell Powder Bowl *£40 - £80*
2146 Card Series Bridge Butter Pat or Ashtray Set *£40 - £80*
2147 Triangular Ash Tray, hollow, 3 rests
2148 Tray *£40 - £65*
2149 Square Bowl, 2 sizes
2150 Jug, 3 sizes
2151 Rectangular Ash Tray, 1 rest
2152 Globular Lamp
2153 Cherry Mug *£30 - £60*
2154 Hydrangea Vase, Tall, 3 sizes *£100 - £160*
2155 Cherry Jug, 2 sizes *£50 - £80*
2156 Leaf Tray *£30 - £40*
2157 Coffee Set
2158 Cherry Toast Rack *£30 - £60*
2159 Round Bowl, 3 sizes *£20 - £30*
2160 Bowl as 1387 Butter, 2 sizes
2161 Hydrangea Tray, 3 sizes *£60 - £120*
2162 Oval Bowl, 3 sizes
2163 Round Bowl, 2 sizes
2164 Bon Bon with Knobs
2165 Hydrangea Flat Bowl, 2 sizes *£70 - £110*
2166 Dewars Jug *£20 - £40*

2167 Hydrangea Vase *£70 - £90*
2168 Bowl with 2 handles
2169 Hydrangea Bon-bon dish *£50 - £80*
2170 Hydrangea Round Bowl *£110 - £170*
2171 Hydrangea Wall Vase *£70 - £110*
2172 Hydrangea Preserve with Cover *£80 - £120*
2173 Hydrangea Sugar & Cream *£60 - £80 each*
2174 Hydrangea Oval Bowl, 2 sizes *£80 - £130*
2175 Bell Handle Butter
2176 Hydrangea Footed Bowl *£100 - £140*
2177 Bell Handle Tray, 3 sizes
2178 Bell Handle Ash Tray, 1 rest
2179 Bell Handle Vase, 2 Bell handles
2180 Bell Handle Cigarette Box
2181 Bell Handle Oval Bowl
2182 Bell Handle Comport
2183 Bell Handle Sugar & Cream
2184 Butter
2185 Lobster Tray, 1 lobster, 3 sizes *£20 - £30*
2186 Lobster Salt & Pepper *£20 - £40*
2187 Triangular Butter
2188 Butter & Knife
2189 Lamp
2190 Lamp
2191 Vase
2192 Ash Tray, 18 rests
2193 Fluted Vase
2194 Embossed Flower Oval Dish, Flower centre
2195 Grape Round Dish *£50 - £70*
2196 Shell Dish *£20 - £40*
2197 Grape Round Dish *£50 - £70*
2198 Bowl, as 2003 Tray
2199 Double Candle Stick
2200 Plain Biscuit Barrel
2201 Ash Tray, green glaze
2202 Cigarette Box with Ash Tray Lid, green glaze
2203 Grape Two Way Tray *£50 - £98*
2204 Vinegar Jar, 4ins
2205 Gondola
2206 Fluted Oval Tray
2207 Fluted Sugar & Cream
2208 Grape Preserve and Stand *£60 - £90*
2209 Hydrangea Two way Tray *£90 - £110*
2210 Hydrangea Five way Tray *£120 - £170*
2211 Grape Jug, 2 sizes *£50 - £90*
2212 Vinegar Jar, 3ins
2213 Vinegar Jar, 3.25ins
2214 Grape Three Way Tray, handled *£70 - £110*
2215 Card Series Ashbowl, Cube, with Dice indents *£25 - £40*
2216 Soup & Stand
2217 Grape Cruet Set *£120 - £160*
2218 Lobster Serving Tray, 2 lobsters, 2 sizes *£30 - £60*
2219 Hydrangea Three way Tray *£100 - £130*
2220 Grape Five Way Tray, handled *£90 - £130*
2221 Grape Planter, Oblong Dish, 2 sizes *£60 - £80*
2222 Guinness Bridge Ash Tray *£20 - £40*
2223 Bon Bon
2224 Grape Cigarette Box, Covered Box *£60 - £90*
2225 Grape Mug or Beaker *£40 - £60*
2226 Grape Sugar & Cream *£40 - £60 each*
2227 Grape Toast Rack *£70 - £100*
2228 Grape Candlestick *£40 - £60*
2229 Swirl Candle Holder
2230 Lobster 3 Way Round Tray *£40 - £70*
2231 Lobster Egg Tray *£60 - £80*
2232 Lobster 5 Way Round Tray *£50 - £80*

2283 SPIRAL DOUBLE CANDLESTICK

2233 Heart Ash Tray, 3 rests
2234 Heart Ash Tray, 3 rests
2235 Spiral Cigarette Box Cover, use 1398 for base
2236 Spiral Vase, as 125/5
2237 Spiral Round Ash Tray
2238 Spiral Round Bowl, 3 sizes
2239 Spiral Oval Ash Tray
2240 Spiral Bon Bon
2241 Open handle Tray, as 2184 Butter, 3 sizes
2242 Lobster 5 Way Round Tray, Low Relief *£40 - £70*
2243 Lobster 3 Way Round Tray, Low Relief *£40 - £70*
2244 Ribbed Cigarette Box
2245 Ribbed Ash Tray
2246 Cigarette Box, as large 2139
2247 Comport, as 2223 Bon Bon
2248 Oval Ash Tray
2249 Rectangular Cigarette Box
2250 Ash Tray
2251 Combined Ash Tray & Cigarette Box
2252 Combined Ash Tray & Cigarette Box
2253 Grape Five Way Tray, unhandled *£80 - £120*
2254 Grape Three Way Tray, unhandled *£60 - £80*
2255 Horse Shoe, 1.5ins
2256 Card Series Ashbowl, Cube *£25 - £40*
2257 Poppy Plate, 3 sizes *£40 - £70*
2258 Scroll Tray, 3 sizes
2259 Lamp base
2260 Oval Vase, 6ins
2261 Hydrangea Wall Vase, Flat Back, 2 sizes *£80 - £120*
2262 Five Way Tray
2263 Poppy Jug *£60 - £90*
2264 Hydrangea Flat Back Lamp Base *£90 - £130*
2265 Ribbed Round Bowl
2266 Card Series Oblong Butter *£10 - £20*
2267 Covered vase, Buddha knob
2268 Grape Round Dish, 13ins *£50 - £70*
2269 Grape Oval Tray *£50 - £70*
2270 Ash Tray
2271 Cigarette Box
2272 Grape Dessert Plate, 5ins *£30 - £40*
2273 Fluted Covered vase, Buddha knob
2274 Ashtray
2275 Clematis Basket Tray, one hole *£35 - £50*
2276 Poppy 3 Way Tray *£60 - £90*

2277 Hazel Nut Tray/Dish £20 - £40
2278 Poppy 5 Way Tray £100 - £150
2279 Spiral Vase, 3 sizes
2280 Spiral Oblong Ash Tray
2281 Poppy Oval Bowl, double poppy, 3 sizes
£50 - £80
2282 Spiral Single Candle Stick
2283 Spiral Double Candle Stick
2284 Poppy Butter & Knife, Jam & Spoon £50
- £80 each set
2285 Poppy Preserve with lid & spoon £70
- £110
2286 Spiral Comport, tall & low
2287 Poppy Bon Bon £40 - £60
2288 Poppy Sugar and Cream £40 - £70 each
2289 Poppy Salad Bowl £90 - £130 with 2291
2290 Poppy Toast Rack, combination £80 - £120
2291 Poppy Servers see 2289
2292 Poppy Tea Pot £140 - £200
2293 Poppy Cruet £100 - £150
2294 Poppy Sauceboat & Stand £60 - £80
2295 Grape Cigarette Box, different to 2224 £60
- £90
2296 Grape Oval Bowl £50 - £70
2297 Grape Ashtray £30 - £50
2298 Guinness Glass & Toucan £250 - £350
2299 Grape Bon Bon £40 - £60
2300 Lamp, Brookes booked 26 May 1955
2301 Grape Comport £50 - £70
2302 Lamp, Elliot & Snears booked 20 August
1955
2303 Grape Turned over Bowl, 16 July 1955 £50
- £70
2304 Grape Candlestick £40 - £60
2305 Coral Vase, 28 July 1955
2306 Hazel Nut Butter or Jam £20 - £40 with
2327 each set
2307 Hazel Nut Sauce Boat and Stand £20
- £40
2308 Guinness Kangaroo £100 - £150
2309 Hazel Nut Salt & Pepper, large £15 - £35
2310 Hazel Nut Oval Serving Dish, 2 sizes £30
- £50
2311 Hazel Nut Jug, 3 sizes £40 - £80
2312 Fluted Bowl
2313 Hazel Nut Salad Bowl £50 - £80 with 2321
2314 Ash Tray
2315 Schweppes Ash Tray £5 - £10
2316 Hazel Nut Oval Bowl, 3 sizes £25 - £50
2317 Guinness Ostrich £100 - £150
2318 Hazel Nut Boomerang Tray, 2 sizes £30
- £60
2319 Guinness Tortoise £100 - £150
2320 Guinness Seal £100 - £150
2321 Hazel Nut Servers see 2313
2322 Guinness Small Glass & Toucan £100
- £150
2323 Kensitas Ash Tray £5 - £10
2324 Hazel Nut Tea Pot £35 - £60
2325 Guinness Toucan Lamp, with shade £300
- £400
2326 Hazel Nut Bon-bon Dish £20 - £40
2327 Hazel Nut Knife & Spoon see 2306
2328 Vase
2329 Bowl, 3 conical legs
2330 Hazel Nut Cruet £25 - £50
2331 Guinness Zoo Keeper £100 - £150
2332 Vase
2333 Bowl, 3 conical legs
2334 Vase
2335 Vase
2336 Leaf Salad Set with Servers, 2 sizes £40
- £70
2337 Coral Vase, 27 April 1956

2338 Tray, 3 sizes
2339 Coral Vase
2340 Oval Bowl with flat end, 2 sizes
2341 Vase
2342 Coral Tray, 3 sizes
2343 Footed Bowl
2344 Coral Ash Tray
2345 Oval Tray, panelled edge, 3 sizes

2346 Leaf Sauce Boat & Stand £15 - £30
2347 Brandyman £60 - £80
2348 Triangular Tray
2349 Vase
2350 Pin Tray
2351 Vase
2352 Gilbey Ash Tray, Round, 9 rests £5 - £10
2353 Ash Tray, 2 sizes
2354 Jug with handle
2355 Bowl, 2 sizes
2356 Tio Pepe, loose hat
2357 Hazel Nut Television Set (Cup & Tray) £40
- £50

2358 Hazel Nut Morning Tea Set (Tea for two)
£120 - £200
2359 Leaf Sauce Boat £10 - £20
2360 Guinness Toucan in flight on Charger £100
- £150
2361 Leaf Butter & Knife, Jam & Spoon £25 -
£40 each set
2362 Crinkled Bowl
2363 Leaf Long Tray £20 - £40
2364 Lamp
2365 Guinness Ash Tray, 13 October 1956 £20
- £40
2366 Leaf Turned-over Leaf Bowl, 2 sizes £20
- £40
2367 Leaf Tray, 4 sizes £10 - £30
2368 Leaf Two way Tray £20 - £40
2369 Leaf Cruet Set (Pepper, Salt, Mustard and
Frame) £30 - £50
2370 Leaf Egg Set £40 - £60
2371 Leaf Covered Cheese £40 - £60
2372 Leaf Preserve Jar and Saucer £30 - £50
2373 Leaf Posy Holder £20 - £30
2374 Leaf Toast Rack £25 - £45
2375 Guinness Menu Holder, 4 November 1956
£20 - £40
2376 Leaf Handled Basket, 2 sizes £15 - £35
2377 Leaf Three way Tray £25 - £45
2378 Guinness Blue Ash Bowl £20 - £40
2379 Service Plate
2380 Lamp Base
2381 Leaf Morning Tea Set (Tea Pot, Sugar, etc)
£80 - £150
2382 Leaf Salt & Pepper, large £10 - £25
2383 Leaf Television Set (Tray with cup) £15-
£25
2384 Plain Tray
2385 Leaf Tea Pot, 2 sizes £25 - £50
2386 Leaf Candlestick £10 - £20
2387 Leaf Bon Bon £10 - £20
2388 Leaf Oval Bowl, 3 sizes £10 - £40
2389 Leaf Pin or Trinket Box £10 - £20
2390 Leaf Handled Basket £15 - £35
2391 Wall Lamp
2392 Ash Bowl
2393 Lamp, as 2335
2394 Windswept Tray £10 - £20
2395 Windswept Jug £10 - £20
2396 Windswept Preserve and Stand £20 - £30
2397 Perforated Lamp Base, as 2152
2398 Guinness Drayman (man pulling horse in
cart) £250 - £350
2399 Guinness 3 Flying Toucans £300 - £400
2400 Pheasant Cruet £40 - £70
2401 Guinness Drayman Plaque £100 - £150
2402 New Daisy Lamp, 2043 upside down £60
- £90
2403 Windswept Cream, Sugar, Cup and
Saucer £10 - £20 each
2404 Windswept 5ins Plate £10 - £20
2405 Windswept Tea Pot, 2 sizes £20 - £45
2406 Windswept Saucéboat and Stand £20
- £35
2407 Windswept Toast Rack £20 - £30
2408 Windswept Butter & Knife, Jam & Spoon
£15 - £25 each set
2409 Windswept Ashtray £10 - £20
2410 Dunhill Table Lighter
2411 Windswept Two way Tray £15 - £25
2412 Gordons Ash Tray, Triangular, 3 rests,
open back £5 - £10
2413 Gordons Ash Tray, Triangular, 3 rests,
open face £5 - £10
2414 Windswept Cruet Set (Pepper, Salt,
Mustard and Frame) £20 - £40

2415 Windswept Cheese Dish and Stand *£15 - £30*

2416 Windswept Cress Dish and Stand *£25 - £40*

2417 Leaf Mayonnaise Bowl, Ladle & Stand *£40 - £60*

2418 Cat Ash Tray *£5 - £10*

2419 Pinstripe Tall Jug *£15 - £25*

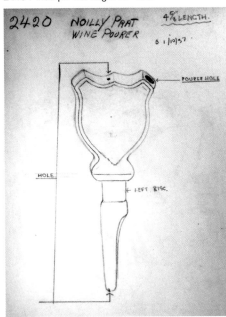

2420 Noilly Prat Wine Pourer

2421 Guinness Toucan Jug *£100 - £150*

2422 Windswept Coffee Set (inc 6 C&S) *£100 - £150*

2423 Windswept Egg Tray *£15 - £30*

2424 Windswept Salad Bowl and Servers *£25 - £50*

2425 Windswept Barbecue Set (4 cups on stand) & Crescent Plate (Side Tray) *£25 - £40 & £15 - £25*

2426 Windswept Plate, large size *£10 - £20*

2427 Hors d'oeuvre Dish

2428 Pinstripe Butter & Knife, Jam & Spoon *£20 - £40 each set*

2429 Pinstripe Plate 5ins *£10 - £20*

2430 Pinstripe Long Tray *£20 - £40*

2431 Fruit Cruet Set (Fruit) *£30 - £50*

2432 Bowl

2433 Haig Ash Tray, as 1381, no rests, oval inside *£5 - £10*

2434 Haig Ash Tray, as 1381, 2 rests, oval inside *£5 - £10*

2435 Pinstripe Cruet Set (Pepper, Salt, Mustard and Frame) *£30 - £50*

2436 Handled Round Jug

2437 Haig Oval Jug *£10 - £15*

2438 Windswept Soup Jug or Hot Water Jug *£20 - £40*

2439 Pinstripe Tray, 2 sizes *£15 - £30*

2440 Modern Cruet *£25 - £45*

2441 Mushroom Cruet *£50 - £75 (£75 - £100 with spots)*

2442 Linen & Other Vase *£20 - £30*

2443 Linen & Other Coffee Pot, Cup & Saucer, Sugar & Cream *£30 - £50, £20 - £40, £30 - £50*

2444 Linen & Other Butter *£10 - £20*

2445 Linen & Other Triangular Plate, 3 sizes *£20 - £60*

2446 Linen & Other Bowl, 2 sizes *£20 - £40*

2447 Linen & Other Tall Narrow Vase *£20 - £40*

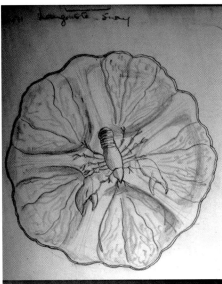

2448 Linen & Other Wall Vase *£20 - £40*

2449 Linen & Other Jug *£30 - £50*

2450 Linen & Other Candle Holders *£25 - £35*

2451 Pinstripe Morning Tea Set (Tea for two) *£80 - £150*

2452 Pinstripe Preserve and Stand *£30 - £50*

2453 Pinstripe Two way Tray *£20 - £35*

2454 Pinstripe Three way Tray *£25 - £45*

2455 Pinstripe Sauceboat and Stand *£20 - £30*

2456 Pinstripe Tall Cup with Saucer *£15 - £25*

2457 Pinstripe Pin Tray *£10 - £20*

2458 Pinstripe Television Set (Tray with cup) *£20 - £30*

2459 Babycham *£50 - £100*

2460 Boothe Ash Tray, 6 rests *£5 - £10*

2461 Pinstripe Cheese Dish and Stand *£40 - £60*

2462 Pinstripe Toast Rack *£30 - £50*

2463 Guinness Miniature Glass *£40 - £60*

2464 Pinstripe Tea Pot *£25 - £50*

2465 Pinstripe Egg Set *£40 - £60*

2466 Pinstripe Salad Set - Bowl with Servers *£40 - £60*

2467 Pinstripe Salt & Pepper, large *£10 - £25*

2468 Wood Tray

2469 Wood Jug

2470 Langouste Serving Dish, 2 lobsters, 2 sizes *£30 - £60*

2471 Langouste 5 Way Round Tray *£50 - £80*

2472 Babycham, no grass *£50 - £100*

2473 Langouste Butter, no lobster *£10 - £20*

2474 Langouste Tray, 1 lobster, 3 sizes *£20 - £50*

2475 Langouste 3 Way Round Tray *£40 - £70*

2476 Langouste Mayonnaise Set with stand & ladle *£30 - £60*

2477 Bullman Morris *£100 - £200*

2478 Babycham, for Ash Tray *£50 - £80*

2479 Childs Drawing Butter

2480 Convolvulus Tray, 3 sizes *£25 - £35*

2481 Langouste Salad Set with servers *£60 - £80*

2482 Wood Carved Wood Tray

2483 Tulip Tray *£30 - £40*

2484 Childs Drawing Tray

2485 Convolvulus Jug *£30 - £50*

2486 Childs Drawing Cruet Set (houses from drawing)

2487 Wood Tea Pot

2488 Convolvulus Preserve Pot and Tray *£30 - £50*

2489 Convolvulus Morning Tea Set (Tea for two) *£90 - £150*

2490 Convolvulus Salt & Pepper *£25 - £40*

2491 Convolvulus Butter & Knife, Jam & Spoon *£25 - £40*

2492 Langouste Plate *£20 - £30*

2493 Langouste Salt & Pepper *£20 - £40*

2494 Convolvulus Two way Tray *£25 - £35*

2495 Convolvulus Cruet *£30 - £50*

2496 Convolvulus Tray, short width, 2 sizes *£20 - £30*

2497 Convolvulus Vinegar and Oil Pots (with stoppers) *£25 - £40*

2498 Convolvulus Three way Tray *£25 - £35*

2499 Convolvulus Salad Bowl and Servers *£50 - £80*

2500 Convolvulus Covered Cheese *£40 - £60*

2501 Convolvulus Bowl, 2 sizes *£30 - £40*

2502 Preserve & Stand

2503 Squirrel Cruet *£40 - £70*

2504 Convolvulus Tea Pot, 2 sizes *£30 - £60*

2505 Haig Round Ash Tray with triangular top *£5 - £10*

2506 Haig Square Ash Tray *£5 - £10*

2507 Convolvulus Tray, long width *£30 - £40*

2508 Convolvulus Sauceboat and Tray *£25 - £40*

2509 Convolvulus Lamp Base *£35 - £50*

2510 Convolvulus Soup Cup *£10 - £20*

2511 Convolvulus Coffee Pot *£40 - £70*

2512 Convolvulus Mayonnaise, Ladle and Tray *£40 - £70*

2513 Convolvulus Toast Rack *£25 - £45*

2514 Fruit Apple Preserve and Stand *£20 - £35*

2515 Magnolia Preserve Pot and Tray *£30 - £50*

2516 Button

2517 Embossed Flower Button

2518 Convolvulus Vase, medium *£20 - £30*

2519 Convolvulus Vase, tall *£25 - £35*

2520 Convolvulus Vase, squat *£20 - £30*

2521 Convolvulus Bowl *£20 - £30*

2522 Lighter Holder

2523 Convolvulus Vase, tall *£25 - £35*

2524 Convolvulus Double Vase, crescent *£25 - £40*

2525 Aladdins Lamp Lighter Holder *£20 - £50*

2526 Fruit Pear Butter *£10 - £20*

2527 Fruit Apple Butter *£10 - £20*

2528 Fruit Lemon Butter *£10 - £20*

2529 Fruit Pineapple Butter *£10 - £20*

2530 Fruit Knife or Spoon for Butter Set *£15*

2589   Zulu

2540   Dutchman

2541   Cossack

2542   Spaniard

259

- £25 each
2531 Magnolia Oval Plate, 2 sizes £20 - £30
2532 Plate, 5ins
2533 Orchid Tray, large size £30 - £50
2534 Sampan Cruet £40 - £70
2535 Mug, Embossed Figure & Thistle

2536 Sir Walter Raleigh Lighter Holder
2537 Convolvulus Hot Water Pot £35 - £60
2538 Shelf Preserve & Stand
2539 Zulu
2540 Dutchman
2541 Cossack
2542 Spaniard
2543 Scotsman
2544 Shelf Cruet Set £30 - £50
2545 Shelf Oval Tray
2546 Langouste Butter, with lobster £15 - £25
2547 Tray
2548 Round Trinket Box, 2 sizes
2549 Rectangular Cigarette Box
2550 Martell Ash Bowl £5 - £10
2551 Pin Tray
2552 Candle Stick
2553 Specimen Vase, 2 sizes
2554 Specimen Vase, 3 sizes
2555 Specimen Vase, 3 sizes
2556 Guinness Salt & Pepper £50 - £80
2557 Colibri Lighter Holder
2558 Magnolia Butter & Knife, Jam & Spoon £25
   - £40 each set
2559 Magnolia Double Candlestick £15 - £30
2560 Magnolia Jug, 1 pint £15 - £30
2561 Magnolia Pin Box, Covered £20 - £30
2562 Magnolia Covered Bon Bon, Trinket Box
   £20 - £30
2563 Magnolia Single Candlestick £10 - £25
2564 Magnolia Long Tray £25 - £35
2565 Single Candlestick
2566 Guinness Toucan Wall Plaque £100 - £150
2567 Double Candlestick
2568 Triple Candlestick
2569 Motor Boat Lighter Holder
2570 Carreras Ash Tray £5 - £10
2571 Magnolia Covered Cheese £50 - £80
2572 Shell Cruet £30 - £50
2573 Octagonal Ash Tray
2574 Orchid Flower Jug £65 - £90
2575 Orchid Cigarette Box £45 - £70
2576 Orchid Trinket Box with legs, including lid
   £45 - £70

2577 Orchid Ashtray £25 - £40
2578 Orchid Bud Vase (no handle) £50 - £80
2579 Orchid Oval Bowl £25 - £40
2580 Orchid Vase, Squat £50 - £80
2581 Octagonal Ash Tray, open top
2582 Orchid Tray, 2 sizes £25 - £40
2583 Flowers Brewmaster Model £50 - £75
2584 Guinness Mug, half pint £50 - £80
2585 Orchid Bon Bon Dish £40 - £60
2586 Orchid Low Vase £40 - £60
2587 Flowers Shakespeare Ash Bowl, figure
   fluxed on £20 - £30
2588 Trinket Set Tall Jug
2589 Trinket Set Long Tray
2590 Trinket Set Bowl, 2 sizes
2591 Fruit Pear Preserve with Apple Preserve
   Stand £20 - £35
2592 Magnolia Cup & Saucer, Sugar, Cream
   £20 - £30 each
2593 Magnolia Two way Tray £25 - £35
2594 Magnolia Double Butter £20 - £30
2595 Magnolia Salad Bowl and Servers £60
   - £80
2596 Magnolia Salt & Pepper £25 - £40
2597 Magnolia Sugar Shaker £25 - £40
2598 Magnolia Dessert Bowl £20 - £30
2599 Magnolia Tea Pot, 2 sizes £90 - £120

2600 Williams & Humbert Sherry Girl
2601 Magnolia Three way Tray £25 - £40
2602 Guinness Waterford Tankard £30 - £50
2603 Trinket Set Lamp Base
2604 Magnolia Coffee Pot, Cup & Saucer £80
   - £100, £20 - £30
2605 Magnolia Tray, 3 sizes £20 - £30
2606 Berhard & Mayes Lighter Holder
2607 Magnolia Bowl, 2 sizes £15 - £30
2608 Preserve
2609 Convolvulus Bud Vase, from large Salt £20
   - £30
2610 Magnolia Hot Milk Jug £80 - £100
2611 Magnolia Sauceboat and Tray £30 - £60
2612 Magnolia Soup Jug £80 - £100
2613 Magnolia Egg Set £40 - £60
2614 Flowers Shakespeare Figure, 10ins £50
   - £75
2615 Magnolia Handled Soup Cup £15 - £30
2616 Magnolia Cruet £40 - £55
2617 Magnolia Oil and Vinegar £30 - £50
2618 Magnolia Mayonnaise, Ladle and Tray £30
   - £60
2619 Guinness Lamp Base, as 1640 £30 - £50

2620 Magnolia Toast Rack £45 - £65
2621 Magnolia Vase, Tall £40 - £60
2622 Magnolia Vase, Squat £30 - £50
2623 Magnolia Vase, Bud £30 - £50
2624 Magnolia Vase, Open Top £30 - £50
2625 Magnolia Covered Butter, rectangular £40
   - £60
2626 Magnolia Large Stand for Oil etc £20 - £30
2627 Guinness Salt, Pepper, Mustard & Spoon
   £60 - £90
2628 Honeysuckle Long Tray, 13.75 ins
2629 Honeysuckle Jug
2630 Fruit Vegetable Cruet Set £30 - £50
2631 Square Ash Bowl
2632 Guinness Candlestick £40 - £60
2633 Honeysuckle Preserve & Stand
2634 Honeysuckle Butter
2635 Fruit Tomato Cruet Set £30 - £50
2636 Cottage Light Holder
2637 Guinness Penguin Lamp, with shade £300
   - £500
2638 Round Ash Bowl, 7ins
2639 Floral Spray Preserve & Stand £20 - £30
2639 Orbit Preserve & Stand £30 - £50
2640 Ash Tray, 3 rests
2641 Floral Spray Butter & Knife, Jam & Spoon
   £20 - £30 each
2641 Orbit Butter & Knife, Jam & Spoon £30
   - £40 each
2642 Floral Spray Plate, 3 sizes £10 - £30
2642 Orbit Plate, 3 sizes £20 - £50
2643 Guinness Bowl £30 - £50
2644 Floral Spray Coffee Pot, Cup & Saucer
   £50 - £90
2644 Orbit Coffee Pot, Cup & Saucer £95 - £170
2645 Carlton Village Inn £40 - £60
2646 Carlton Village Smithy £40 - £60
2647 Carlton Village Water Mill £40 - £60
2648 Carlton Village Wind Mill £150 - £300
2649 Carlton Village Church £40 - £60
2650 Carlton Village Cottage £40 - £60
2651 Carlton Village Butter Market £100 - £170
2652 Carlton Village Shop £40 - £60
2653 Carlton Village Hall £40 - £60
2654 Floral Spray Cruet Set (Frame is Magnolia)
   £30 - £50
2654 Orbit Cruet Set (Frame is Magnolia) £50
   - £80
2655 Floral Spray Sauce Boat (Stand is 2629)
   £20 - £30
2655 Orbit Sauce Boat (Stand is 2629) £30
   - £50
2656 Floral Spray Mayonnaise Bowl & Ladle
   (Stand is 2629) £30 - £40
2656 Orbit Mayonnaise Bowl & Ladle (Stand is
   2629) £40 - £60
2657 Floral Spray Egg Frame (Cups are
   Magnolia) £30 - £40
2657 Orbit Egg Frame (Cups are Magnolia) £40
   - £60
2658 Floral Spray Salad Bowl & Servers £30
   - £40
2658 Orbit Salad Bowl & Servers £40 - £60
2659 Floral Spray Tray, Triangular, 3 sizes £15
   - £30
2659 Orbit Tray, Triangular, 3 sizes £25 - £55
2660 Haig Triangular Ash Tray, 1 rest £5 - £10
2661 Fruit Apple Salt and Pepper £20 - £30
2662 Fruit Pear Salt and Pepper £20 - £30
2663 Guinness Sea Lion Lamp Base &
   Revolving Shade £400 - £600
2664 Floral Spray Cheese Dish & Stand £25
   - £45
2664 Orbit Cheese Dish & Stand £45 - £65

2665 Floral Spray Long Tray, Elongated *£20 - £30*
2665 Orbit Long Tray, Elongated *£30 - £40*
2666 Floral Spray Sugar, Cream, Tea Cup & Saucer *£10 - £20 each*
2666 Orbit Sugar, Cream, Tea Cup & Saucer *£25 - £35 each*
2667 Floral Spray Oil & Vinegar *£20 - £30*
2667 Orbit Oil & Vinegar *£30 - £50*
2668 Floral Spray Two way Tray *£20 - £35*
2668 Orbit Two way Tray *£30 - £50*
2669 Floral Spray Three way Tray *£20 - £35*
2669 Orbit Three way Tray *£30 - £50*
2670 Floral Spray Soup Jug *£30 - £50*
2670 Orbit Soup Jug *£50 - £70*
2671 Floral Spray Double Butter *£10 - £20*
2671 Orbit Double Butter *£20 - £30*
2672 Floral Spray Salt & Pepper, large *£20 - £30*
2672 Orbit Salt & Pepper, large *£35 - £60*
2673 Petlick Ash Tray *£5 - £10*
2674 Floral Spray Individual Fruit *£10 - £20*
2674 Orbit Individual Fruit *£20 - £30*
2675 Floral Spray Sugar Shaker *£20 - £30*
2675 Orbit Sugar Shaker *£40 - £60*
2676 Floral Spray Jug, 2 sizes *£20 - £40*
2676 Orbit Jug, 2 sizes *£40 - £60*
2677 Floral Spray Bowl, 2 sizes *£10 - £25*
2677 Orbit Bowl, 2 sizes *£20 - £35*
2678 Floral Spray Soup Cup & Barbecue Tray *£20 - £30*
2678 Orbit Soup Cup & Barbecue Tray *£30 - £45*
2679 Floral Spray Tea Pot, 2 sizes *£40 - £70*
2679 Orbit Tea Pot, 2 sizes *£50 - £80*
2680 Floral Spray Hot Water Jug or Small Coffee Pot *£30 - £50*
2680 Orbit Hot Water Jug or Small Coffee Pot *£50 - £70*
2681 Floral Spray Covered Butter *£20 - £30*
2681 Orbit Covered Butter *£40 - £65*
2682 Floral Spray Five way Tray *£20 - £35*
2682 Orbit Five way Tray *£30 - £50*
2683 Floral Spray Vegetable Dish *£20 - £35*
2683 Orbit Vegetable Dish *£30 - £45*
2684 Floral Spray Powder Bowl *£20 - £35*
2684 Orbit Powder Bowl *£30 - £50*
2685 Floral Spray Salt, Pepper & Stand, small *£20 - £30*
2685 Orbit Salt, Pepper & Stand, small *£35 - £60*
2686 Floral Spray Candlestick *£15 - £30*
2686 Orbit Candlestick *£25 - £45*
2687 Floral Spray Divided Bowl *£15 - £30*
2687 Orbit Divided Bowl *£25 - £35*
2688 Floral Spray Toast Rack *£20 - £35*
2688 Orbit Toast Rack *£30 - £50*
2689 Guinness Flower Pot *£30 - £50*
2690 Guinness Cheese Containers, 2 sizes *£45 - £80*
2691 Vase, large & small
2692 Bowl
2693 Craven A Ash Bowl *£5 - £10*
2694 Vase
2695 Lamp Base, as 2691
2696 Bon Bon
2697 Bud vase, 8ins
2698 Round Cigarette Box
2699 Ash Tray
2700 Tapestry & Daisy Chain Tray *£10 - £20*
2701 Covered Vase
2702 Mackeson Ash Tray *£5 - £10*
2703 Guinness Pickle Jar *£30 - £50*
2704 Guinness Store Jar *£30 - £50*
2705 Guinness Miniature Penguin *£100 - £150*

2706 Flowers Ash Bowl *£5 - £10*
2707 Tapestry & Daisy Chain Preserve, Cover & Stand *£20 - £30*
2708 Gold Border Lighter Holder
2709 Guinness Vase *£30 - £50*
2710 Tapestry & Daisy Chain Coffee Pot, Cup & Saucer *£20 - £30, £10 - £20*
2711 Tapestry & Daisy Chain Sugar Shaker *£20 - £30*
2712 Tapestry & Daisy Chain Cruet *£25 - £40*
2713 Tapestry & Daisy Chain Long Tray *£10 - £20*
2714 Tapestry & Daisy Chain Round Plate, 3 sizes *£10 - £30*
2715 Tapestry & Daisy Chain Two way Tray *£10 - £20*
2716 Tapestry & Daisy Chain Three way Tray *£15 - £25*
2717 Tapestry & Daisy Chain Double Butter *£10 - £20*
2718 Tapestry & Daisy Chain Cheese & Stand *£20 - £30*
2719 Tapestry & Daisy Chain Vegetable Dish *£10 - £20*
2720 Guinness Hors d'oeuvres, set of 4 *£30 - £50*
2721 Tapestry & Daisy Chain Five way Tray *£15 - £25*
2722 Guinness Crowson Cheese Jar *£30 - £50*
2723 Square Vase *£5 - £10*
2724 Tapestry & Daisy Chain Butter & Knife, Jam & Spoon *£20 - £30 each set*
2725 Tapestry & Daisy Chain Mayonnaise Bowl, Stand & Ladle *£20 - £30*
2726 Tapestry & Daisy Chain Oil & Vinegar *£20 - £30*
2727 Ash Tray *£5 - £10*
2728 Guinness Ash Tray *£20 - £40*
2729 Tapestry & Daisy Chain Platters, 3 sizes *£10 - £20*
2730 Tapestry & Daisy Chain Salad Bowl & Servers *£20 - £30*
2731 Tapestry & Daisy Chain Tea Pot, 2 sizes, Cup & Saucer, Sugar, Cream *£20 - £40 TP, £10 - £20 others each*
2732 Tapestry & Daisy Chain Salt & Pepper, large *£20 - £30*
2733 Tapestry & Daisy Chain Oval Bowl, 2 sizes *£10 - £25*
2734 Tapestry & Daisy Chain Individual Fruit *£10 - £20*
2735 Schweppes Cricketers
2736 Schweppes Golfer
2737 Tapestry & Daisy Chain Soup Cup *£10 - £20*
2738 Tapestry & Daisy Chain Covered Bon Bon *£15 - £25*
2739 Schweppes Ascot
2740 Schweppes Sculptor
2741 Schweppes Skier
2742 Tapestry & Daisy Chain Sauce Boat & Stand *£15 - £25*
2743 Tapestry & Daisy Chain Hot Milk Jug *£20 - £30*
2744 Tapestry & Daisy Chain Jug *£20 - £30*
2745 Tapestry & Daisy Chain Salt, Pepper & Stand *£15 - £25*
2746 Tapestry & Daisy Chain Egg Frame *£20 - £30*
2747 Tapestry & Daisy Chain Divided Bowl *£10 - £20*
2748 Tapestry & Daisy Chain Covered Butter *£15 - £25*
2749 Tapestry & Daisy Chain Toast Rack *£20*

- £30
2750 Guinness Keg Harp Ash Bowl *£20 - £40*
2751 Guinness Square Ash Tray *£20 - £40*
2752 Guinness Miniature Toucan *£50 - £80*
2753 Vase
2754 Tapestry & Daisy Chain Sugar, small size *£10 - £20*
2755 Johnson Mathey Ash Tray *£5 - £10*
2756 Guinness Dish *£20 - £40*
2757 Guinness Inn Sign Vase *£45 - £80*
2758 Guinness Inn Sign Vase *£45 - £80*
2759 Guinness Horse Drawn Bus Ash Tray *£50 - £80*
2760 Guinness Continental Ash Bowl *£30 - £50*
2761 Candles & Snuffer Cruet
2762 Chessman Cruet
2763 Onion Preserve Pot with Face *£10 - £20*
2764 Lantern Cruet
2765 Guinness Cube Cruet *£30 - £50*
2766 Owl & Pussycat Cruet *£15 - £25*
2767 Guinness Pudding Bowl *£30 - £50*
2768 Guinness Antique Plate *£30 - £50*
2769 Fruit Banana Split Tray *£10 - £20*
2770 Guinness Antique Bottle *£30 - £50*
2771 Fruit Apple Individual Preserve *£15 - £25*
2772 Fruit Lemon Individual Fruit Dish *£10 - £20*
2773 Fruit Apple Salad Bowl and Servers *£30 - £50*
2774 Fruit Banana Long Tray *£15 - £25*
2775 Fruit Pear Egg Frame and Apple Egg Frame *£40 - £60*
2776 Fruit Range Centre Piece *£35 - £55*
2777 Fruit Knob for covered Butter *£20 - £35*
2778 Fruit Apple and Pear Three Way Tray *£25 - £40*
2779 Fruit Banana Salt and Pepper Stand *£20 - £30*
2780 Fruit Banana Two Way Tray *£15 - £25*
2781 Fruit Lemon Cream or Sauceboat *£15 - £25*
2782 Fruit Combination Toast Rack, Pear *£60 - £80*
2783 Fruit Lemon Individual Preserve *£15 - £25*
2784 Fruit Individual Apple and Lemon Preserve Stand *£10 - £20*
2785 Jiggered Dishes, 3 sizes
2786 Oval Dish, 4.75ins
2787 Tray
2788 Jiggered Fluted Round Dish
2789 Mouse covered Cheese Dish
2790 Cow covered Butter
2791 Gold Scroll Cigarette Box, round
2792 Squirrel Acorn Preserve *£40 - £70*
2793 Guinness Double Tray *£30 - £50*
2794 Athena Salt, Pepper *£15 - £25 with 2796*
2795 Athena Egg Set *£20 - £30*
2796 Athena Salt & Pepper Stand *see 2794*
2797 Cup
2798 Bamboo Coffee Pot
2799 Bamboo Two way Tray
2800 Athena Covered Butter *£15 - £25*
2801 Athena Long Tray *£10 - £20*
2802 Athena Butter *£10 - £20*
2803 Athena Vinegar Jug *£15 - £25*
2804 Skye Coffee Pot, Coffee Mug *£20 - £30, £10 - £15*
2805 Athena Preserve & Stand *£15 - £25*
2806 Athena Coffee Mug *£10 - £20*
2807 Athena Cheese *£15 - £25*
2808 Athena Coffee Pot, Cup & Saucer, Cream, Sugar *£15 - £25 CP, £10 - £20 others each*
2809 Athena Hot Milk Jug *£15 - £25*
2810 Athena Bowl, 2 sizes *£10 - £20*
2811 Athena Tray, 2 sizes *£10 - £20*

2812 Athena Toast Rack £15 - £25
2813 Skye Long Rectangular Tray £10 - £15
2814 Skye Circular Dish £10 - £15
2815 Persian Coffee Pot
2816 Persian Coffee Cup & Saucer
2817 Persian Tea Pot
2818 Persian Preserve
2819 Persian Hot Water Jug
2820 Persian Cream & Sauce Boat
2821 Persian Plate, 5ins

2822 Figure 10 Royal Hussars

2822 Military Figures Royal Hussar £90 - £140
2823 Persian Sugar
2824 Military Figures Royal Horse Guard £90 - £140
2825 Persian Long Tray
2826 Persian Tray
2827 Persian Cruet Set (Salt, Pepper, Mustard, Frame)
2828 Persian Covered Butter
2829 Persian Salt & Pepper Stand
2830 Military Figures 12th Royal Lancers £90 - £140
2831 Persian Egg Cup Frame
2832 Persian Individual Butter
2833 Persian Large Plate
2834 Persian Oil/Vinegar Bottle
2835 Military Figures Coldstream Guard £90 - £140
2836 Athena Tea Pot £15 - £25
2837 Athena Plate, 5ins £10 - £20
2838 Coffee Percolator
2839 Cube Lighter Base
2840 Low Square Cigarette Box
2841 Tall Square Cigarette Box
2842 Small Square Ash Tray, 4 rests
2843 Large Square Ash Tray, 4 rests
2844 Tea Pot Percolator
2845 Monk Cruet Set
2846 Skye Square Tray, small £10 - £15
2847 Skye Three way Tray, oblong £10 - £15
2848 Elephant Cruet set
2849 Skye Five way Tray, round £10 - £15
2850 Skye Television Set (with cup) £15 - £20
2851 Bird Sweet Tray

2852 Skye Two way Tray, oblong £10 - £15
2853 Skye Triangular Tray £10 - £15
2854 Skye Coffee Jug £20 - £30
2855 Bird Sweet Tray
2856 Skye Butter £5 - £10
2857 Skye Salt & Pepper £10 - £15
2858 Elephant Salt & Pepper Stand
2859 Bird Egg Set (Salt, Pepper, Egg Cup, Frame)
2860 Bird Pepper, Salt & Stand
2861 Military Figures Beefeater Yeoman £50 - £80
2862 Ash Bowl, Large Size, Mackesons £5 - £10
2863 Monk Salt & Pepper Stand
2864 Beaker
2865 Bird Tray
2866 Bird Tray
2867 Warwick Urn, large
2868 Coffee Percolator
2869 Booths Ash Tray £5 - £10
2870 Colibri Lighter Base
2871 Coffee Percolator
2872 Vine or Canterbury Coffee Pot, Cup & Saucer, Cream, Sugar £25 - £40 CP, £10 - £15 others each
2873 Warwick Jardiniere
2874 Warwick Rose Bowl
2875 Warwick Urn, medium
2876 Warwick Urn, small
2877 Warwick Jardiniere, small
2878 Vine or Canterbury Tea Cup £15 - £20
2879 Haig Ice Jug £10 - £15
2880 Oslo Coffee Set £75 - £100
2881 Vine or Canterbury Cruet £20 - £30
2882 Vine or Canterbury Egg Set £10 - £15
2883 Oslo Tea Cup £15 - £20
2884 Vine or Canterbury Plate, 5ins £10 - £15
2885 Vine or Canterbury Three way Tray £10 - £15
2886 Haig Ash Bowl £5 - £10
2887 Vine or Canterbury Long Tray £10 - £15
2888 Skye Cream £10 - £15
2889 Skye Covered Sugar £10 - £15
2890 Oslo Beaker £10 - £15
2891 Vine or Canterbury Butter £10 - £15
2892 Oslo Oil/Vinegar Jug £10 - £15
2893 Oslo Preserve, as 2902 without embossment £15 - £20
2894 Vine or Canterbury Salt & Pepper Stand, large, also for Oslo £10 - £15
2895 Oslo Cheese Cover & Stand, as 2910 £20

2835 Coldstream Guard figure

- £30
2896 Oslo Long Tray, as 2887 £15 - £20
2897 Oslo Three way Tray, as 2885 £15 - £20
2898 Oslo Plate, 5ins, as 2884 £15 - £20
2899 Vine or Canterbury TV Tray £10 - £15
2900 Heinekin Salt & Pepper £10 - £15
2901 Vine or Canterbury Vinegar Jug £10 - £15
2902 Vine or Canterbury Preserve, with cover £15 - £20
2903 Oslo Sauce Boat, as 2920 £15 - £20
2904 Vine or Canterbury Sauce Boat Stand, also for Oslo see 2920
2905 Oslo Tea Pot, 2 cup, as 2917 £25 - £40
2906 Heinekin Clog Ash Tray £10 - £15
2907 Vine or Canterbury Covered Butter £20 - £25
2908 Heinekin Salt & Pepper, large £10 - £15
2909 Vine or Canterbury Beaker £10 - £15
2910 Vine or Canterbury Covered Cheese £20 - £30
2911 Oslo Cruet, as 2881 £20 - £30
2912 Oslo Egg Cup, as 2882 £15 - £20
2913 Tahiti Tall Lighter Base
2914 Tahiti Low Lighter Base
2915 Tahiti Round Ash Tray, 3 sizes
2916 Tall Cigarette Box
2917 Vine or Canterbury Tea Pot £25 - £40
2918 Small Bowl
2919 Oslo TV Tray, as 2899 £15 - £20
2920 Vine or Canterbury Sauce Boat £15 - £20 with 2904
2921 Oslo Covered Butter, as 2907 £20 - £25
2922 Money Box - Flat Back Owl £35 - £50
2923 Money Box - Flat Back Horse £35 - £50
2924 Haig Ash Bowl, centre rests £5 - £10
2925 Mustard, Heinekin £10 - £15
2926 Oblong Pencil Box
2927 Covered Vase, large
2928 Vase, 2 covers, small
2929 Box/Ash Tray, large
2930 Box, small, hole in top
2931 Box, small, 4 holes in top
2932 Coffee Pot
2933 Haig Ice Jug £10 - £15
2934 Pin Box
2935 Candle Stick
2936 Cancelled
2937 Bud Vase, 3 sizes
2938 Covered Jar
2939 Bathroom Squat Ginger Jar, 2 sizes
2940 Bathroom Pin Box
2941 Bathroom Bud Vase, 2 sizes
2942 Bathroom Powder Bowl
2943 Bathroom Candle Stick
2944 Money Box - Flat Back Cat £35 - £50
2945 Bathroom Oval Tray
2946 Money Box - Flat Back Ark £35 - £50
2947 Bathroom Beaker
2948 Bathroom Pedestal Soap Dish
2949 Bathroom Low Soap Dish
2950 Money Box - Flat Back Engine £35 - £50
2951 Embossed Fruit Pepper & Salt, large £20 - £45
2952 Ash Tray
2953 Pepper & Salt
2954 Wellington Pepper & Salt £15 - £25
2954 Sunflower Pepper & Salt £5 - £10
2955 Cruet Set
2956 Bowl
2957 Cruet Set
2958 Sugar
2959 Cup for TV Tray 2962
2960 Vase, small
2961 Cancelled

2962 TV Tray for Cup 2959
2963 Urn
2964 Pin Tray, 6ins
2965 Cream
2966 Coffee Jug
2967 Cancelled
2968 Three Way Tray
2969 Vase, narrow neck
2970 Pin Box, oval
2971 Covered 4 sided Vase
2972 Fluted Bowl with tall or low foot and handles
2973 Wellington Vase, 3 sizes £20 - £30
2973 Sunflower Vase, 3 sizes £10 - £20
2974 Wellington Lighter Holder £10 - £20
2974 Sunflower Lighter Holder £5 - £10
2975 Wellington Tray £10 - £20
2975 Sunflower Tray £5 - £10
2976 Wellington Footed Mug £15 - £20
2976 Sunflower Footed Mug £5 - £10
2977 Wellington Cup & Saucer £10 - £20
2977 Sunflower Cup & Saucer £5 - £10
2978 Wellington Ashtray £10 - £20
2978 Sunflower Ashtray £5 - £10
2979 Wellington Lighter Holder, tall £10 - £20
2979 Sunflower Lighter Holder, tall £5 - £10
2980 Wellington Cigarette Box £20 - £30
2980 Sunflower Cigarette Box £10 - £15
2981 Wellington Candle Stick (5 flanges) £10 - £15
2981 Sunflower Candle Stick (5 flanges) £5 - £10
2982 Wellington Candle Stick (3 flanges) £10 - £15
2982 Sunflower Candle Stick (3 flanges) £5 - £10
2983 Wellington Coffee Pot, Cream, Sugar £40 - £60
2983 Sunflower Coffee Pot, Cream, Sugar £20 - £40
2984 Wellington Ashtray, large £10 - £20
2984 Sunflower Ashtray, large £5 - £10
2985 Fluted Urn
2986 Wellington Preserve £10 - £15
2986 Sunflower Preserve £5 - £10
2987 Plain Percolator
2988 Wellington Spice Jar £10 - £15
2988 Sunflower Spice Jar £5 - £10
2989 House of Lords Ash Tray
2990 Wellington Oil & Vinegar £15 - £25
2990 Sunflower Oil & Vinegar £10 - £15
2991 Wellington Soup Cup £10 - £20
2991 Sunflower Soup Cup £5 - £10
2992 Wellington Tea Cup £10 - £20
2992 Sunflower Tea Cup £5 - £10
2993 Ball Cruet
2994 Wellington Cruet £20 - £30
2994 Sunflower Cruet £10 - £15
2995 Wellington Butter Tray £10 - £20
2995 Sunflower Butter Tray £5 - £10
2996 Long Tray
2997 Wellington Covered Cheese £20 - £30
2997 Sunflower Covered Cheese £10 - £15
2998 Wellington Covered Butter £20 - £30
2998 Sunflower Covered Butter £10 - £15
2999 Roman covered Vase
3000 Wellington Two way Tray £10 - £20
3000 Sunflower Two way Tray £5 - £10
3001 Childs Plate, Vintage Ash Tray
3002 Penguin Salt & Pepper £20 - £45
3003 Cancelled
3004 Cancelled
3005 Double Pepper & Salt
3006 Owl Pepper & Salt £20 - £45

3007 Elephant Pepper & Salt £20 - £45
3008 Poodle Pepper & Salt £20 - £45
3009 New Buttercup and Somerset Butter £10 - £20
3010 Vase Lamp
3011 Vase Lamp (Fishtail)
3012 Jug (Inverhouse)
3013 Ash Tray (Inverhouse)
3014 Bird Pepper & Salt £20 - £45
3015 Ash Tray
3016 New Buttercup and Somerset Sauce Boat £20 - £40
3017 Jug
3018 Tortoise Pepper & Salt £20 - £45
3019 Bowl or Ash Tray
3020 Cancelled
3021 New Buttercup and Somerset Five way Tray £35 - £55
3022 Goblet
3023 Mug with Face
3024 New Buttercup and Somerset Preserve £20 - £30
3025 New Buttercup and Somerset Two way Tray £30 - £50
3026 New Buttercup and Somerset Butter £10 - £20
3027 New Buttercup and Somerset Coffee Set (Coffee for two) £90 - £150
3028 New Buttercup and Somerset Salt & Pepper £10 - £20
3029 New Buttercup and Somerset Covered Butter £20 - £40
3030 New Buttercup and Somerset Jug £20 - £40
3031 New Buttercup and Somerset Sauceboat and Stand £25 - £45
3032 New Buttercup and Somerset Plate, 5ins £15 - £30
3033 New Buttercup and Somerset Tea Pot £40 - £60
3034 Cancelled
3035 New Buttercup and Somerset Tray or Oval Dish, large £20 - £25
3036 New Buttercup and Somerset Tray or Oval Dish, small £15 - £20
3037 New Buttercup and Somerset Beaker £15 - £30
3038 New Buttercup and Somerset Cheese & Cover with Stand £30 - £50
3039 Perth Pepper & Salt
3040 Carlsburg Ash Bowl £5 - £10
3041 Perth Coffee Pot
3042 Cancelled
3043 Tanqueray Ice Jug £30 - £50
3044 ICTC Artichoke Dish
3045 ICTC Corn on the Cob Tray
3046 ICTC Avocado Dish
3047 Ballantyne Ice Jug £30 - £50
3048 Perth Sugar with Lid
3049 Focus Lighter Base
3050 ICTC Egg Cup
3051 Perth Cream Jug
3052 Perth Saucer
3053 Perth Covered Dish, large size
3054 Perth Covered Dish, small size
3055 ICTC Cake Stand
3056 Money Box Cube £20 - £30
3057 Tangier Ash Tray
3058 Cancelled
3059 Tangier Candle Stick
3060 Tangier Pepper & Salt
3061 Toby Jug Dormouse
3062 Tangier Low Vase
3063 Fruit Strawberry Preserve £20 - £40

3064 Fruit Pineapple Preserve £20 - £40
3065 Fruit Blackberry Preserve £20 - £40
3066 Fruit Raspberry Preserve £20 - £40
3067 Fruit Peach or Plum Preserve £20 - £40
3068 Tangier Cigar Jar
3069 ICTC 5 bar Toast Rack
3070 Tangier Bud vase
3071 Tangier Tray
3072 Tangier Pomanda
3073 Rio Ash Tray
3074 Picture Frame Posy Holder, large
3075 Picture Frame Posy Holder, small
3076 Tangier Powder Bowl
3077 Tangier Lighter base
3078 Tangier Cigarette Box, as 3068 but shorter
3079 Tangier Tall vase
3080 Money Box - Flat Back Face £35 - £50
3081 Fish Platter, small
3082 Fish Platter, large
3083 ICTC Salad Plate
3084 ICTC Grapefruit Dish
3085 Lighter Holder
3086 Money Box - Flat Back Pig £35 - £50
3087 Honey Pot, with Bee £25 - £45
3088 Parsley Sauce Boat, with Fish Head £10 - £20
3089 Bread Sauce Jar £10 - £20
3090 Horse Radish Preserve Pot, with Face £10 - £20
3091 String Holder
3092 Red Cabbage Preserve Pot, with Face £10 - £20
3093 Beetroot Preserve Pot, with Face £10 - £20
3094 Lampbase Cat £75 - £100
3095 Lampbase Ark £75 - £100
3096 Lampbase Owl £75 - £100
3097 Lampbase Engine £75 - £100
3098 Lampbase Horse £75 - £100
3099 Annabelle
3100 Percolator
3101 Goblet
3102 Cancelled
3103 Spectrum Water Jug
3104 Money Box - Flat Back Soldier £35 - £50
3105 Spectrum Cruet
3106 Annabelle
3107 Small Vase
3108 Spectrum Beaker
3109 Spectrum Coaster
3110 Egg Cup
3111 Beaker
3112 Goblet
3113 Spectrum Salt & Pepper
3114 Embossed Posy Vase
3115 Annabelle & Cat
3116 Goblet with base
3117 Wine Decanter
3118 Cover for Ginger Jar
3119 Embossed Soup Bowl
3120 Embossed Soup Tureen
3121 Face Salt & Pepper £20 - £45
3122 Alphabet Bowl
3123 Annabelle with Flowers
3124 Annabelle with Doll
3125 Annabelle with Birds
3126 Annabelle with Teddy
3127 Cancelled
3128 Money Box - Bug Eyes Owl £35 - £55
3129 Money Box - Bug Eyes Snail £35 - £55
3130 Money Box - Bug Eyes Bird £35 - £55
3131 Money Box - Bug Eyes Frog £35 - £55
3132 MG Car £100 - £200
3133 Elgin Coffee Set

3134 Gordons Gin Ash Tray *£5 - £10*
3135 Bottle
3136 Salt
3137 Salt
3138 Salt
3139 Salt
3140 Pepper
3141 Money Box - Flat Back Boot *£35 - £50*
3142 Money Box - Flat Back Peacock *£35 - £50*
3143 Walking Ware First Range Cup *£30 - £50*
3143 Walking Ware First Range Egg Cup *£25 - £40*
3143 Walking Ware First Range Milk *£30 - £50*
3143 Walking Ware First Range Sugar with lid (standing), *£45 - £65*
3143 Walking Ware First Range Tea Pot (small) *£80 - £120*
3143 Walking Ware First Range Tea Pot (miniature) *£150 - £200*
3144 Curling Stone *£10 - £20*
3145 1st Kiwi Figure
3146 Gordons Gin Ash Tray *£5 - £10*
3147 Toby Jug, 3 sizes
3148 Daisy Bowl, 2 sizes
3149 Money Box Tram Car *£40 - £70*
3150 Money Box Carousel *£30 - £40*
3151 2nd Kiwi Figure
3152 Pepper, Female eyes
3153 Salt, Male Eyes
3154 Goblin Tea Pot
3155 Coffee Cup Set
3156 Lady Powder Bowl, low oval
3157 Lady Powder Bowl, round
3158 Lady Powder Bowl, tall
3159 Money Box Rocking Horse *£35 - £50*
3160 Gourmet Grapefruit
3161 Gourmet Pear Dish, 3 parts
3162 Gourmet Corn on the Cob
3163 Gourmet Single Egg Cup
3164 Gourmet Double Egg Cup
3165 Gourmet Artichoke
3166 Golf Ball
3167 Gourmet Escargot
3168 Gourmet Toast Rack
3169 Gourmet Salad Plate
3170 Curling Stone *£10 - £20*
3171 Hen Egg Dish
3172 Hen Pepper & Salt *£20 - £45*
3173 Celery Tray
3174 Money Box Pig *£30 - £50*
3175 Apple Blossom - AW Sauceboat and Stand *£40 - £60*
3176 Apple Blossom - AW Individual Butter *£20 - £30*
3177 Flow Blue - AW Toothbrush Jar *£10 - £20*
3178 Apple Blossom - AW Long Tray *£30 - £50*
3179 Apple Blossom - AW Covered Butter *£50 - £75*
3180 Apple Blossom - AW Jug - 1 pint *£40 - £70*
3181 Flow Blue - AW Candlestick *£15 - £25*
3182 Apple Blossom - AW Pepper and Salt *£25 - £40*
3183 Apple Blossom - AW Preserve *£50 - £80*
3184 Flow Blue - AW Heart Box *£10 - £20*
3185 Apple Blossom - AW Cheese and Stand *£75 - £125*
3186 Apple Blossom - AW Crescent Tray *£25 - £40*
3187 Flow Blue - AW Footed Box *£10 - £20*
3188 Apple Blossom - AW Salad Bowl *£30 - £50*
3189 Apple Blossom - AW Leaf Tray *£25 - £35*
3190 Flow Blue - AW Tray *£5 - £10*
3191 Flow Blue - AW Soap Dish *£5 - £10*
3192 Apple Blossom - AW Toast Rack *£40 - £70*

3193 Flow Blue - AW Chamber Pot, 2 sizes *£5 - £15*
3194 Walking Ware First Range Salt & Pepper *£50 - £80*
3195 Walking Ware First Range Tea Pot, large *£100 - £150*
3196 Walking Ware First Range Coffee or Water Jug *£70 - £130*
3197 Walking Ware First Range Sugar with lid, sitting cross legged *£55 - £85*
3198 Walking Ware First Range Plate *£60 - £90*
3199 Walking Ware First Range Soup Bowl with lid *£55 - £85*
3200 Flow Blue - AW Clog *£5 - £10*
3201 Plant Pot Holder
3202 Flow Blue - AW Apothecary Jar *£10 - £20*
3203 Flow Blue - AW Tankard *£5 - £10*
3204 Flow Blue - AW Basin and Ewer *£25 - £35*
3205 Flow Blue - AW Kettle *£10 - £20*
3206 Flow Blue - AW Trinket Box *£5 - £10*
3207 Gourmet Sugar Shaker
3208 Gourmet Salt & Pepper
3209 Gourmet Boat Stand
3210 Gourmet Preserve
3211 Gourmet Cheese & Stand
3212 Gourmet Covered Butter
3213 Gourmet Coffee Jug
3214 Gourmet Coffee Cup
3215 Gourmet Coffee Filter
3216 Flow Blue - AW Iron *£5 - £10*
3217 Books
3218 Embossed Salad Vinegar Jar
3219 Walking Ware Other Items Cow in Bath Butter *£40 - £60*
3220 Pint Tankard with Figure
3221 Embossed Salad Tureen
3222 Ginger Jar, medium
3223 Ginger Jar, small
3224 Flow Blue - AW Caravan Cigarette Box *£10 - £20*
3225 Half Pint Mug with Figure
3226 Kaning Pepper & Salt
3227 Walking Ware Other Items Kneeling Jubilee Mug *£60 - £90*
3228 Walking Ware First Range Tea Pot, miniature *£150 - £200*
3229 Walking Ware First Range Biscuit Barrel *£70 - £130*
3230 Toby Jug Huntsman
3231 Toby Jug Bandit
3232 Salad Range Soup Bowl *£10 - £20*
3233 Flow Blue - AW Tumbler or Goblet *£5 - £10*
3234 Penguin Pepper & Salt, with plinth *£20 - £45*
3235 Covered Dish with Figure Knob
3236 Fox Covered Dish & Ladle
3237 Roman Tea Cup
3238 Boss Egg Cup
3239 Duck Spout Tea Pot *£20 - £40*
3240 Walking Ware Other Items Cow Milk *£30 - £50*
3241 Valentine Mug
3242 Goose Bowl
3243 Denim Preserve Jar *£10 - £20*
3244 Denim Covered Sugar *£10 - £20*
3245 Denim Coffee Mug *£10 - £20*
3246 Denim Tea Pot & Coffee Pot, large *£20 - £40*
3247 Denim Biscuit Barrel, small *£15 - £30*
3248 Denim Cream *£10 - £20*
3249 Denim Ash Tray *£10 - £20*
3250 Denim Biscuit Barrel, large *£15 - £30*
3251 Tuba Egg Cup
3252 Elephant Tea Pot *£20 - £40*

3253 Haig Round Water Jug *£10 - £20*
3254 Haig Antique Water Jug *£10 - £20*
3255 Green Apple Range Tea Pot, Cheese, etc
3256 Bow Tie Pepper, Salt & Mustard *£10 - £20*
3257 Cosy Egg Cup, stacking
3258 Disney Tea Cup
3259 Disney Egg Cup
3260 Duck Egg Cup
3261 Camel Tea Pot *£20 - £40*
3262 Dovecote Range Coffee Pot *£40 - £60*
3262 Dovecote Range Cream *£20 - £30*
3262 Dovecote Range Sugar *£30 - £50*
3262 Dovecote Range Cup & Saucer *£20 - £30*
3263 Tuba Mug
3264 Double Bags Pepper & Salt
3265 Store Jar
3266 Drum Preserve
3267 Dovecote Range Tea Pot *£40 - £60*
3268 Hare Mug
3269 Duck Mug
3270 Frog Mug
3271 Pig Water Jug, 2 sizes *£45 - £75*
3272 Orange Pepper & Salt
3273 Hovis Toast Rack *£15 - £30*
3274 Tortoise Mug
3275 Figure Cup
3276 Whisky Dirk
3277 Fruit Banana Tray *£10 - £20*
3278 Brown & Poulson Cream *£10 - £20*
3279 Dolls Head & Hands
3280 Fred Man Pepper, Salt & Mustard
3281 Walking Ware Other Items Child of the Year Mug *£35 - £70*
3282 Wine Bottle, Beaujolais
3283 Dust Bin
3284 Large Flower Man
3285 Egg Cup & Tray
3286 Fred Pie Funnel
3287 Bird Custard Jug
3288 Money Box Fred *£35 - £55*
3289 Bilton Pepper & Salt
3290 Walking Ware Running Jumping Standing Cup *£45 - £70*
3290 Walking Ware Running Jumping Standing Egg Cup *£30 - £50*
3290 Walking Ware Running Jumping Standing Milk *£45 - £70*
3290 Walking Ware Running Jumping Standing Sugar with lid *£55 - £85*
3290 Walking Ware Running Jumping Standing Tea Pot *£90 - £160*
3290 Walking Ware Caribbean Series Cup *£50 - £75*
3290 Walking Ware Caribbean Series Egg Cup *£35 - £55*
3290 Walking Ware Caribbean Series Milk *£50 - £75*
3290 Walking Ware Caribbean Series Sugar with lid *£50 - £80*
3290 Walking Ware Caribbean Series Tea Pot *£100 - £160*
3291 Ice Cream Wafer *£10 - £20*
3292 Milk Shake Preserve (October 1979) *£10 - £20*
3293 Dolls Head, no hands
3294 Walking Ware Other Items Santa Cup *£60 - £90*
3295 Dragon Tea Pot *£15 - £30*
3296 Fruit Apple Tea Pot *£40 - £60*
3297 Fruit Pear Tea Pot *£50 - £65*
3298 Hovis Covered Butter (January 1980) *£10 - £20*
3299 Cat Cheese
3300 Plant Pots

3301 Walking Ware Other Items Birthday Cream £35 - £55
3302 Water Jug, 100 Pipers
3303 She Mug
3304 Walking Ware Other Items Valentine/ Hearts Cup £45 - £75
3305 Glen Water Jug
3306 Hovis Plate (January 1980) £10 - £20
3307 Bow Tie £10 - £20
3308 Walking Ware Other Items Easter Egg Cup £45 - £70
3309 Walking Ware Other Items Birthday Cup £35 - £55
3310 Culter handle
3311 Round Sided Ice Jug
3312 Fruit Orange Preserve £20 - £40
3313 Mustard Bottle
3314 Cooks Tea Pot, etc
3315 Tap Tea Pot £15 - £30
3316 Beans on Toast Toast Rack & Egg Cup £15 - £30
3317 Pie & Pea Plaque
3318 Lady Book Ends £20 - £40
3319 Plug Ash Tray £10 - £20
3320 Nut & Bolt Vase £10 - £20
3321 Nail & Screw Pepper & Salt £10 - £20
3322 Legs Toast Rack, on Lettuce Rack £10 - £20
3323 Chocolate Box
3324 Bean Cheese, Mug & Preserve
3325 Michelle Vase, 3 sizes
3326 Potts Family, Face Range, Egg Cup, Dish & Beaker £10 - £20
3327 Sweet Pea Desk Set
3328 Lamb Mint Sauce Boat & Stand
3329 Lamb Store Jar
3330 Guinness Tankard Egg Cup
3331 P K Franks Pepper, Salt, Egg Cup & Mug
3332 Walking Ware Other Items Charles & Di Cup £45 - £70 each
3333 Ash Tray & Ice Jug £10 - £20
3334 Asparagus Tray
3335 Mini Whisky Flask
3336 Dove or Pillar Range Pepper, Salt, Ash Tray, Egg Cup, Sugar
3337 Tea Rose
3338 Circus Clown Sugar/Preserve £100 - £200
3339 Strong Man
3340 Fruit Apple Sugar, Cream, Cup and Saucer £20 - £30, £20 - £30, £25 - £40
3341 Circus Women Wrestlers Butter £400 - £600
3342 Circus Clown Cream on Duck £100 - £200
3343 Circus Clown Cream on Pantomime Horse £100 - £200
3344 Sweet Pea Bath Salt Jar
3345 Walking Ware Other Items Wellington Cup £50 - £80
3346 Walking Ware Other Items Maid or Waitress Cup £80 - £110
3347 Alice through the Looking Glass Book Ends (February 1982) £20 - £40
3348 Early Bird Egg Pepper & Salt £10 - £15
3349 Cadburys Mug
3350 Walking Ware Other Items Adam Cup £75 - £110
3351 Circus Clown Tea Pot £100 - £200
3352 Early Bird Egg Cup £5 - £10
3353 Early Bird Beaker £5 - £10
3354 Early Bird Toast rack £10 - £15
3355 Circus Double Egg Cup £50 - £100
3356 Walking Ware Other Items Eve Cup £75 - £110
3357 Playing Card Man Toast Rack £10 - £20

3358 Lady with Mirror Plaque £5 - £10
3359 Haig Square Ash Tray £5 - £10
3360 Lady Mirror £5 - £10
3361 Toby Plaque
3362 Tooth Cup
3363 Wisdom Tooth Cup
3364 Toothbrush Holder
3365 World Cup Ball
3366 Rugby Ball
3367 Alice Mirror £5 - £10
3368 Bath Towel Soap
3369 Half Pint Beer Tankard
3370 Cushion Spoon Rest
3371 Sandcastle Tooth Brush Holder
3372 Hamburger
3373 Walking Ware Big Feet Bookend £50 - £90
3373 Walking Ware Big Feet Candlestick £55 - £90

3373 Walking Ware Big Feet Clock £70 - £110
3373 Walking Ware Big Feet Cup £30 - £55
3373 Walking Ware Big Feet Egg Cup £25 - £45
3373 Walking Ware Big Feet Cream £35 - £60
3373 Walking Ware Big Feet Napkin Ring £25 - £40
3373 Walking Ware Big Feet Nut Bowl or Soap Dish £40 - £70
3373 Walking Ware Big Feet Sugar with lid £45 - £70
3373 Walking Ware Big Feet Tea Pot £80 - £150
3373 Walking Ware Big Feet Toast Rack £80 - £140
3373 Walking Ware Big Feet Toothbrush Mug £30 - £55
3374 Shark Tidy Safe
3375 Pelican Tidy Safe
3376 Venice range of Table Ware

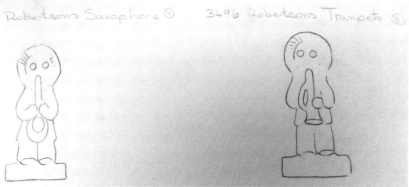

3377 Money Box Rumbelows £35 - £55
3378 Pelican Spoon Rest
3379 Sheep Toast Rack
3380 Lip Egg Cup
3381 Egg Cup
3382 Money Box Rumbelows £35 - £55
3383 Tetley Tea Carrier Bag
3384 J & B Ash Bowl £5 - £10
3385 Money Box Access £35 - £55
3386 Corset Mug
3387 Gourmet Wedge Cheese
3388 Gourmet Napkin Ring
3389 Napoleon Clock

3430 Boots Mustard, small
3431 Boots Salad Bowl, small
3432 Boots Crescent Tray
3433 Boots Cream
3434 Boots Serving Tray
3435 Boots Gateaux Plate, 12ins
3436 Boots Sauce Boat & Stand
3437 Boots Mayonnaise & Stand
3438 Lucerne Sewing Tray
3439 Lucerne Sauce Boat & Stand
3440 Shoe Book Ends
3441 Heart Powder Box
3442 Rolls Royce Range Tea Pot, Sugar, Cream

3480 Bovril Mug
3481 Russell Hobbs Percolator
3482 Sainsbury Toast Rack
3483 Sainsbury Cruet
3484 Sainsbury Preserve
3485 Sainsbury Egg Cup
3486 Sainsbury Cheese & Cover
3487 Sainsbury Butter & Cover
3488 Hovis Egg Cup £5 - £10
3489 Robertsons Golly Singer £30 - £50
3490 Robertsons Golly Flute £30 - £50
3491 Robertsons Golly Accordion £30 - £50
3492 Robertsons Golly Double Base £30 - £50
3493 Robertsons Golly Guitar £30 - £50
3494 Robertsons Golly Drums £30 - £50
3495 Robertsons Golly Saxophone £30 - £50
3496 Robertsons Golly Trumpet £30 - £50
3497 TV Mug
3498 Hovis Covered Sugar £10 - £20
3499 Hovis Cream £10 - £20
3500 Hovis Tea Pot £25 - £40
3501 Hovis Salt & Pepper £10 - £20
3502 Robertsons Golly Band Stand £30 - £50
3503 Poppy & Daisy (New Interior) Vase, as 2057 £60 - £160
3504 Corporate Ash Tray, large
3505 Corporate Ash Tray, small
3506 Whistle Whiskey Container
3507 Poppy & Daisy (New Interior) Bowl, as 2010 £60 - £90
3508 Whitbread Tankard
3509 Corporate Tankard
3510 Flowers Ash Bowl £5 - £10
3511 Face Tea Pot £10 - £20
3512 Maid Tea Pot £10 - £20
3513 Orange Mug £10 - £20
3514 Coronation Street Stan Ogden £30 - £50
3515 Coronation Street Albert Tatlock £30 - £50
3516 Coronation Street Ena Sharples £30 - £50
3517 Coronation Street Hilda Ogden £30 - £50
3518 Coronation Street Mike Baldwin £30 - £50
3519 Coronation Street Bett Lynch £30 - £50
3520 Corporate Tankard, cancelled
3521 Hovis Storage Jar or Biscuit Barrel £20 - £30
3522 Hippopotamus Tea Pot £10 - £20
3523 Hippopotamus Handled Mug £10 - £20
3524 Rabbit Egg Cup £10 - £20
3525 Hippopotamus Egg Cup £10 - £20
3526 Seal Egg Cup £10 - £20
3527 Calf Egg Cup £10 - £20
3528 Ram Egg Cup £10 - £20
3529 Hippopotamus Preserve £10 - £20
3530 Cat Tea Pot £40 - £60
3531 Spitting Image Egg Cups £20 - £30
3531 Spitting Image Tea Pots £50 - £80
3532 Round Bath, 2 sizes
3533 ITCT Toast Rack
3534 Trophy Special Ash Bowl
3535 Rectangular Ash Bowl
3536 Pig Book Ends £10 - £20
3537 Mini Tea Pots
3538 Elephant (Jumbo) Range: Cruet, Toast Rack, Tea Pot, etc £10 - £20 each
3539 Long John Whiskey Bottle
3540 Clock Tea Pot
3541 Scandinavian A B Range
3542 Handled Tankard
3543 Alligator Range: Teapot, Sugar, Cream, Eggcup, Toast Rack, Butter Dish, Preserve, Salt and Pepper £10 - £20 each
3544 Clock Tea Pot
3547 Tea Pots, Bi-plane, Red Baron, Lucy May, Blue Max, etc £60 - £120

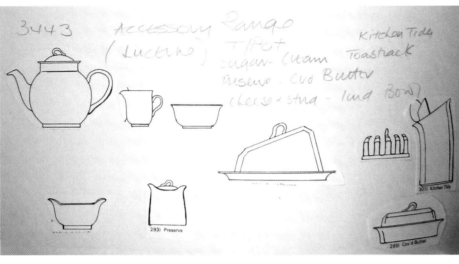

3390 Napoleon Low Clock
3391 Ridgeway Clock
3392 Talles Candle Stick
3393 Chambury Clock
3394 Can Can Mug
3395 School House Clock
3396 Gourmet Gravy Boat
3397 Queen of Hearts Preserve £15 - £30
3398 Mad Hatter Egg Cup £10 - £20
3399 Gourmet Cream
3400 Caterpillar Sugar
3401 Mouse Egg Cup
3402 Cat Butter Dish £10 - £20
3403 Card Pepper & Salt £10 - £20
3404 Shell Jar
3405 Cat & Mouse Toast Rack £10 - £20
3406 Boots Cheese & Stand
3407 Boots Pepper & Salt
3408 Boots Toast Rack
3409 Guinness One Pint Tankard £45 - £80
3410 Boots Butter
3411 Boots Preserve
3412 Small Bath
3413 Large Bath
3414 Tally Clock
3415 Tally Clock
3416 Tally Clock
3417 Hexagonal Napkin Ring
3418 Boots Egg Cup
3419 Boots Toast Rack
3420 Small Cadbury Mug
3421 Large Duck Egg Cup
3422 Small Duck Egg Cup
3423 Cherub Dish with Figure
3424 Singapore Airlines Whiskey
3425 Cherub Round Tray
3426 Cherub Barrel
3427 Cherub Posy Holder
3428 Boots Salad Bowl, large
3429 Cherub

3443 Lucerne Tea Pot, Sugar, Cream, etc
3444 Queen Anne Tea Pot
3445 Castlemaine Ash Tray £5 - £10
3446 Bisto Gravy Boat & Stand £10 - £20
3447 Whiskey Flask
3448 Thompson Man Cruet
3449 Hovis Mug £10 - £15
3450 Utility Ware Baking Tray, small
3451 Utility Ware Baking Tray, large
3452 Utility Ware Goblin Tea Pot
3453 Utility Ware Percolator & Stand, 10 parts
3454 Utility Ware Sugar, Cream, Cup, etc
3455 Utility Ware Vegetable Dish, large
3456 Utility Ware Vegetable Dish, small
3457 Singapore Airlines Tail Fin
3458 Trinket Range Jug, Preserve, Plant Holder, etc
3459 Handles for Beakers, Puffin, Pelican, Flamingo, Toucan, Parrot
3460 Jack Tray
3461 Cook Range Cooking Items
3462 Sheep range (Vicar, Bikini Girl, etc)
3463 Percolator with Cover
3464 Percolator with long Spout & Cover
3465 Rugby Bar
3466 Pickwick Plate
3467 No details
3468 Cook Range Soup
3469 Cook Range Flan, 10ins & 8ins
3470 Percolator
3471 Guinness Egg Cup, Store Jar, Pepper, Salt, Sugar, Shaving Mug, etc £50 - £80
3472 Plants Pots, 2 sizes
3473 Boots Cheese
3474 Fryer Tuck Plate
3475 Dish
3476 BHS Casserole
3477 Harrods Van, large & small £10 - £20
3478 Pirate Plate
3479 BHS Beaker

List of Shape Numbers by Shape Name

Acorn: 1048
Advertising Ware: 1127, 1128, 1257, 1258, 1281, 1329, 1462, 1463, 2166, 2315, 2323, 2347, 2352, 2356, 2410, 2412, 2413, 2420, 2459, 2460, 2472, 2477, 2478, 2550, 2557, 2570, 2583, 2587, 2600, 2606, 2614, 2673, 2693, 2702, 2706, 2723, 2727, 2735, 2736, 2739, 2740, 2741, 2755, 2862, 2869, 2870, 2900, 2906, 2908, 2925, 3040, 3043, 3047, 3134, 3146, 3278, 3302, 3305, 3333, 3335, 3349, 3361, 3365, 3366, 3383, 3384, 3420, 3424, 3445, 3446, 3447, 3448, 3457, 3476, 3477, 3479, 3480, 3481, 3482, 3483, 3484, 3485, 3486, 3487, 3508, 3510, 3539
Aladdins Lamp: 2525
Anemone: 925, 928, 932, 933, 935, 945, 946, 970, 975, 976, 978, 979, 983, 997, 1014, 1015, 1026, 1027, 1028, 1029, 1030, 1031, 1032, 1033, 1041, 1042, 1067, 1068, 1069, 1096, 1097, 1174, 1184, 1753, 1761, 1762
Animals: 1423, 1424, 1425, 1426, 1427, 1430, 1437, 1438, 1440, 1441, 1442, 1445, 1446, 1447, 1448, 1449, 1450, 1451, 1466, 1467, 1468, 1469, 1470, 1471, 1475, 1480, 1481, 1506, 1507, 1508, 1509
Apple Blossom: 1614, 1617, 1618, 1621, 1638, 1648, 1649, 1650, 1651, 1652, 1653, 1654, 1655, 1663, 1664, 1665, 1668, 1669, 1670, 1671, 1680, 1686, 1687, 1688, 1689, 1696, 1697, 1700, 1701, 1704, 1707, 1710, 1714, 1720, 1723, 1728, 1729, 1756, 1799, 2008
Apple Blossom - AW: 3175, 3176, 3178, 3179, 3180, 3182, 3183, 3185, 3186, 3188, 3189, 3192
Arum Lily: 1740, 1855
Athena: 2794, 2795, 2796, 2800, 2801, 2802, 2803, 2805, 2806, 2807, 2808, 2809, 2810, 2811, 2812, 2836, 2837
Bamboo: 2798, 2799
Basket: 1764, 1775, 1803, 1810, 1876, 1907, 1908, 1909, 1910, 1911, 1912, 1913, 1922, 1944
Bathroom: 2939, 2940, 2941, 2942, 2943, 2945, 2947, 2948, 2949
Bee: 1527
Begonia: 1768
Bell: 1715
Bell Handle: 2175, 2177, 2178, 2179, 2180, 2181, 2182, 2183
Bird: 2851, 2855, 2859, 2860, 2865, 2866
Blackberry/Raspberry: 1266, 1473, 1477, 1515, 1516, 1545, 1546, 1547, 1548, 1559, 1560, 1564, 1565, 1570, 1580, 1581, 1584, 1586, 1593, 1598, 1599, 1602, 1662
Bluebell: 1099
Boots: 3406, 3407, 3408, 3410, 3411, 3418, 3419, 3428, 3430, 3431, 3432, 3433, 3434, 3435, 3436, 3437, 3473
Buttercup: 1395, 1402, 1478, 1479, 1482, 1483, 1486, 1501, 1510, 1511, 1512, 1513, 1514, 1522, 1523, 1524, 1525, 1526, 1528, 1529, 1530, 1531, 1532, 1533, 1534, 1558, 1574, 1583, 1585, 1587, 1595, 1597, 1613, 1661, 1709
Campion: 1771, 1873
Card Series: 2146, 2215, 2256, 2266
Carlton Village: 2645, 2646, 2647, 2648, 2649,

2650, 2651, 2652, 2653
Cat: 1132, 1158, 1159, 1160, 1206
Cherry: 1991, 2109, 2126, 2127, 2128, 2129, 2130, 2133, 2134, 2135, 2136, 2137, 2153, 2155, 2158
Chestnut: 1946, 1954, 1955, 1956
Circus: 3338, 3341, 3342, 3343, 3351, 3355
Clematis: 1953, 1957, 1958, 1959, 1960, 1961, 1962, 1963, 1964, 2275
Clover/Shamrock: 1754, 1869, 1874
Cone: 1639
Convolvulus: 2480, 2485, 2488, 2489, 2490, 2491, 2494, 2495, 2496, 2497, 2498, 2499, 2500, 2501, 2504, 2507, 2508, 2509, 2510, 2511, 2512, 2513, 2518, 2519, 2520, 2521, 2523, 2524, 2537, 2609
Cook Range: 3461, 3468, 3469

Coral: 2305, 2337, 2339, 2342, 2344
Coronation Street: 3514, 3515, 3516, 3517, 3518, 3519
Cottage: 1725, 1745, 1848
Crab: 1270
Crab & Lobster: 1280, 1334, 1335, 1338, 1339, 1348, 1350, 1354, 1364
Crinoline: 1087
Crinoline Lady: 1705
Crocus: 1552, 1553, 1747, 1759, 1760, 1765, 1766, 1808, 1809, 1832
Curled Lettuce: 1367, 1372, 1374, 1375, 1380, 1382, 1383, 1385, 1386, 1389, 1390, 1391, 1392, 1412, 1542
Daffodil: 1732, 1780
Daisy: 1472, 1476, 1947, 1951
Delphinium: 2000, 2013, 2014, 2015, 2016,

2017, 2018, 2019

Denim: 3243, 3244, 3245, 3246, 3247, 3248, 3249, 3250

Dimple: 1133, 1134

Dogshead: 1866, 1914, 1915, 1916, 1917, 1918

Dolls Head: 1274, 1276, 1279, 1288, 1312, 1331, 1344, 1349, 1368

Dove or Pillar Range: 3336

Dovecote Range: 1263, 3262, 3267

Embossed: 3114, 3119, 3120

Embossed Birds: 2031

Embossed Flower: 1993, 2024, 2194, 2517

Embossed Flowers: 2035

Embossed Fruit: 2951

Embossed Salad: 3218, 3221

Engine Turned: 1487, 1488, 1489, 1490, 1491, 1492, 1493, 1494, 1495, 1496, 1497, 1498, 1499, 1500, 1502, 1561, 1562, 1573, 1590

Face: 3121

Fish: 1370

Fish Band: 1020, 1021, 1022, 1023, 1024, 1025

Floral Spray: 2639, 2641, 2642, 2644, 2654, 2655, 2656, 2657, 2658, 2659, 2664, 2665, 2666, 2667, 2668, 2669, 2670, 2671, 2672, 2674, 2675, 2676, 2677, 2678, 2679, 2680, 2681, 2682, 2683, 2684, 2685, 2686, 2687, 2688

Flow Blue - AW: 3177, 3181, 3184, 3187, 3190, 3191, 3193, 3200, 3202, 3203, 3204, 3205, 3206, 3216, 3224, 3233

Flower: 1544

Fluted: 2193, 2206, 2207, 2273, 2312

Forget-me-not: 1769

Foxglove: 1870, 1875, 1879, 1881, 1882, 1883, 1884, 1885, 1886, 1887, 1888, 1895, 1896, 1897, 1898, 1903, 1904

Fruit: 331, 1226, 1550, 1556, 1739, 2431, 2514, 2526, 2527, 2528, 2529, 2530, 2591, 2630, 2635, 2661, 2662, 2769, 2771, 2772, 2773, 2774, 2775, 2776, 2777, 2778, 2779, 2780, 2781, 2782, 2783, 2784, 3063, 3064, 3065, 3066, 3067, 3277, 3296, 3297, 3312, 3340

Fruit Basket: 245, 711, 760, 761, 830, 876, 995

Gazelle: 1217, 1223

Gladioli: 1744

Gourmet: 3160, 3161, 3162, 3163, 3164, 3165, 3167, 3168, 3169, 3207, 3208, 3209, 3210, 3211, 3212, 3213, 3214, 3215, 3387, 3388, 3396, 3399

Grape: 2195, 2197, 2203, 2208, 2211, 2214, 2217, 2220, 2221, 2224, 2225, 2226, 2227, 2228, 2253, 2254, 2268, 2269, 2272, 2295, 2296, 2297, 2299, 2301, 2303, 2304

Green Apple Range: 3255

Guinness: 1255, 1282, 1464, 1485, 1681, 2060, 2222, 2298, 2308, 2317, 2319, 2320, 2322, 2325, 2331, 2360, 2365, 2375, 2378, 2398, 2399, 2401, 2421, 2463, 2556, 2566, 2584, 2602, 2619, 2627, 2632, 2637, 2643, 2663, 2689, 2690, 2703, 2704, 2705, 2709, 2720, 2722, 2728, 2750, 2751, 2752, 2756, 2757, 2758, 2759, 2760, 2765, 2767, 2768, 2770, 2793, 3330, 3409, 3471

Gum Nut: 949, 950, 952, 1009, 1010, 1011, 1035, 1036, 1037, 1038, 1040, 1043, 1044, 1045, 1063, 1064, 1066, 1082, 1084, 1086, 1089, 1100, 1101, 1126

Haig: 1271, 1406, 2433, 2434, 2437, 2505, 2506, 2660, 2879, 2886, 2924, 2933, 3253, 3254, 3359

Hazel Nut: 2277, 2306, 2307, 2309, 2310, 2311, 2313, 2316, 2318, 2321, 2324, 2326, 2327, 2330, 2357, 2358

Honeysuckle: 2628, 2629, 2633, 2634

Hovis: 3273, 3298, 3306, 3449, 3488, 3498, 3499, 3500, 3501, 3521

Hydrangea: 2086, 2154, 2161, 2165, 2167, 2169, 2170, 2171, 2172, 2173, 2174, 2176, 2209, 2210, 2219, 2261, 2264

Incised: 1290, 1291, 1292, 1293, 1294, 1295, 1296, 1297, 1298, 1299, 1300, 1301, 1302, 1303, 1304, 1305, 1306, 1307, 1308, 1309, 1310, 1320, 1321, 1322, 1323, 1324, 1325, 1326, 1853, 1856, 1871, 1889, 1890, 1891, 1892, 1893, 1894, 1923, 1924, 1925, 1926, 1927, 1928, 1929, 1930, 1931, 1932, 1933, 1934, 1935, 1936, 1937, 1938, 1939, 1940, 1941, 1942

Jaffa: 1065, 1088

Lampbase: 3094, 3095, 3096, 3097, 3098

Langouste: 2470, 2471, 2473, 2474, 2475, 2476, 2481, 2492, 2493, 2546

Late Buttercup or Buttercup Garland: 2030,

2046, 2047, 2055, 2061, 2062, 2063, 2064, 2065, 2066, 2068, 2069, 2074

Leaf: 1537, 1538, 1539, 1772, 2156, 2336, 2346, 2359, 2361, 2363, 2366, 2367, 2368, 2369, 2370, 2371, 2372, 2373, 2374, 2376, 2377, 2381, 2382, 2383, 2385, 2386, 2387, 2388, 2389, 2390, 2417

Lemon: 1170

Lily: 1868

Linen & Other: 2442, 2443, 2444, 2445, 2446, 2447, 2448, 2449, 2450

Lobster: 1267, 1269, 1272, 1273, 1277, 1278, 2125, 2185, 2186, 2218, 2230, 2231, 2232, 2242, 2243

Lucerne: 3438, 3439, 3443

Magnolia: 2515, 2531, 2558, 2559, 2560, 2561, 2562, 2563, 2564, 2571, 2592, 2593, 2594, 2595, 2596, 2597, 2598, 2599, 2601, 2604, 2605, 2607, 2610, 2611, 2612, 2613, 2615,

2616, 2617, 2618, 2620, 2621, 2622, 2623, 2624, 2625, 2626

Margarite: 1867

Military Figures: 2822, 2824, 2830, 2835, 2861

Moderne: 1245, 1246

Money Box: 3056, 3149, 3150, 3159, 3174, 3288, 3377, 3382, 3385

Money Box - Bug Eyes: 3128, 3129, 3130, 3131

Money Box - Flat Back: 2922, 2923, 2944, 2946, 2950, 3080, 3086, 3104, 3141, 3142

Mugs & Jugs, Musical: 1213, 1260, 1284, 1285, 1289, 1330, 1543, 1549, 1685, 1972

Narcissus: 1767

New Buttercup and Somerset: 3009, 3016, 3021, 3024, 3025, 3026, 3027, 3028, 3029, 3030, 3031, 3032, 3033, 3035, 3036, 3037, 3038

New Daisy: 2043, 2044, 2045, 2056, 2402

Novelty: 1002, 1004, 1005, 1006, 1007, 1008, 1012, 1138, 1197, 1313, 1314, 1315, 1316, 1355, 1624, 1625, 1698, 1699, 1702, 1703, 1711, 1716, 1770, 2400, 2418, 2440, 2441, 2479, 2484, 2486, 2503, 2534, 2535, 2536, 2569, 2572, 2636, 2761, 2762, 2763, 2764, 2766, 2789, 2790, 2792, 2845, 2848, 2858, 2863, 3002, 3006, 3007, 3008, 3014, 3018, 3087, 3088, 3089, 3090, 3092, 3093, 3099, 3106, 3115, 3122, 3123, 3124, 3125, 3126, 3144, 3145, 3147, 3148, 3151, 3152, 3153, 3154, 3155, 3156, 3157, 3158, 3166, 3170, 3171, 3172, 3173, 3217, 3220, 3225, 3226, 3234, 3235, 3236, 3237, 3238, 3239, 3241, 3242, 3251, 3252, 3256, 3257, 3258, 3259, 3260, 3261, 3263, 3264, 3265, 3266, 3268, 3269, 3270, 3272, 3274, 3275, 3276, 3279, 3280, 3282, 3283, 3284, 3285, 3286, 3287, 3289, 3291, 3292, 3293, 3295, 3299, 3300, 3303, 3307, 3310, 3311, 3313, 3314, 3315, 3316, 3317, 3318, 3319, 3320, 3321, 3322, 3323, 3324, 3325, 3326, 3327, 3328, 3329, 3331, 3334, 3337, 3339, 3344, 3347, 3348, 3352, 3353, 3354, 3357, 3358, 3360, 3362, 3363, 3364, 3367, 3368, 3369, 3370, 3371, 3372, 3374, 3375, 3376, 3378, 3379, 3380, 3381, 3386, 3389, 3390, 3391, 3392, 3393, 3394, 3395, 3397, 3398, 3400, 3401, 3402, 3403, 3404, 3405, 3412, 3413, 3414, 3415, 3416, 3417, 3421, 3422, 3423, 3425, 3426, 3427, 3429, 3440, 3441, 3442, 3444, 3459, 3460, 3462, 3465, 3466, 3474, 3478, 3497, 3511, 3512, 3513, 3522, 3523, 3524, 3525, 3526, 3527, 3528, 3529, 3530, 3531, 3532, 3536, 3537, 3538, 3540, 3543, 3544, 3547

Oak Tree: 1098, 1143, 1144, 1145, 1146, 1147, 1148, 1149, 1155, 1162, 1163, 1164, 1165, 1166, 1167, 1168, 1169, 1175, 1183, 1185, 1186, 1187, 1188, 1189, 1190, 1191, 1192, 1193, 1194, 1208, 1214

Old Salad: 620

Old Water Lily: 1540, 1541

Orbit: 2639, 2641, 2642, 2644, 2654, 2655, 2656, 2657, 2658, 2659, 2664, 2665, 2666, 2667, 2668, 2669, 2670, 2671, 2672, 2674, 2675, 2676, 2677, 2678, 2679, 2680, 2681, 2682, 2683, 2684, 2685, 2686, 2687, 2688

Orchid: 2533, 2574, 2575, 2576, 2577, 2578, 2579, 2580, 2582, 2585, 2586

Ornament: 1003, 1016, 1017, 1018, 1019, 1046, 1047, 1049, 1050, 1051, 1052, 1056, 1061, 1083, 1085, 1090, 1091, 1092, 1093, 1102, 1130, 1202, 1203, 1204, 1261, 1517, 1518, 1519, 1520, 1521, 1535, 1536, 1726, 1731, 1802, 1812, 1813, 1814, 1815, 1816, 1817, 1818, 1819, 1821, 1822, 1823, 1824, 1825,

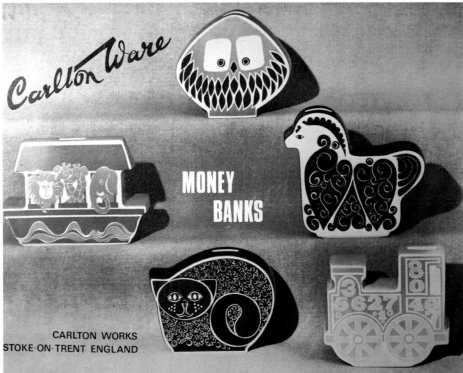

1826, 1827, 1828, 1829, 1830, 1831, 1833, 1834, 1835, 1836, 1837, 1838, 1839, 1840, 1841, 1842, 1843, 1844, 1845, 1846, 1847, 1849, 1850, 1851, 1852, 1854, 1857, 1858, 1859, 1860, 1861, 1862, 1863, 1864, 1865, 2082, 2083, 2255, 2539, 2540, 2541, 2542, 2543, 3132

Ornament Stand: 1899, 1900, 1901, 1902

Oslo: 2880, 2883, 2890, 2892, 2893, 2895, 2896, 2897, 2898, 2903, 2905, 2911, 2912, 2919, 2921

Oven Ware: 1094

Pear: 1039, 1474

Persian: 2815, 2816, 2817, 2818, 2819, 2820, 2821, 2823, 2825, 2826, 2827, 2828, 2829, 2831, 2832, 2833, 2834

Perth: 3039, 3041, 3048, 3051, 3052, 3053, 3054

Pig: 3271

Pinstripe: 2419, 2428, 2429, 2430, 2435, 2439, 2451, 2452, 2453, 2454, 2455, 2456, 2457, 2458, 2461, 2462, 2464, 2465, 2466, 2467

Plain: 1557

Poppy: 1746, 1872, 2257, 2263, 2276, 2278, 2281, 2284, 2285, 2287, 2288, 2289, 2290, 2291, 2292, 2293, 2294

Poppy & Daisy (New Interior): 3503, 3507

Poppy and Daisy: 2010, 2033, 2034, 2042, 2051, 2053, 2054, 2057, 2079

Primula: 1975, 1982, 2005, 2012, 2036, 2038, 2039, 2040, 2041, 2048, 2049, 2052

Pyrethrum: 1751, 1757

Rabbit: 1137

Red Currant: 1603, 1605, 1606, 1607, 1637, 1656, 1657, 1658, 1659, 1660, 1679, 1708, 1730

Ribbed: 2244, 2245, 2265

Rings: 1356, 1357, 1358, 1359, 1360, 1361

PIN STRIPE DESIGN

4609 Lime Green
4610 Brown
4611 Sand

Robertsons Golly: 3489, 3490, 3491, 3492, 3493, 3494, 3495, 3496, 3502
Rock Garden: 1237, 1238, 1239, 1240, 1241, 1243, 1244, 1247, 1248, 1249, 1250, 1251, 1252, 1253, 1254, 1262, 1264, 1265, 1287, 1336, 1337, 1353
Rope: 1616, 1640, 1641, 1642, 1643, 1644, 1645, 1646, 1647, 2058
Rope Pattern: 2097, 2100, 2101, 2102, 2103, 2104, 2105, 2106, 2107, 2110, 2111, 2112
Royalty: 1328, 1332, 1414, 1432, 1434, 1435
Salad Range: 3232
Salad Ware: 2092, 2093, 2094, 2095, 2096, 2099, 2131
Scroll: 2258
Shelf: 2538, 2544, 2545
Shell: 1973, 1976, 1978, 1979, 1980, 1981, 1992, 1994, 1996, 1997, 1998, 1999, 2087, 2145, 2196
Skye: 2804, 2813, 2814, 2846, 2847, 2849, 2850, 2852, 2853, 2854, 2856, 2857, 2888, 2889
Spectrum: 3103, 3105, 3108, 3109, 3113
Spiral: 2235, 2236, 2237, 2238, 2239, 2240, 2279, 2280, 2282, 2283, 2286
Stone Ware: 1070, 1071, 1072, 1073, 1074, 1075, 1076, 1077, 1078, 1079, 1080, 1081, 1103, 1104, 1105, 1106, 1107, 1108, 1109, 1110, 1111, 1112, 1113, 1114, 1115, 1116, 1117, 1118, 1119, 1120, 1121, 1122, 1123, 1124, 1140, 1161, 1171, 1172, 1177, 1178, 1179, 1180, 1181, 1182, 1205, 1211, 1212, 1567
Strawberry: 1396
Sunflower: 2954, 2973, 2974, 2975, 2976, 2977, 2978, 2979, 2980, 2981, 2982, 2983, 2984, 2986, 2988, 2990, 2991, 2992, 2994, 2995, 2997, 2998, 3000
Swirl: 1974
Tangier: 3057, 3059, 3060, 3062, 3068, 3070, 3071, 3072, 3076, 3077, 3078, 3079
Tapestry & Daisy Chain: 2700, 2707, 2710, 2711, 2712, 2713, 2714, 2715, 2716, 2717, 2718, 2719, 2721, 2724, 2725, 2726, 2729, 2730, 2731, 2732, 2733, 2734, 2737, 2738, 2742, 2743, 2744, 2745, 2746, 2747, 2748, 2749, 2754
Thistle: 1576, 1577, 1578, 1579
Toby Jug: 3061, 3230, 3231
Tomato: 1748
Trinket Range: 3458
Trinket Set: 2588, 2589, 2590, 2603
Tulip: 1403, 1404, 1416, 1417, 1418, 1419, 1420, 1421, 1422, 1439, 1453, 1457, 1459, 1461, 1736, 1811, 2483
Utility Ware: 3450, 3451, 3452, 3453, 3454, 3455, 3456
Vine or Canterbury: 2872, 2878, 2881, 2882, 2884, 2885, 2887, 2891, 2894, 2899, 2901, 2902, 2904, 2907, 2909, 2910, 2917, 2920
Walking Ware Big Feet: 3373
Walking Ware Caribbean Series: 3290
Walking Ware First Range: 3143, 3194, 3195, 3196, 3197, 3198, 3199, 3228, 3229
Walking Ware Other Items: 3219, 3227, 3240, 3281, 3294, 3301, 3304, 3308, 3309, 3332, 3345, 3346, 3350, 3356
Walking Ware Running Jumping Standing: 3290
Wallflower: 1752, 1758, 1763, 1995, 2020, 2021, 2022, 2023, 2025, 2026, 2027, 2028, 2029, 2032
Warwick: 2867, 2873, 2874, 2875, 2876, 2877
Water Lily: 1588, 1718, 1738, 1741, 1750, 1773, 1774, 1776, 1777, 1778, 1779, 1781, 1782,

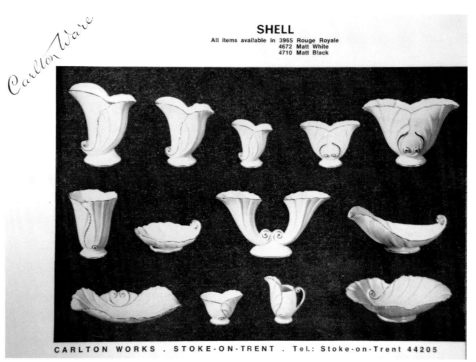

SHELL

All items available in 3965 Rouge Royale
4672 Matt White
4710 Matt Black

Carlton Ware

CARLTON WORKS . STOKE-ON-TRENT . Tel.: Stoke-on-Trent 44205

1783, 1784, 1786, 1787, 1788, 1789, 1798, 1801, 1804, 1805, 1806, 1820, 1952
Wedding Cake: 1717, 1742, 1743, 1785, 1790, 1791, 1793, 1794, 1795, 1796, 1797, 1800, 1905, 1906, 1948, 1949
Wellington: 2954, 2973, 2974, 2975, 2976, 2977, 2978, 2979, 2980, 2981, 2982, 2983, 2984, 2986, 2988, 2990, 2991, 2992, 2994, 2995, 2997, 2998, 3000
Wild Rose: 1551, 1554, 1555, 1724, 2108, 2114, 2115, 2116, 2117, 2118, 2119, 2120, 2121, 2122, 2123, 2124, 2132
Windswept: 2394, 2395, 2396, 2403, 2404, 2405, 2406, 2407, 2408, 2409, 2411, 2414, 2415, 2416, 2422, 2423, 2424, 2425, 2426, 2438
Wood: 2468, 2469, 2482, 2487

Carlton Ware

CARLTON WORKS
STOKE-ON-TRENT ENGLAND

SKYE

Available in ROMAN GREEN
SUNGLOW, THISTLE

Index